NATIONALISM, NATIONAL IDENTITY AND DEMOCRATIZATION IN CHINA

T0362360

Dedication

This book is dedicated to the new generation of Chinese national democrats, or democratic nationalists, in the hope that they can find a new way in which to become national democrats, or democratic nationalists, and, in so doing, reduce or dissolve the tensions between nationalism and democracy.

Nationalism, National Identity and Democratization in China

BAOGANG HE
Associate Professor, School of Government
University of Tasmania, Australia
YINGJIE GUO
School of Government, University of Tasmania, Australia

Routledge
Taylor & Francis Group

LONDON AND NEW YORK

First published 2000 by Ashgate Publishing

Reissued 2018 by Routledge
2 Park Square, Milton Park, Abingdon, Oxon OX14 4RN
711 Third Avenue, New York, NY 10017, USA

Routledge is an imprint of the Taylor & Francis Group, an informa business

Publisher's Note
The publisher has gone to great lengths to ensure the quality of this reprint but points out that some imperfections in the original copies may be apparent.

Disclaimer
The publisher has made every effort to trace copyright holders and welcomes correspondence from those they have been unable to contact.

A Library of Congress record exists under LC control number: 99076354

ISBN 13: 978-1-138-63431-2 (hbk)
ISBN 13: 978-1-138-63428-2 (pbk)
ISBN 13: 978-1-315-20547-2 (ebk)

Contents

List of Tables

Preface

1. Political Background to the Study

A booming Chinese economy has fuelled speculations about the potential global impact of a new giant emerging on the world stage in the 21st century - a Greater China whose territory stretches over the PRC, Taiwan, Hong Kong, Macao, and ethnic communities in the Chinese Diaspora, and which is presumed to be permeated or underpinned by some essential 'Chineseness' or 'pan-Chinese nationalism'. At the same time, there is speculation about what is seen as a national identity crisis. Some ethnic groups in the PRC do not, for example, identify themselves as 'Chinese' and demand independence. Some in Taiwan are actively involved in constructing a separate identity, thereby undermining the 'Pan-Chinese' identity. Not only do these ethno-national movements represent the people and offer evidence of their ability to develop their culture and identity, and demonstrate the growing demand for new rights, such as the right to be different and the right to control a specific living space, but they also raise the question of whether or not China will disintegrate, as happened in the Soviet Union, Yugoslavia, Czechoslovakia, Ethiopia and elsewhere. They also highlight the multi-faceted and interrelated nature of the national identity problem. For instance, in the case of Tibet, the national identity question is one concerned with an awakening nation without a state. For China, on the other hand, it is to develop a new set of national identities strong enough to maintain and expand the Chinese nation state, while for Taiwan, it is focused on the issue of independence (chapter 1).

A number of serious questions are raised through a consideration of the national identity problem in the context of China. What does it mean, for example, to be Chinese? Is there a national identity crisis in China? What is the new Chinese nation being imagined by Chinese historians and the literati? Who is imagining the nation? Who is included or excluded? What is this new nation like? Where is the nation going? What transpires in the transformation of national identity? How does the new 'imagined community', and the imagining of it, exert pressure on the Party-state? How does the government respond to pan-Chinese nationalism? How does a monolithic political structure respond to problems of national identity, and what effects does suppression have on national identity? How does the government try to dissolve anti-Han sentiment among minority groups through a new ideology of nationalism? How do economic reforms impact on national identity and the unity of the Chinese state? Do economic reforms strengthen or weaken national identity? Is the sequence (economic reform followed by political reform) favourable to Chinese nation-building? And, how does uneven economic development create tensions between the Han and ethnic minorities? Is Chinese nationalism an ally or enemy for Chinese democratization? Under what conditions will Chinese nationalism hinder Chinese democratization? Or, under specific circumstances, will it favor democratization? These are just some of the questions this book will attempt to answer.

Baogang He has already addressed the national identity problem in his previous two books. In his first book, *The Democratisation of China*, he encountered the problem in the context of his treatment of the right to secede and the question of Tibet's secession movement. In his second book, *The Democratic Implications of Civil Society in China*, Baogang He discussed the role of civil society in defining national boundaries and described the dilemma in which Chinese democrats have been caught as they deal with the tensions between nationalism and democratization.

Since then, Baogang He has thought more and more about this issue and was joined in this intellectual enterprise by Yingjie Guo, who studied in detail the rise of nationalism and its impact on the development of new national identities. This book is an attempt to answer some of the myriad questions raised above and to remedy the deficiencies of Baogang He's previous two books in which he was able to touch only briefly upon these issues. If *The Democratic Implication of Civil Society in China* is regarded as an essay on driving forces for Chinese democratization, this book can be seen as a treatise on the obstacles and the difficulties China's democratization confronts. It is also our hope that this book will fill in some of the gaps in the study of Chinese nationalism in relation to Chinese democratization.

2. Intellectual Background of the Study

There is a growing body of literature dedicated to the study of Chinese nationalism and national identity. Various aspects of nationalism in modern

China are covered in *Chinese Nationalism,* edited by Jonathan Unger. Many studies of the contemporary scene focus mainly on 'official nationalism' and radical nationalist expressions such as *China Can Say No.*[1] One of the underlying concerns for the bulk of this literature is the potential and actual threat posed by Chinese nationalism. Ying-shih Yu, Allen Whiting and Michel Oksenberg see state nationalism in China respectively as 'fascist', 'assertive' and 'confident'. Wang Gungwu's term of 'restoration nationalism' seems much broader and multi-layered, including at least some elements of state, popular and cultural nationalisms. Other adjectives frequently used to qualify 'Chinese nationalism' include arrogant, dogmatic, expansionist, irrendentist, jingoistic, potboiler, reactionary, revolutionary, visceral and xenophobic, although it is rarely made clear what is, in fact, meant by 'Chinese nationalism'. Given the negativity associated with nationalism, both in theory and practice, Chinese scholars on the mainland and overseas, seem generally more interested in prescriptions for 'Chinese nationalism' than descriptions of it. The proposed alternative nationalisms are wide ranging and include pragmatic, rational, moderate, constructive, wise and romantic approaches.

The major studies of national identity in the Chinese field have contributed significantly to our understanding of the issue. In his essay 'Chinese Nationalism', Townsend has conceptually identified four 'Chinese nations': 'the official one of state nationalism', composed of all the PRC citizens; a 'Han nation'; a nation that comprises the PRC and the 'compatriots' of Taiwan, Hong Kong, and Macao; and one that includes Chinese who reside elsewhere around the world but retain some idea of dual nationality. Prasenjit Duara 'deconstucts' 'the Chinese nation' into 'a plurality of sources of identifications'.[2] Some have added potential 'nations' such as Tibet, Mongolia, Xinjiang to this list of nations and identifications. In *China's Quest for National Identity*, Lowell Dittmer and Samuel Kim focus on official identity, seeing national identity as 'the relationship between nation and state that obtains when the people of that nation identify with the state'.[3] In *National Identity and Democratic Prospects in Socialist China*, Edward Friedman examines Chinese national identity from the perspective of the South-North dichotomy. He argues that a newly imagined China is being reinvented in terms of a south tied to an Asian-Pacific economic dynamism that brings in most of China's foreign exchange earnings and investment.[4] He goes on to contrast the open south-oriented national identity with the features of the northern-oriented national identity which he describes as anti-imperialist, conservative, chauvinistic, and agrarian. He also raises the question of China's democratic national identity.[5]

Chinese writings on nationalism are burgeoning. Some writers in discussing the basic concept, make a distinction between different types of nationalism.[6] Others attempt to justify the need for Chinese nationalism in terms of the nation-state system and current international order, with nationalism being perceived and promoted as China's only road to political security.[7] This view is also reconfirmed by overseas Chinese intellectuals who advocate a constructive and rational nationalism as the means of dealing with what is called 'China's problem' or the Tibet problem.[8] At the same time, many intellectuals criticize and warn against the rise of Chinese nationalism, pointing to its failure in modern history.[9]

Although providing us with rich theories, useful insights and empirical findings, the bodies of literature referred to above have offered little to facilitate our understanding of the essential question concerning the impact of the national identity issue on democratization in China. Seldom do Chinese writings on nationalism discuss the questions concerning 'democracy' or 'democratization', let alone examine the complex relationship between nationalism and democratization. We attempt to add to the existing literature on Chinese nationalism in two main ways. First, we will offer a detailed analysis which critically examines the various approaches towards a new imagining of the Chinese nation. Second, through a systematic, analytical and comparative study, we will examine the impact of the national identity question on political transition, focusing particularly on the question of transformation towards democratization in China and the potential effect of democratization on the resolution of the national identity question. Our focus is different from works which analyze the foreign policy implications of Chinese nationalism.[10] It is hoped that, through an in-depth analysis of the above issues, the book will provide a clearer understanding of the complex relationship that exists between nationalism, national identity, the state and democratization, the direction and trend of China's transition and the subsequent prospects for democratization. Such an understanding is timely, given China's growing stature on the world stage, and it is hoped this intellectual enterprise proves to be of interest to ordinary citizens, scholars and politicians around the world, as well as useful in the context of business, trade, international relations and defense considerations. In particular, it is hoped that this may promote mutual understanding between the seemingly antagonistic nationalist and democratic camps: while pro-democracy people would improve their understanding of the impact of the national identity problem on nationalists; nationalists can improve their understanding of why democrats insist on democratic solution to the national identity question.

3.   Aims and Methods of the study

Three key words - nationalism, national identity and democratization - indicate the focus and theme of the book, which aims to provide a systematic way of accounting for the national identity question and democratization issue. It attempts to offer an analysis of the tensions and contradictions between the democratization of China and nationalist strategies in trying to address the challenge of national identity problems. In so doing it seeks three main objectives. First, to critically describe the rise of Chinese nationalism and examine the poverty of this approach in adequately treating the national identity question in the age of democratization. Second, the book aims to examine the formation and characteristics of a new Pan-Chinese national identity, identifying the underlying forces and dynamics that are shaping it. Third, it seeks to analyze forces and factors that could hinder China's movement towards democracy in the 21st century, and highlight the tensions between nationalism and democratization which are likely to ensue.

To achieve these aims, the book will conduct a comparative analytic study, covering the period 1989 - 1998, which will compare China, Taiwan and the Soviet Union/Russia, mapping the different forms and features of national identity problems as they manifest in each case. It will also analyze the impact of reform strategies on national identity, and the impact of the national identity problem on democratization. It is our contention that an adequate understanding of Chinese nationalism is hindered by a lack of knowledge about nationalism in Taiwan and Russia. It is hoped that a study, which compares nationalism and democratization between Taiwan and China, and between the Soviet Union/Russia and China, can offer some sort of remedy, by providing a contrasting context which will allow us to see how different forms of the national identity question and nationalism have impacted on democratization, and thus have offered differing paths to democracy.

Soviet Union/Russia and Taiwan have been selected because their geographical proximity to China means that Chinese leaders are influenced by what happens in these countries. Drawing lessons from the democratization experiences in Taiwan and the Soviet Union/Russia, the Chinese leadership currently rejects democratic solutions to the Tibet issue and Taiwan question. They obviously fail to understand that democratization has prevented and contained secession in more remote countries, such as Spain, South Africa and the Philippines, which are less influential than the Soviet Union/Russia and Taiwan.

While relying principally on empirical data, this study will also examine influential literary texts, TV programs and films, as fundamental to our understanding of nations is Benedict Anderson's inspirational notion that nations are 'imagined communities' and they depend for their existence on an apparatus of cultural fictions in which imaginative literature plays a decisive role.

4.   Structure of the Book

A central argument of this book, signified by the words in the title - nationalism, national identity and democratization, is that the Chinese nationalist solution to the national identity problem is logically and inherently opposed to the contemporary trend towards democracy. With this idea uppermost in mind, the book is organized into two sections. The first part comprises three chapters which describe the rise of Chinese nationalism and the accompanying discourse on Chinese national identity. The second part is composed of three chapters which focus on the national identity question and its impact on democratization.

In the introductory chapter the conceptual framework for the whole book is set out. It defines the key concepts for the study and spells out the conceptual and practical linkages between nationalism, the national identity question, nationalist strategies and democratization.

Chapter 2 describes the content and strategies of the CCP's patriotic indoctrination against the backgrounds of the rise of Chinese nationalism, and details its central concerns. It then examines the content of state nationalism, and analyzes the problematic against its professed objectives.

Chapter 3 looks at the rise of Chinese nationalism and explores its content and various discourses on Chinese national identity from a literary perspective. It also explores the role played by Chinese writers in shaping Chinese nationalism, questioning whether they have a hidden agenda and what might be the political implications of such an agenda.

Chapter 4 gives consideration to nationalist efforts which have been made to construct a new notion of what constitutes Chinese identity through an examination of the debate over Zeng Guofan. It analyzes the modern and cultural conceptions of the Chinese nation-state in the debate, and points out the strengths and weaknesses of new notions of Chinese national identity put forward by Chinese nationalists.

Chapter 5 examines and compares the national identity question and the rise of nationalism in both Taiwan and China. It investigates the impact of the Taiwan question on the democratization process in Taiwan, and the impact of democratization on the Taiwan question, ending with a discussion of the democratic management of the Taiwan question.

Chapter 6 compares and contrasts the national identity question and the rise of nationalism in the Soviet Union/Russia and China. In particular, it examines the impact of ethnic composition, elite divisions and structure, and the sequencing of reforms on the national identity question. Finally it discusses the prospects for democracy in both Russia and China in light of troublesome questions of national identity.

Chapter 7 focuses on the issue of how Chinese nationalism clashes with democracy over the national identity question. It begins with a general discussion of the relationship between nationalism and democracy, followed by a historical review of specific clashes between Chinese democracy and the national identity question. It further analyzes this clash over the questions of Hong Kong, Tibet and Taiwan in today's China. The asymmetric effect of democratization is identified and employed as a theoretical tool to help explain why there is such a conflict between democracy and nationalism over the national identity question in China.

Chapter 8 discusses the nature and poverty of Chinese nationalism, and considers whether China can be both greater and democratic. It further examines the tension between nationalism and democracy and considers a democratic solution to the national identity problem. Finally, it discusses the prospect for democratic national identity in China, and considers what lessons may be learned by Chinese democrats from Australia's tradition of democratic civic nationalism.

Notes

1   Song Qian, Zhang Zangzang, and Qiao Bian, *Zhongguo keyi shuo bu [China Can Say No]*, (Beijing: *Zhonghua gongshang lianhe chubanshe*), 1996.

2   See J. Unger (ed.), *Chinese Nationalism*, M.E. Sharpe, Armonk, New York, 1996, p. 44.

3   Lowell Dittmer and Samuel S. Kim, (eds.), *China's Quest for National Identity*, Cornell University Press, Ithaca, 1993, p. 13.

4   Friedman, E., *National Identity and Democratic Prospects in Socialist China*, M. E. Sharpe, New York, 1995, p. 59.

5   Friedman, *National Identity and Democratic Prospects*, 77-86.

6   Li Xing, 'Lun guojia minzu zhuyi gainian' (On the concept of state nationalism), *Beijing daxue xuebao (zhexue shehui kexue ban)*, No. 4, pp. 74-80, 1995; Song Quan, 'Guanyu minzu zhuyi de jige wenti' (On Several Topics about nationalism), *Heilongjiang congkan* (Harbin), No. 2, 1996, pp 31-34; Tian Tong, 'Guanyu minzu zhuyi lilung de ruogan jiexi' (Various analyses on nationalism theory), *Shixue yuekan* (Kaifeng) No. 5, 1997, p. 9-13; Xong Kunxin, 'Guanyu minzu zhuyi zhenglun zhong de jige redian wenti' (On several hot topics concerning nationalism), *Guizhou minzu yanjiu* (Guiyang), No. 4, 1996, pp. 1-6.

7   Tang Yongsheng, 'Minzu zhuyi yu guoji zhixu' (Nationalism and international order), *Strategy and Management*, (March issue, 1996), pp. 76-79; Chen Mingming, 'Zhengzhi fazhan shijiao zhong de minzu yu minzu zhuyi' (Nation and nationalism from the angle of political development), *Strategy and Management*, Feb., 1996, pp. 63-71; Jiang Yihua, 'Lun 20 shiji zhongguo de minzu zhuyi' (On Chinese nationalism in the 20th century), *Fudan xuebao (shehui kexue ban)*, No. 3, 1993, pp. 8-13; Cai Xiaoping, 'Lun minzu zhuyi yu quanqiu yitihua de guanxi' (On the relationship between nationalism and globalisation), *Qinghai minzu xueyuan xuebao: Sheke ban*, No. 3, 1996, pp.26-31; Zhang Wenbiao, 'Zhonghua minzu yishi yu shehui fazhan' (National consciousness of China and society development), *Fujian luntan*: Wenshizhe ban (Fuzhou) 1, 1996, p. 15-21; Cao Yueming, 'Zhongguo xiandaishi shang de sanda sichao yu minzu zhuyi yundong' (Three big trends of thought and nationalism movements in Chinese modern history), *Tianjin Social Science*, No. 1, 1992, pp. 84-89.

8   Zhong Weiguang, 'Minzu, minzu zhuyi he zhongguo wenti' (Nation, nationalism and the China problem), *Modern China Studies*, No. 2, 1997, p. 128-142; Song

Liming, 'Minzu zhuyi yu xizang wenti' (Nationalism and Tibet problem), *Modern China Studies*, No. 2, 1997, pp. 159-167; Wang Pengling, 'Zhongguo minzu zhuyi de yuanliu – jianlun cong geming de minzu zhuyi zhuanxiang jianshe de minzu zhuyi' (Source of Chinese nationalism – On the Transformation from revolutionary nationalism to constructive nationalism), *Modern China Studies*, No.2, 1997, p. 101-127.

9   See Tao Dongfeng, 'Xiandai Zhongguo de minzu zhuyi' (Nationalism in Modern China), *Academic Monthly*, June issue, 1994, pp. 6-9; Jiang Niantao, 'Dui minzu ziwo zhongxin de fanbo' (A Critique of the Selfcentralism of Nationality), *Jianghan Tribune*, No. 3, 1996, pp. 33-35; Ge Hongbing, 'Jingti xiaai de minzu zhuyi' (On guard against narrow nationalism), *Zhongguo qingnian yanjiu* (*China Youth Studies*) No. 1, 1998, p. 32-33; Liu Junning (1997), 'Minzu zhuyi simianguan' (Four Dimensions of Nationalism), *Nanfang wenhua*, No. 6, 1997, pp. 25-28; Wu Chuke, 'Dui Dangdai minzu zhuyi sichao fanlan de pingxi' (Comment and analysis on the spreading of the trend of thought of nationalism in the present age), *Neimenggu shehui kexue, Wenxueshi ban* (Huhehaote), No. 3, 1996, pp. 6-12; Chen Shaoming, 'Minzu zhuyi: fuxing zhi dao?' (Nationalism: the route to renaissance?), *Dongfang* (Beijing) No. 2, 1996, pp. 74-76; Pi Mingyong, 'Minzu zhuyi yu rujia wenhua' (Nationalism and Confucian culture), *Strategy and Management*, Feb., 1996, pp. 51-57.

10   On this question, see Michael Oksenberg, 'China's Confident Natioanlism', *Foreign Affairs*, Vol. 65, No. 3, 1987, 501-523; Allen Whiting, 'Assertive Nationalism in Chinese Foreign Policy', *Asian Survey, Vol. 23, No. 8, 1983, 913-33;* Allen Whiting, 'Chinese Nationalism and Foreign Policy after Deng', *The China Quarterly*, No. 142, 1995, pp. 295-316.

Acknowledgments

We feel much indebted to Professor Jan Pakulski for permitting us to use some of our co-authored article; to Della Clark for formatting the book; to Jack Hogan, Christine Standish, Amy Wheaton, Lang Youxing, Shaw Wang and Bai Xin for their assistance in the research and collection of materials, and the editing of parts of the draft, in particular for Christine Standish's proof-reading; to the School of Government at the University of Tasmania where we have been supported by colleagues in our research work; to Professors John Fitzgerald, Bruce Jacobs and C. L. Chiou for their comments on Taiwanese nationalism; to Professors Edward Friedman, Arif Dirlik and Prasenjit Duara for their suggestions and comments on Chinese nationalism; to Dr. Jonathan Unger for his unfailing ecouragement and guidance to Yingjie Guo during his research at the ANU between June and September 1997; to the Contemporary China Centre at the Australian National University for providing us with the facilities to access the library and the photocopying machine; and to the Australian Research Council and the ANU for granting Baogang He large and small grants and Yingjie Guo a National Visiting Scholarship. These enabled us to gain new information on current developments in China, and speed up the production of the book. We also thank Kirstin Howgate, the commissioning editor at Ashgate publishing. It was her invitation that encouraged us to put our works together and reorganize them into a coherent book. Finally, Baogang would like to thank his wife, Suxing, and his daughter, Mao Mao, for their daily support and Yingjie thanks Shang Wei and Olivia.

Yingjie Guo wrote the drafts of chapters 2 and 3, while Baogang He wrote those of chapters 1, 5, 6, 7 and 8. He and Guo co-authored the Preface and chapter 4. Both have looked at each other's drafts, making suggestions, comments, changes and corrections. Guo checked the spelling, grammar, notes and bibliography.

We thank the editors and publishers below for permitting us to reproduce the following materials and passages from our papers, which they originally published.

'Patriotic Villains and Patriotic Heroes: Chinese Literary Nationalism in the 1990s', *Nationalism and Ethnic Politics* Vol. 4, Spring/Summer, No 182, 1998, pp. 163-88.

'Reimagining the Chinese Nation: The Zeng Guofan Phenomenon', *Modern China* (Uni. of California), Vol. 25, No. 2, April 1999, pp. 142-170.

'National Integrity, Elites and Democratization: Russia and China Compared', *The Journal of Communist Studies and Transition Politics*, Vol. 15, No. 2, June 1999, pp. 69-87.

1 Conceptual Introduction

This chapter aims to define key concepts, explore their implications in a Chinese context, and spell out the linkages between nationalism, national identities, the national identity question, the nation-state system, and the relationship between the national boundary/identity question and democratization. It also aims to outline the central questions and themes of the book, as well as its theoretical and analytical framework. In short, the chapter serves as a conceptual foundation for the book as a whole and provides a brief preview of its central concerns.

1.   Nationalism and its Four Forms

According to Anthony Smith, nationalism refers to the whole process of the growth of nations and nation states, sentiments of attachment to and pride in the nation, an ideology and language (or discourse) extolling the nation, and a movement with national aspirations and goals.[1] The components of the ideology of nationalism can be briefly summarized in the following way: the world is divided into nations, each with its own character and destiny; the nation is the sole source of political power, and loyalty to it overrides all other loyalties; everyone must belong to a nation, if everyone is to be truly free; to realize themselves, nations must be autonomous; and nations must be free and secure if there is to be peace and justice in the world. The goals of nationalist movements are national identity, national unity and national autonomy.[2]

We would like to emphasize that Chinese nationalism provides legitimation for the Chinese nation-state, and stresses individual loyalty to the state and the priority of the political community over individual rights. To Chinese nationalists, the most important human unit is the nation; all others, especially individuals, are insignificant, and national interests can even be carried out at the cost of personal sacrifice. Chinese nationalism can be seen as a special way of organizing and distributing political power in a way which favors Han nationality.

The core goal of Chinese nationalism is not only to promote and protect the national interests of China, but also to restore its 'greatness'. Mao Zedong, Deng Xiaoping and Jiang Zemin are all nationalists in the sense that they were, or are, ambitious for China to regain pre-eminence in power and influence as quickly as possible. 'This was restoration nationalism at its most romantic and Nietzschean, and it has not been wholly discarded', as Wang Gungwu puts it.[3] In the 1990s, Chinese nationalism reflects a growing national confidence that, as a result of the economic development of the 'big dragon' and the spread of the concept of 'Greater China', China can provide a successful model for developmental states.

Nationalism takes many forms. Snyder classifies nationalism into fissiparous nationalism in Europe, black nationalism in Africa, anticolonial nationalism in Asia, politico-religious nationalism in the Middle East, popular nationalism in Latin America, melting-pot nationalism in the US, and messianic nationalism in the former Soviet Union.[4] Chinese intellectuals distinguish assertive, aggressive and narrow nationalism from rational, responsible and constructive nationalism. Lucian Pye praises the Shanghai-type nationalism that was buried by Mao's anti-imperialist nationalism but has risen again in recent years.[5]

For the purpose of this book, we classify nationalism into state versus popular nationalism; and super versus ethno nationalism. Chinese nationalism can be divided into two categories: state and popular. State (or official) nationalism refers to any doctrine, ideology or discourse in which the Chinese Party-state strives to identify itself as the nation, or claims that its goals embody those of the nation and are essential to its nationhood. It also denotes a process whereby the Chinese state sponsors, controls, and invents the content of patriotism and cultural symbols of the Chinese nation (chapter 2). Another interpretation of state nationalism is that the interests of the state are identical with those of the nation, and therefore the state is an instrument to represent and protect national interests in international relations.[6]

Popular nationalism comes from 'below' and represents unsystematic, popular national sentiments. Popular nationalism is reflected in, for instance, folk music and literature. While the formation of popular nationalism is always a natural process, the ideas and beliefs of state nationalism must be actively promoted. A concrete example of popular nationalism is the massive protest against a group of right-wing Japanese who built a lighthouse in the disputed Diaoyu Islands. Ordinary Chinese in

Hong Kong and Taiwan organized mass demonstrations in response to what was perceived as an aggressive action by the Japanese. By contrast, the Chinese government did not actively protest, and university officials at Shanghai's Fudan University in Mainland China, ripped down posters critical of Japan.[7]

One version of popular nationalism in China is cultural nationalism, whose carriers and interpreters are mostly intellectuals. They may have close relations with the government, but they also attempt to represent the will of the people. Cultural nationalists see the Chinese nation and Chinese people as being rooted in Confucian tradition and philosophy. Cultural nationalism emphasizes the ideological function of traditional Chinese culture in maintaining political order.[8] While state nationalism and cultural nationalism overlap and influence each other in practice, they may however also undermine each other with conflicting hidden agendas. The complex relationship between them will be explored in our discussion of the politics of national identity (chapters 2-4).

There is a further distinction between super and ethno-nationalisms. In the process of maintaining the existing 'empire', a super or pan-Chinese nationalism invents and promotes the notion of *da zhonghua minzu*, a set of shared values and cultural identities that could hold the Chinese peoples (including 55 ethnic minorities as well as the Han) together.[9] It emphasizes a Chinese national identity which is beyond any modern political ideological differences, and attempts to overcome the narrow definition of the Chinese as Han.

One particular version of Chinese super-nationalism is overseas Chinese nationalism, or a *borderless nationalism* that is common among overseas Chinese. Overseas Chinese patriots are regarded as a constructive force for China's economic development, and as a 'bridge' across the Taiwan Strait that will lead toward political unification.[10] At various international conferences, in recent years, Chinese scholars overseas have presented many more papers on Chinese nationalism than on Chinese democracy.[11] Many Chinese students have become more nationalistic than democratic, as shown by the decrease in students' participation in overseas democratic movements and the increase in their defense and protection of China's international image.[12] Many overseas Chinese students were angry and disappointed at NBC's negative coverage of the Chinese Team in 1996. A committee of Chinese engineering and science graduate students at Harvard and Berkeley has through the Internet gathered more than 3,500 e-mailed 'signatures' in order to wage a cyberspace campaign against the television reporting of the Chinese Team. They have also raised over $36,000 from supporters in the U.S.[13] This reflects heightened overseas Chinese nationalism.

By contrast, in China in the process of moving from 'empire' to nation ethno-nationalism has emerged.[14] Ethno-nationalisms always emphasize one ethnic nationality, based on a unique culture and history, and always stress identity difference, as in the now-familiar claim that, 'We are different from the Han (*Hanren*)'. Ethno-nationalism reflects the cultural reconstruction of ethnic identities as, for example, in Tibet and Xinjiang. Ethno-nationalism has been greater during the 1980s and 1990s than in any previous decade, with some significant exceptions, such as Xinjiang in the 1930s and 1940s.[15] The rise of ethno-nationalism and the resurgence of feelings of national cultural identity among minorities was, in part, a reaction against the savage assimilation with China and the Han that occurred during the Cultural Revolution. It was also the result of the collapse of the Marxist-Leninist governments in Eastern Europe and of a worldwide culture in which indigenous people everywhere have begun to play an increasingly prominent role.[16]

Nationalism can also be characterized as either 'hot' or 'cool'. 'Hot' nationalism is more emotional and irrational, while 'Cool' nationalism is more rational and less emotional. Chinese liberal-minded scholars, including those overseas, propose a *rational* nationalism in which China would maintain its openness and compete with other nation-states in a civilized and cooperative way.[17] It is argued that Chinese industrialization requires a strong nationalism and that if nationalism is related to capitalism, it is more likely to be rational and cooperative, as shown in the case of today's South Korea and Japan.[18] For Chinese nationalists, Chinese nationalism was and still is weak and defensive when compared with Western nationalism. As Wang Gungwu has observed:

> This form of nationalism [a constructive face of nationalism in the post-colonial states] was used to rally disparate peoples to create new nations. It was often highly defensive, but over time, it has matured considerably in most of these new nation-states. The word can still arouse some enthusiasm but now rarely produces the violent emotions that had originally been such an essential part of it. Why does it still remind us of fearsome power when it applies to China?[19]

2. National Identities

As noted above, nationalism consists, in part, of a sense of belonging to the nation, a sense of security, a feeling of national pride and attachment to the nation. All of these are inextricably linked to national identity. There are several contending views of Chinese national identity.

Statist and Socialist Identity

In constructions of statist and socialist identity, the Chinese nation is identified with the Chinese Party/state, the CCP and socialism. The key element of Chinese nationalism is loyalty to communist Party-state institutions, which forms an essential part of the Chinese national identity (chapter 2).

Han Identity

In an exclusivist Han view of national identity, 'the Chinese' are defined as 'the Han', a nationality said to encompass the PRC and the 'compatriots' of Taiwan, Hong Kong, and Macao. Moreover, China is seen as a Han-dominated nation-state, with the Han identified as the 'core' of the Chinese nation, entitled to their own state. It has been taken for granted by most people, including Sun Yat-sen and Mao Zedong, that the country is rightfully dominated by the Han, even if official state policy has condemned Han chauvinism and defined China as a poly-ethnic political community. (For a critique of this view see chapter 4.) A point which should be made clear is that Han identity is not defined in terms of race, simply because the so-called 'yellow race' is thought to include Japanese, Koreans and others. Unlike some other nationalisms, Chinese nationalism does not link its nation to the notion of race.

Cultural Identity

In the model of Chinese cultural identity, 'the Chinese' are defined as a community of Chinese speakers who share Chinese culture, in particular Confucianism, regardless of their ethnic origins and political beliefs (chapter 4). This includes Chinese elsewhere around the world. This Confucian definition of Chinese identity, based on culture rather than ethnicity, strives to incorporate other peoples into a Confucian civilization.[20] Nevertheless, a cultural definition of 'the Chinese' may elide substantial political divisions, as in the debate over the Taiwan question (chapter 5).

Civic and Territorial Identity

In a view of national identity, based on civic and territorial identity, all people living in the territories of the PRC are seen as Chinese citizens, regardless of their ethnic, cultural and 'racial' background (chapter 4). This definition of 'the Chinese' contains a modern liberal element of national identity: the liberal notion of modern citizenship. We can trace this definition back to Liang Qichao, who urged that a 'greater nationalism' *(da minzuzhuyi)* be created to bring the Manchus, Mongols, Uighur, and Tibetans into the nation; to Sun Yat-sen, who spoke about the need to rise above existing ethnic identities to create a new 'national people'; and to Chiang Kai-shek, who argued that ethnic minorities could have no separate identity since they inhabited peripheral regions which were already part of the greater Chinese race.[21] One Chinese scholar argues, that today, when ninety-five percent of Chinese people accept China's civic and territorial national identity, a modern notion of the Chinese nation-state should be well established. For this scholar, China's problem is not the separatism of Tibet and Xinjiang, but rather the failure of the Chinese Party/state to develop a modern notion of the Chinese nation-state. In this sense, China must still be regarded as a nationless state.[22]

The above four definitions of national identity can be categorized according to two dimensions: the relative strengths of national identity: weak versus strong; and the sources of national identity: tradition versus modernity. (see Table 1.1)

Although these four versions of Chinese national identity below are neatly pigeon-holed here, the complex practices of national identity in China always defy such a systematic intellectual definition. The four manifestations of national identity are overlapping, and national identity should be seen as an ongoing process rather than a fixed set of boundaries. Today, for example, Hong Kong and Taiwanese popular culture has a significant role to play in the re-definition of 'Chineseness'. Indeed, Hong Kong and Taiwanese popular culture, including music, film, television, literature, advertisements, décor and attire, are flooding the Mainland market. A 1993 survey, in Beijing, revealed that, of the students surveyed,

47.4 percent preferred foreign or dubbed films; 44.9 percent indicated a liking for Hong Kong or Taiwanese films; whereas only 6.6 percent preferred Mainland films.

Table 1.1   Characters of National Identity Constructs

		Sources of National identity	
		Traditional	Modern
The Strengths of National Identity	Weak	Han national identity	Socialist national identity
	Strong	Confucian cultural national identities	Civic and territorial national identity

The influence of Hong Kong and Taiwanese popular culture is reflected in the following trends: the new 'giant stars' of Hong Kong and Taiwan outsell their Mainland counterparts; Hong Kong and Taiwanese-style karaoke, KTV, bars, restaurants and shops are sweeping across the Mainland; Taiwan and Hong Kong writers, Qiong Yao, San Mao, Yi Shu, Gu Long and Jin Yong are some of the most widely read authors on the Mainland. Also. mainland Chinese increasingly use the non-simplified characters typically used in Hong Kong and Taiwan; and an increasing number of words derived from Hong Kong English [such as *leishe* (laser), *dishi* (taxi), and *bashi* (bus), etc.], and a mock Hong Kong accent, are being used in China.

One may argue that the geographically peripheral Chinese societies of Hong Kong and Taiwan, as well as other overseas Chinese communities, are mounting a challenge to the centre. More importantly, the statist and socialist national identity of China has been challenged by the return of Hong Kong to China, because it is difficult to ask the people of Hong Kong to accept this socialist definition of 'the Chinese' and the Chinese state which is no longer useful in dealing with Taiwan. Likewise, the rise of Taiwanese nationalism raises questions about the notion of a pan-Chinese identity, with the concept of Han-Confucian-Chinese at its centre (chapter 5). The most serious challenge to the statist, socialist, and Han national identities comes from ethno-nationalism and secessionist movements, that have denied Chinese national identity and invented their own national identities, and from Taiwan, where a new Taiwanese national identity has emerged in opposition to Chinese national identity (chapter 5). This gives rise to the national identity question in China.

3. National Identity Problems in China

The national identity problem challenges the unity and legitimacy of China, highlighting the tenuous relationship between the center and the peripheries. It is a problem concerning the boundaries of China, and a problem of secession or unification which involves the modification of national boundaries. The key issue of China's national identity problem is that certain sections of peoples, such as some Tibetans, do not identify themselves with the existing Chinese nation-state where they live, but seek an independent entity through the construction of their cultural and ethnic identities.

Growing secessionist movements in Tibet and Xinjiang highlight the exigency of the national identity problem, and raise the question of whether China will follow the Soviet Union and Yugoslavia in the direction of disintegration (chapter 6). Particular attention should be paid to the Tibetan secessionists who 'manufacture a picture of past glories which accord more with current political needs than with realities'.[23] Unlike the secessionists in Xinjiang, the Tibetans constitute a 'centralized' rather than a 'dispersed' ethnic system, with the Dalai Lama as their spiritual and political leader. In fact, the clergy took the lead in the separatist demonstrations between 1987 to 1989.[24] Unlike the Yi and Bai in Yunnan, the Tibetans are not only 'centralized' but also 'awakened'. And, unlike the Inkatha Freedom Party in South Africa, they have a good international image as an admirably spiritual people and non-violent victims to be sympathized with. Moreover, they strive to build a democratic Tibet; and the Tibetan government in exile elected an assembly in 1960, and has speeded up the democratic process since 1991.

It should be noted that there are quite a few minorities who do not have separatist aspirations, for example, those in Guizhou, Guangxi and

Yunan and Western Hunan. The Yi, for instance, have a notion of national identity, but no conception of state. In popular legend, the Yi and the Han are believed to be brothers. The Dai, on the other hand, are dispersed across China, Burma and Thailand. The group is too diverse to form a political power demanding an independent state; and, more importantly, the Dai did not develop a modern notion of nation-state until the 1960s. In the past, the Dai people crossed national borders with relative freedom. In the 1960-1970s, however, border controls were tightened, and those crossing borders without permission were regarded as 'traitors'. New passport requirements and the raising of the PRC flag at border crossings have contributed to the development of a sense of national identity.

4. The National Identity Problem and the Rise of Nationalism

The book focuses on the national identity question which it considers a fundamental source of the rise of nationalism.[25] It will examine in detail the close association between the national identity problem and the rise of Chinese nationalism and identifies the national identity problem as the substantive issue facing China. Certainly, in this context, we disagree with Whiting's argument that 'the varying virulence of assertive nationalism is more a function of factional politics than of substantive issues'.[26]

In the 1990s, the Chinese nation-state has confronted the most serious national identity problem: the possibility of disintegration. The collapse of communism in the Soviet Union and Eastern Europe forced Chinese Communist leaders to redefine and re-adjust Communist ideology by supplementing it with more nationalist characteristics so that it could be a more persuasive and more effective means of defending the legitimacy of the government. Wang Huning, former Professor of the Political Science Department at Fudan University and now one of President Jiang Zemin's newest strategists, has suggested that 'nationalism is a useful tool' in state building.[27] Yan Zhu, a researcher at the General Staff Department of the People's Liberation Army, has argued that China should combat America's strategy to split China by launching new drives to 'promote a combination of loyalty and patriotism' among its peoples.[28] In fact, the first international conference on culture after the 1989 Tiananmen event was about Confucian thought.[29]

It is clear now that Chinese neo-nationalism is an attempt to defend the unity of the Chinese nation-state through the invention of a pan-

Chinese national identity. For Chinese nationalists, China's unity must largely be maintained by the strength and content of a modern national identity, or a set of shared values and goals, or a world view that unites the Chinese people as a nation in an era of increasing economic engagement with the world, and far-reaching social and political changes. Furthermore, Chinese nationalism provides an alternative ideology to the declining official doctrine. More fundamentally, neo-Chinese nationalism delivers a justification for the foundation of the Chinese nation-state and for reunification with Taiwan. Chinese nationalism is officially sponsored and sanctioned by the state, which considers political and cultural reconstruction as China's only road to political and economic security.

Chinese nationalism can also be seen as a response to the sympathy the USA expresses towards Tibet and Taiwan (this will be discussed in section 6). It is also a reaction to the rise of ethno-nationalisms and secessionist movements. Super-nationalism and ethno-nationalism are mutually interactive. While ethno-nationalism and secessionist movements stimulate and promote pan-Chinese nationalism, Chinese pan-nationalism also promotes and stimulates the development of ethnic nationalism.

To support the above argument, let us look at some Chinese writings on nationalism. Zhao Jun, for example, clearly states that when we study Chinese nationalism, we are actually studying all the most important domestic problems of the Chinese nation. Nowadays, the political and economic realities of everyday life make people feel that nationalism is an urgent matter. For today's China, the danger of separation comes not only from Taiwanese and Tibetan exiles, but also from regional differences and from the social-psychological imbalances caused by substantial economic changes in some areas. For the author, no matter what type of political system China may develop, the nation must maintain its national integrity. Without political unification, China will be a disintegrating country.[30]

Shi Zhong comments that many Western scholars blithely predict the disintegration of China, and suggest that separation is better than unification. They even play up the 'new archaeological discovery' that originally China was not one nation. Many scholars in China have also been influenced by such Western viewpoints. They regard separation as beneficial, and publish 'creative suggestions' to this end one after another. However, Shi Zhong throws some doubts on these ideas and suggestions. He asserts that the Chinese will take seriously the situation in the former Yugoslavia, and carefully explore the new possibilities opened up by Chinese nationalism.[31]

5. The National Identity Question, Historical Legacies and the 'Empire Thesis'

The national identity problem that today's China faces has to be understood in historical terms. China was itself incorporated into the Qing empire that spanned Inner Asia and East Asia. The Qing was the most successful of China's dynasties in terms of its territorial expansion. Under the Qing empire, ethnic minorities were colonized. When the Qing was overthrown in the 1911 Revolution, loyalty to the Qing dynasty did not automatically translate into loyalty to the Republic of China; for example, the Mongols never considered themselves part of a *Zhongguo* (China).[32] From the outset, the new republic struggled to retain all the Qing territories in the new nation-state. Like its predecessors, the People's Republic of China worked hard to retain the inherited Qing's territories through the consistent repression of independence movements in Tibet, Xinjiang, and Inner Mongolia.[33]

There are two opposite processes in the building of the Chinese nation-state. One involves the retention of territories of the former Qing 'empire' while building a new modern nation-state. In such a move, super or pan-nationalism always employs visions of a broad political community binding together different ethnic groups and nationalities, and preventing the disintegration of the nation. Liang Qichao invented a pan-Chinese identity in order to retain the Qing peripheries. As Rawski points out, 'Only a definition of the nation that transcends Han identity can thus legitimately lay claim to the peripheral regions inhabited by non-Han peoples, since these claims rest on the empires created by the Mongols and the Manchus'.[34] Following Liang, today's Chinese nationalists continue to construct a pan-Chinese national identity (chapter 4).

Another process moves from 'empire' to nations and often involves ethno-nationalism, which is said to lead inevitably to the proliferation of smaller and more ethnically homogeneous states. And so we come to the 'empire thesis'. The core idea of this thesis is that China is the 'last empire', as all other empires (such as the British, Ottoman and Russian) have collapsed. The rise and continuing persistence of ethnic nationalisms and independence movements in the PRC are seen as part of the logic of the breakdown of the world's 'last empire' into several nations.

There are different versions of this thesis. Victor Louis, a member of the KGB, presented his version of the empire thesis as a rationale intended to justify a Soviet 'war of liberation' against the People's Republic of

China, in 1979. Louis outlined three key ideas of this thesis. First, the present Chinese leadership, continuing the traditional imperial expansionist line, was laying claim to vast areas of the Soviet Far East, Siberia, and Central Asia. Second, for several decades the peoples of the outlying regions of China, all along the Sino-Soviet border, had been waging an unrelenting struggle for their national self-determination and independence.[35] Third, the solution, according to Louis, was to grant independence to the peoples of Manchuria, Mongolia, Eastern Turkestan, and Tibet. For him, this was a just solution of the national identity problem (in his terms, the 'nationalities question'), and this would largely remove the threat of Chinese expansion toward the adjacent territories.[36] Louis predicted that future developments would show how soon the national aspirations of the Manchu, Mongols, Uighurs and Tibetans could become reality.[37]

Zhuang Wanshou, a Taiwanese scholar, presents another version of the empire thesis. He argues that Taiwan's independence movement is historically determined by the inevitable breakdown of the Chinese empire.[38] Similarly, it is often said that Tibetan independence should be seen as a just and ineluctable outcome of this same historical trajectory.

Chinese nationalists certainly dislike the empire thesis, and are keen to learn a lesson from the Soviet Union, where the emergence of Russian ethnic nationalism played a decisive role in generating centrifugal forces which tore the Soviet Union apart.[39] According to S.N. Eisenstadt, given the centre-periphery relations in the former U.S.S.R., a collapse of the Soviet empire was inevitable. Historically, a highly active Russian centre exercised centralized control over a politically passive periphery. However, during the Soviet period the political centre mobilized the periphery and activated it socially and politically to such a degree that it changed the balance between the centre and the periphery. The totalitarian regime maintained effectively tight controls, forbidding the formation of autonomous subsystems, but legitimating national cultures within a universalistic framework. Once the totalitarian controls weakened, ethnic tensions were enhanced by the rise of ethno-nationalism, leading to the break-down of the empire system (chapter 6).[40]

6.   The National Identity Problem and the Nation-State System

The national identity question can be further understood in terms of the nation-state system. It is fundamentally produced and reproduced by the nation-state system in which the world is divided into nations, and which, as Anthony Smith argues, is likely to remain the only realistic widespread popular ideal of community.[41] In the nation-state system, political boundaries should be clearly defined and exclusively controlled by one state, and the separation of countries ought to be maintained and supported by distinctive national identities. No matter how much cosmopolitanism, with the aid of the Internet and cultural exchange, doubts and despises nationalism, the Chinese sense of national belonging is likely to be reproduced and reinforced when Chinese travel around the world. For world travel requires the preparation of passports, which are ultimately certificates of national belonging, and encounters with the often intractable 'Other' when applying for visas to enter foreign lands. It is absolutely true that feelings of nationalism do exist. It is not reasonable to deny their existence. Indeed, rising Chinese nationalism is likely to be a permanent structural political condition and a driving force in twenty-first century China.

The rise of Chinese nationalism can be further understood through a brief elaboration of Chinese nationalist perceptions of the USA. Chinese nationalists suggest that the USA's policies toward China are part of an effort to contain China and prevent it from becoming a superpower to challenge its dominant position in the current international system.

Wars of words were waged between China and the US over such issues as: American criticism of China's human rights record; American sales of weapons to Taiwan; American reluctance to grant China Most Favoured Nation Status; American sanctions on China after the military crackdown on students in 1989; American pressure on China over Chinese sales of missiles to Pakistan and Iran; disputes over intellectual property rights, which started in 1990 and culminated at the beginning of 1995; the American show of force in the Taiwan Straits during China's military exercises in 1996; American opposition to Beijing's bid for the 2000 Olympic Games,[42] and, what was seen to be a hostile reception of the Chinese Olympic team at the opening ceremony of the Atlanta Olympic Games; the American blockade of China's entry to GATT; American policies towards Tibet and Taiwan; and last, but not least, strategies for containing China, which were devised by a circle of US intellectuals, but widely believed in China to be official American policy, not merely academic views.

Chinese nationalists' suspicion of the West deepened after the publication of Professor Samuel P. Huntington's article, 'The Clash of Civilizations'.[43] In it Huntington argues that modern geopolitical struggles are not ideologically motivated, but are better described as clashes of different civilizations. He suggests that the biggest threat to Western civilization is Islamic and Confucian culture, and thus the West should be alert to a Confucian and Islamic alliance. Mainland intellectuals were especially outspoken in their opposition to Huntington's theory.[44]

Some Chinese nationalists believe that Western countries have done everything they can to weaken Russia's standing, and have refused to provide Russia with sufficient assistance as it struggles internally with its reform program. They are worried that if China were to initiate the political reform promoted by the West, it would share a similar fate to that of Russia. Coincidentally, from 1994 to 1995, arguments supporting a policy to contain China appeared in America.[45] This led some Chinese nationalists to the conclusion that containing China on all fronts has become a fundamental policy of the United States government, and that a new cold war aimed at China is being initiated by the United States.[46] Typical anti-Western opinions can be seen in Wang Shan's *Viewing China with a Third Eye* as well as the follow-up *Viewing China with a Fourth Eye*. The most important work in this genre is Song Qiang et al., in their book *China Can Say No*.[47] It should be noted that articles in the increasingly popular genre of chest-thumping nationalist literature are largely written by officials, army officers and government researchers, rather than a mere band of nettled intellectuals.[48]

7. A Nationalist Solution to the National Identity Question[49]

A nationalist approach to the national identity question emphasizes the priority of the political community, and focuses on the inability of democracy to solve the problem of what constitutes the membership of a political community.

From a nationalist perspective, when there is a dispute about the membership of a political community, democracy is seemingly unable to provide a universally-accepted criterion for deciding which people and territories are to be included in the polity.[50] The nationalist approach, therefore, appeals to the common tradition, history and culture of a 'nation', relying on commonalties in biology, psychology and spirituality. Why do nationalists appeal to history? It is the uniqueness of history which legitimates claims over territories, and grants at least some power to eradicate disputes.

The Chinese nationalist management of the national identity problem establishes an axiomatic rule that citizens and politicians must acknowledge the priority of the right of the community over individuals, and that the boundary of the nation-state should be maintained through the promotion of a strong national identity and cultural nationalism. Nationalists stress the will of the national community, rather than individualism and consent, as the source of governmental legitimacy and are likely to oppose the democratic principles that will be used by sub-ethno-nationalists for their independence movements. A nationalist approach justifies the power of the state to do whatever is necessary to preserve the integrity of national boundaries, and endorses the use of force if required to defend the superiority of national interests and the national territory. As Hertz remarks:

> The idea of the national territory is an important element of every modern national ideology. Every nation regards its country as an inalienable sacred heritage, and its independence, integrity, and homogeneity appear bound up with national security, independence and honor. This territory is often described as the body of the national organism and the language as its soul.[51]

In the Chinese context, the former Chinese Foreign Minister Qian Qichen has warned,

> The United States is a major power and has its own dignity, and so does China. For the Chinese people who suffered grievously from aggression and bullying by foreign powers throughout modern times, state sovereignty and territorial integrity are of paramount importance. When it comes to acts of encroachment upon China's sovereignty and obstructing its peaceful reunification, the Chinese government has no choice but to react strongly. I would like to reiterate that on the Taiwan question, a question of important principle bearing on China's fundamental interests, the Chinese government

remains firm and unshakable....Some proponents are still nostalgic of the Cold War strategy of containment and confrontation against China. This is, no doubt, reactionary and retrogressive.[52]

8. The Centrality of the National Identity Question for Democratization[53]

Constrained by the framework of the nation-state system, democratic development, in fact, presupposes and requires a national setting. Mill argued long ago that, 'It is in general a necessary condition of free institutions that the boundaries of [representative] governments should coincide in the main with those of nationalities'.[54] Following Mill, Emerson pointed out that democracy requires a national setting, or at least flourishes best where the people concerned are knit together by emotional and traditional bonds. Ghia Nodia recently endorsed this view in the context of the democratization of Eastern Europe, where nationalism, as a historical force, has provided a foundation for the political units of new democratic governments.[55]

The national identity question has enormous implications for democratization. One of the earliest political scientists to seriously call attention to the national identity issue in the context of democratization was Dankwart Rustow. In *A World of Nations*, he explored a whole range of sequences of political modernization and argued that the political ingredients of the modern nation-state, namely unity (identity), authority and equality 'are effectively assembled one by one rather than at once, and that political participation and equality should be last'.[56] Similarly, Robert Dahl believes that agreements about the national boundary are prior to democratization:

> We cannot solve the problems of the proper scope and domain of democratic units from within democratic theory. Like the majority principle, the democratic process presupposes a unit. The criteria of the democratic process presuppose the rightfulness of the unit itself. If the unit itself is not proper or rightful - if its scope or domain is not justifiable - then it cannot be made rightful simply by democratic procedures.[57]

In their recent book, Juan Linz and Alfred Stepan concur with Rustow and Dahl's that the resolution of the national identity problem, or 'stateness' as they term it, is logically prior to the creation of democratic institutions. As Linz and Stepan put it, paraphrasing the well-known Barrington Moore formula: 'No state, no democracy', or, in their other words, 'Without a state, there can be no citizenship; without citizenship, there can be no democracy'.[58] For them, an integral state capable of upholding its laws in its territory is a precondition for democracy.

One of the key threats to such a state - and, therefore, one of the key obstacles to democratization - is 'ethnic conflict in a multinational state'. It is particularly dangerous when ethnic minorities are large and concentrated, and when ethnic divisions are deep and routinized. Diamond, Linz and Lipset have also pointed out, in *Democracy in Developing Countries*, that ethnic divisions 'have presented a stiff challenge to democratic regimes; the greater the cultural differences, socioeconomic imbalances, historic rivalries, and the centralization of demographic structure, the stiffer the challenge has been'.[59] Democratization, in fact, aggravates such divisions by 'awakening' national consciousness, enfranchising minorities and stimulating political competition. As Huntington points out,

> The initiation of elections forces political leaders to compete for votes. In many situations, the easiest way to win votes is to appeal to tribal, ethnic, and religious constituencies. Democratization thus promotes communalism and ethnic conflict, and relatively few new democracies have structured their institutions to minimize incentives to make such appeals.[60]

In such a context, authoritarian leaders have often resisted democratization for fear of national disintegration because democratic transitions often put the polis/demos questions at the centre of politics.[61] This is well analyzed by Mark R. Thompson:

> Non-democratic regimes in countries with nation-stateness problems hesitate to democratize because protecting rulers' common interests is more difficult if the state in which they are served ceases to exist. The rise of anti-state nationalism in the Soviet Union and Yugoslavia is one of the main reasons why democratization failed at the union level in these two countries. Gorbachev's 'shift to the right' in 1990 has been explained by his concern that separatism in the Baltics and the Caucasus endangered the territorial integrity of the Soviet Union. The rejection of democratic reforms by the League of Communists of Yugoslavia in January 1990 after most of the revolutions of Eastern Europe had already begun is only understandable when the independence movements in Croatia and Slovenia are considered.

> The Honecker regime in the German Democratic Republic (GDR) was unwilling to negotiate an exit from communism at a time when this was already taking place in Hungary and Poland.... due to the East German leadership's fear for the survival of the state.[62]

Yet one reservation about the discussion of the significance of the national identity problem in democratization is that it is often used as an excuse by dictators to deter democracy. For example, the ruling parties in South Korea and Taiwan for years denied democracy to their people on the grounds of potential national division and Communist menace. But a more important cause for the insufficient discussion of the national identity issue is the tendency for it to be seen as no more than an accidental, trivial and second-order issue.

While it is true that totalitarian and authoritarian regimes have often played on the fear of national disintegration as a deterrent from democratization, few would argue that the fear is groundless. The fact that some non-democratic regimes have succeeded in delaying democratization under the pretext of safeguarding national identity and territorial integrity, in itself gives us some reason to examine the role of the national identity problem in democratization, and offer some clues as to how to avoid having democratization frustrated by ethnic divisions.

The national identity problem can be seen as a long term background factor to the whole process of democratization. If the political and economic problems concerning the allocation and distribution of power and resources persist for years, and constitutional problems for decades, then the problem of national identity persists for centuries. However, in so far as successful democratization depends on the resolution of the national identity problem, it is a first-order issue. Disputes over the national identity question concern the size and membership of a political community, and they can jeopardize the unity of a nation-state. What might be involved is reunification or independence, citizenship, official language policy and a range of other issues, all of which, due to perceptions of zero-sum games, are often resistant to resolution through compromise. The national identity question touches upon the essential and difficult question of the distribution of power and resources among nationalities.

The secessionist movement poses a thorny question, and creates difficulties for Chinese democratization, but does not make it impossible. In order to avoid misunderstanding, let us first acknowledge that the Party-state's refusal to share powers and resources is a bigger obstacle to democratization in China than secessionism;[63] and that the Party-state may use the national boundary problem as an excuse to delay democratization. Nevertheless, secessionism makes democratization more difficult in China than in situations where there is no such national identity problem (chapter 7).

The national identity question in China indicates the special circumstances under which nationalism conflicts with democracy. The nature and forms of the national identity question also influence and shape the course of democratization and affects the consolidation of democracy, for, other things being equal, it is much easier to initialize and consolidate democratization in a state without national identity problems than in a state with such problems. It is not surprising then that democratization has proceeded more smoothly in Poland, Portugal, Greece, Chile, Uruguay and Argentina than in the former Soviet Union, Yugoslavia and Romania (chapter 7).

Notes

1   Anthony D. Smith, 'The Problem of National Identity: Ancient, Medieval and Modern?' in *Ethnic and Racial Studies*, Volume 17, Number 3, July 1994, pp. 375-99.

2   Ibid.

3   Wang Gungwu, 'The Revival of Chinese Nationalism', Lecture Series 6, International Institute for Asian Studies, Leiden 1996, p. 20.

4   Louis L. Snyder, *The New Nationalism*, Ithaca, Cornell University Press, 1968.

5   Lucian Pye, 'How China's Nationalism was Shanghaied', in J. Unger (ed.), *Chinese Nationalism*, New York, M.E. Sharpe, Inc., 1996, pp. 86-112.

6   Li Xing, 'Lun guojia minzu zhuyi gainian' (On the concept of state nationalism), *Beijing daxue xuebao (jiexue shehui kexue ban)*, 1995, No. 4, pp. 74-80.

7   Bruce Gilley, 'Potboiler Nationalism', Vol. 159, No. 40, *Far Eastern Economic Review*, 3 October 1996, p. 24.

8   Chen Xi, 'Nationalism Among Chinese Intellectuals', in *China Strategic Review*, Vol. 1, No. 6, 1996, p. 10.

9   By comparison, Japanese nationalism advocated Pan-Asianism with regional implications. The issue of Japanese national identity has often been located in foreign relations, for example, re-Asianization and irredentist claims over territory lost to Russia.

10   *The Peoples' Daily* (overseas edition), 26 January 1999, p. 5.

11   Baogang He's experience in various international conferences in recent years.

12   For a brief description of overseas Chinese nationalism in Australia, see Edmund Fung and Chen Jie, 'Changing Perceptions: The Attitudes of the PRC Chinese towards Australian and China, 1989-1996', Australia-Asia Papers, No. 78, Griffith University, 1996, pp. 21-22.

13   Pixley, 'Chinese Nationalists Rush the Net', *The Asian Wall Street Journal*, Monday, August 26, 1996, p. 10.

14   For the best account of this process, see Emerson, *From Empire to Nation.* Also see Wang Gungwu's discussion on the by-products of nationalism and Kamanka's ideas on proto-nationalism; see E. Kamenka (ed.), *Nationalism: The Evolution of the Idea*, London: Edward Arnold, 1976, p.14.

15   Mackerras, *China's Minority Cultures*, London, Melbourne, p. 207.

16   Ibid., pp. 214-5.

17   Wu Guoguang, 'Rational Nationalism as a Counterbalance against "Containing China"', *Twenty-First Century*, No. 34, April 1996, pp. 25-33; Chen Yan, 'On the Danger of Nationalism as a Dominant Ideology', *Twenty-First Century*, No. 38, December 1996, pp. 128-134.

18   As Fukuyama asserts, 'nationalism can coexist quite well with liberalism as long as the former becomes tolerant (in the sense that national identity and culture is open to other people). That is to say, national identity has to be pushed off into the realm of private life and culture, rather than being politicised and made the basis of legal rights. Alternatively, national pride can be sublimated into economic competition, as in the case of Japanese supercomputers.' Francis Fukuyama, 'Comments on Nationalism and Democracy', in L. Diamond and Marc F. Flattner, *Nationalism, Ethnic Conflict, and Democracy*, the Johns Hopkins Press, 1994, p. 26. European Sinologists are sceptical about rational nationalism, seeing it as potentially

dangerous (for example, Japanese and Nazi nationalisms were not rational), stressing the Han nationality as an ideological construction, and worrying that Chinese nationalism may take an offensive action to deal with the territorial issue of the South China Sea.

19   Wang Gungwu, 'The Revival of Chinese Nationalism', p. 6.

20   Evelyn S. Rawski, 'Presidential Address: Reenvisioning the Qing: The Significance of the Qing Period in Chinese History', *The Journal of Asian Studies*, vol. 55, no. 4, November 1996, p. 839.

21   Ibid., p. 839.

22   This view was expressed by Liu Suli, the manager of the Wanshan bookshop in our conversation in 1993. Professor John Fitzgerald has also concluded that China is a 'nationless state' since successive modern Chinese states have failed to create one 'imagined community' that would constitute the Chinese nation. See Fitzgerald, 'The Nationless Sate: The Search for a Nation in Modern Chinese Nationalism', in Jonathan Unger (ed.), *Chinese Nationalism*, New York, M.E. Sharpe, Armonk, 1996.

23   Mackerras, *China's Minority Cultures*, p. 217.

24   Ibid., p. 209.

25   A. Whiting identifies two sources of assertive nationalism in China: the leftist ideological faction and components of the PLA. See Whiting, 'Chinese Nationalism and Foreign Policy after Deng', *The China Quarterly*, No. 142, 1995, p. 15.

26   Whiting, 'Chinese Nationalism and Foreign Policy after Deng', p. 315.

27   Quoted by Chen Xi, 'Nationalism among Chinese intellectuals', *China Strategic Review*, Vol. 1, No. 6, 1996, pp. 9-10.

28   Bruce Gilley, 'Potboiler Nationalism', *Far Eastern Economic Reivew*, Vol. 159, No. 40, 3 October 1996, p. 23.

29   Chen Xi, 'Nationalism Among Chinese Intellectuals', in *China Strategic Review*, Vol. 1, No. 6, 1996, p. 10.

30   Zhao Jun, ' "Tianxia weigong" yu shiji zhijiao de zhongguo minzu zhuyi' ('Justice under the heaven' and Chinese nationalism at a centurial turn). *Strategy and Management*, January issue, 1996, pp.1-3.

31 Shi Zhong, 'Xifangren yanzhong de zhongguo minzu zhuyi' ('Chinese nationalism' in the eyes of Western people), *Strategy and Management*, January issue, 1996, pp. 20-26.

32 Rawski, 'Presidential Address', p. 840.

33 Ibid., p. 841.

34 Ibid., p. 841.

35 Victor Louis, *The Coming Decline of the Chinese Empire*, New York, Times Books, 1979, p. 186.

36 Ibid., p. 186.

37 Ibid., p. 187.

38 See Cheng-Feng Shih, ed., *Taiwan Nationalism*, Taipei: Qianfeng, 1994, pp. 276-7.

39 Wang Weimin and Yi Xiaohong, 'Minzu yishi: lijie qiansulian minzu wenti de guanjian' (National consciousness: understanding the crux of the national problem of the former Soviet Union), *Shanxi shida xuebao, Sheke ban* (Linfen), No. 4, 1996, pp. 17-21.

40 Teresa-Rakowska Harmstone, 'Soviet Nationalities and Perestroika', *Canadian Review of Studies in Nationalism*, XXIV, 1-2, 1997, p. 92.

41 Anthony Smith, *Nations and Nationalism in a Global Era*, Cambridge: Polity Press, 1995, pp. 147-160.

42 There is a widely accepted theory in China that Beijing's failure to win the 2000 Olympic Games was the result of a conspiracy by the English-speaking world to frustrate China. An upsurge of nationalism among Chinese intellectuals sprang up immediately after the failure of Beijing's bid.

43 S. Huntington 'The Clash of Civilizations?', *Foreign Affairs* Vol. 72, No. 3, Summer 1993, pp. 22-49.

44 Chen Xi, 'Nationalism Among Chinese Intellectuals', in *China Strategic Review*, Vol. 1, No. 6, 1996, p. 13.

45 Ibid., p. 13.

46 He Beilin, Preface to *China Can Say No*, *China Strategic Review*, Vol, 1 No. 8, 1996, pp. 11-12.

47 Chen Xi, 'Nationalism', p. 11.

48   Bruce Gilley, 'Potboiler Nationalism', p. 23.

49   The nationalist approach to the secessionist and independence problem is analytically distinguished from the democratic approach. It needs democratic support but at the same time will contradict and undermine democracy. Democratic management alone cannot fix the national identity problem either. It needs to be supplemented by economic measures and diplomatic efforts and cannot work without nationalism either.

50   See Frederick G. Whelan, 'Prologue: Democratic Theory and the Boundary Problem' in J. Roland Pennock and John W. Chapman (eds.), *Liberal Democracy: Nomos XXV.* NY: New York University Press, 1983.

51   Hertz, *Nationality in History and Politics*, pp. 150-1.

52   'Qian: Progress Made in Ties, But More Must Be Done', *Beijing Review*, Vol. 38, No. 43, (October 23-29, 1995), p. 14, in Hidenori Ijiri, 'The China-Taiwan Problem in Lieu of U.S.-Japan Leadership Sharing', *Issues and Studies*, 33, No. 5, May 1997, pp. 51-79.

53   The term 'centrality' of the national boundary/identity question does not refer to the first priority of national issues perceived by people. People in Taiwan, for example, may think the most important question is not unification, but rather security, stability, economic development, or whatever it may be. The results of one survey show that democracy and stability issues have the greatest impact on voters' evaluations of parties, followed by economic and national identity issues, with environmental issues having the smallest impact. See John Fuh-sheng Hsieh and Emerson M.S. Niou, 'Issue Voting in the Republic of China on Taiwan's 1992 Legislative Yuan Election', *International Political Science Review*, vol. 17, no. 1, 1996, pp. 13-27: 13.

54   Emerson, *From Empire to Nation*, p. 219. David Miller has also defended the principle of nationality, that is, that each nation should have its own sovereign state. See David Miller, *On Nationality*, Oxford, Clarendon Press, 1995.

55   Ghia Nodia, 'Nationalism and Democracy', in Diamond et al., *Nationalism, Ethnic Conflict, and Democracy*, pp. 7-9.

56   Dankwart A. Rustow, *A World of Nations: Problems of Political Modernization*, Washington, D.C.: the Brookings Institute, 1967, p. 126.

57   R. Dahl, *Democracy and Its Critics*, New Haven, Yale University Press, 1989, p. 207.

58   Juan J. Linz and A. Stepan, *Problems of Democratic Transition and Consolidation: Southern Europe, South America, and Post-Communist Europe*, Baltimore, The John Hopkins University Press, 1996, p. 26.

59   Juan J. Linz and Seymour Martin Lipset, *Democracy in Developing Countries: Asia*, Colorado: Lynne Rienner Publishers, 1987.

60   S. Huntington, 'Democracy for the Long Haul', *Journal of Democracy*, vol. 7, no. 2, 1996, p. 6.

61   See Juan J. Linz and A. Stepan, *Problems of Democratic Transition*, p. 29.

62   Mark R. Thompson, 'No Exit: 'Nation-stateness' and Democratization in the German Democratic Republic', *Political Studies*, vol. XLIV, 1996, pp. 267-8.

63   Vanhanen reaches the conclusion that the concentration of economic and intellectual resources in many countries explains the modest positive correlation between the Index of Ethnic Homogeneity and the Index of Democratization. Tatu Vanhanen, *Politics of Ethnic Nepotism: India as an Example*, Berkshire, Sterling Publishers Ltd, 1992, p. 28.

2 State Nationalism in Post-4th June China

This chapter aims to describe the content and strategies of the CCP's patriotic indoctrination; examine how state nationalism is shaped by factional politics within the CCP; and analyse the dilemma of Chinese state nationalism against its professed objectives. The first section describes the CCP's strategies to create a patriotic atmosphere. The second examines the instrumental nature of the CCP's promotion of traditional culture. Section three discusses the Party's strategy to create a sense of crisis among the people. While state nationalism is treated as more or less static and examined substantively in the first two sections, section 3 attempts to examine it both substantively and chronologically, so as to reveal how state nationalism in China is influenced by factional politics, as demonstrated by the fluctuation in the case of anti-peaceful-evolution. Section four then outlines the definitive features of state nationalism. This is followed, in section 5, by an exploration of how state nationalism is dogged by the class concept, and how the CCP plays down 'class' in order to establish a broader base of authority. In the concluding section, we examine the overall dilemma of state nationalism and venture to offer an explanation as to why it is not achieving its set goals of nation-state building.

1.   Creating a Patriotic Atmosphere: Saturation Bombardment

Jiang Zemin launched the patriotic campaigns, soon after the Tiananmen crackdown, in a speech entitled 'Carry on and Develop the Tradition of Patriotism in New Historical Circumstances'. Li Ruihuan, head of the CCP's Ideological Leading Small Group, followed this up with his speech, on 10 January 1990, in the People's Daily, 'Some Questions Relevant to Enhancing the Outstanding Elements of National Culture'. Deng Xiaoping boosted the campaigns with his speech 'Revive the Chinese Nation', which was published on 7 April 1990. The campaign reached its peak in 1994 with the publication of the CCP's 'Outline for the Implementation of Patriotic Education' and received another boost from the handover of Hong Kong in July 1997.

Patriotic education is intended for all Chinese citizens alike, but the main target of the campaign, as emphasised by Jiang Zemin, Li Ruihuan and Wang Renzhi, is the younger generation. This focus on the young is premised on the CCP's diagnosis that a major cause of the students' protest is the waning of patriotism under the influence of 'cultural nihilism', or 'national nihilism' which permeated intellectual debates in the 1980s, and 'bourgeois liberalisation' within the CCP under Hu Yaobang and Zhao Ziyang, which encouraged 'national nihilism' in the society. On 16 July 1989, at the closing session of the Standing Committee of the Chinese Communist League, Jiang reiterated that young people should be educated in patriotism, socialism and national self-respect in order to produce 'a new socialist generation with high ideals and moral standards, educated and disciplined' who can restore to China its past glory.[1] Needless to say, such a new generation would be more obedient and dedicated to the Party than the Tiananmen generation. However, patriotic education alone is not enough. It is complemented by tighter control of college students through a code of conduct, which came into effect on 17 November 1989, the very first article of which says that students must 'safeguard the interests of the motherland' and are forbidden to take part in 'any activities that harm the dignity and honour of the motherland'.[2]

With regard to society in general, patriotic education aims to cultivate 'patriotic sentiment', 'enhance political consciousness, and guide the Chinese people to establish correct ideals, convictions, a proper perspective of life and values'.[3] The national spirit is, so goes the argument, most significant in 'concentrating the strength of the nation and uniting people of all Chinese nationalities to fight for the rejuvenation of China'.[4] Perhaps another way of putting this is that all energies would be harnessed for the realisation of a more attractive national ideal instead of merely a socialist one, so that no energy would turn into actions that might harm the Party or its social order. This does not mean, of course, that the dream of national revival is not taken seriously. After all, China's modernisation drive in the last two decades is generally seen as another attempt after the Opium War to turn that dream into reality. But few would be so naive as to believe that the CCP fails to see the usefulness of the revivalist slogan in terms of legitimacy for its rule and mobilisation: what once was can be and will be again. Its appeal is such that it has become a clarion call for nationalists all over the world.

The CCP's basic campaign strategy can be described as a saturation bombardment aimed at maximising exposure of the patriotic message and hammer it into the young. Or as it is put in the *Beijing Review,* 'We will take a concerted effort in various quarters to create a strong atmosphere in which the entire Chinese people will be influenced by the patriotic ideas and spirit'.[5] This is achieved by mobilising schools, families and society, and making use of all possible media and occasions - opportunities include newspapers, radio, TV, cinemas, theatres, publications, national day, anniversaries and festivals.

Major state projects include the 'hundred books program' and the 'hundred films program', jointly designed and implemented in 1993-1994 by the Party's Department of Propaganda, the state Education Committee, the Ministry of Broadcasting, TV and Films, and the Ministry of Culture. For a period of over three months, a film with patriotic themes was screened on TV every day all over the country; and group viewing and follow-up discussion were often organised in the schools. Major publications include *The Spiritual Great Wall - the Chinese Patriotic Tradition*, edited by renowned conservative professor, Zhang Dainian; the 20-volume, state-sponsored *Love My China*; *Patriotic Education Series*, by Marxist historian Gong Shuduo and others; and *An Encyclopedia of National Disgrace*, which acknowledges support from Hu Qiaomu, Chen Muhua, Ma Wenrui, and the state council.

A second state project is the 'bases for patriotic education' conducted in a large number of Chinese cities, in the form of museums, memorial halls, historical sites or major construction projects. Nanjing boasts the largest number of such bases; and since September 1996, every primary and secondary school student in the city has been required to visit 40 compulsory and optional bases before they can graduate.[6] A third project is the daily raising of the national flag from the Tiananmen Square to the schools in the villages. When they reach 18, young people take an oath in front of the national flag at 'coming-of-age' ceremonies. At the same time, hundreds and thousands of seminars, public lectures, concerts and exhibitions have taken place throughout the country in order to drum up patriotic enthusiasm; and the mass media are filled with patriotic propaganda.

Patriotic education is wide-ranging in its content, including, as outlined in the Beijing Review:

> ...the long history of China, the development course of the Chinese nation which has pursued greater strength and indominability, and the country's outstanding contributions to the civilisation of humanity; China's broad and profound traditional culture; basic national conditions; the political line of the Communist Party of China and construction achievements; democracy

and legality; national defence and security; national unity; and the principles of peaceful reunification, and one country two systems.[7]

This composition covers three main domains: history and traditional culture; the Party line; and institutions, laws and civic culture. Of those three domains, history and culture assume a more prominent role, whereas the Party line remains the overriding agenda. The promotion of 'people's democracy', political institutions and laws has little effect given the widespread cynicism about them. The socialist education is also confronted with insurmountable difficulties now that 'socialism with Chinese characteristics' is becoming little different from capitalism. For this reason, the Party line is often promoted, most earnestly by the conservatives, through a negative campaign that revives Mao's 'theory of peaceful evolution', rather than justified on its own merit.

For the same reason, the Party has to be content with less. Instead of attempting to indoctrinate the whole people in socialism and Marxism, it is taking a graded approach, scaling the requirement down for non-Party members and overseas Chinese. It is this approach that underlies Deng's well-known comment that 'We can't ask the patriotic compatriots of Hong Kong, Macao and Taiwan to support socialism... As for all the youth and citizens of the People's Republic of China, our requirement is certainly somewhat higher'.[8] Even the requirement for citizens varies. As Jiang Zemin put it, 'We should persistently educate the whole people, especially the young, in patriotism, collectivism, socialism...and educate the members of the Party, Communist Youth League and advanced elements in Communism'.[9] What is not acceptable is 'opposition to the socialist new China': 'What is love for the motherland', Deng once asked, 'if one is opposed to the socialist new China?'.[10] But not to oppose the socialist new China does not mean to support it. It would seem reasonable to conclude from this that the CCP's minimum requirement for patriotism is not to condemn socialism or challenge the Party. Other than that, the CCP no longer attempts to impose the Party's ideology on society at large although it does not tolerate open challenges to it.

2.   Instrumental Culture

The use of history in patriotic education is characterised by a balance between past glory and humiliation, and between the CCP's achievements and the country's historical constraints, or backward national conditions which the nation has to face. To stress both the Party's achievements and 'national conditions' is to say that the Party is the legitimate leader of the nation on account of those achievements; but historical conditions, not the Party, are to blame if it cannot achieve what is expected, and people should be more realistic in their expectations.

The role of traditional culture became increasingly prominent as a main component of patriotic education after Li Ruihuan's speech, 'Some Questions Relevant to Enhancing the Outstanding Elements of the National Culture'. In this speech, Li instructed the mass media and publishers to set up special columns and programs devoted to national culture and publish encyclopedias, dictionaries and books which will 'help people understand their cultural tradition correctly'.[11] A second instruction was to promote folk art - regional operas, dance, acrobatics, painting, calligraphy, etc. - by holding local and national competitions and concentrated performances. Cultural sites and relics, ancient texts and manuscripts are to be preserved, protected or restored. In addition, Li stressed the importance of creating a physical environment that exhibits distinct national features, which should be taken into account when building and renovating libraries, museums, theatres, schools, parks, bridges and so on.[12]

Furthermore, Li wants more books to be written for the younger generations about national heroes, historical figures, poets and writers; and substantially increase the weight of traditional culture in the textbooks for primary and tertiary students alike, particularly in four key subjects: Chinese, history, geography and politics. Since Jiang Zemin added cartoons to the ambit of his 'spiritual civilisation', the Department of Propaganda has instructed leading publishers of children's books to develop cartoons that 'express Chinese traditions and values', so that the likes of the Japanese *City Hunter* and Walt Disney's *The Lion King* could be abolished from China.[13]

This, of course, does not mean culture for culture's sake. Arts and culture serve two practical functions for the Party: as a tool for stability, which under the circumstances in post-Tiananmen China overrides anything else; and as an 'indicator of stability', or a showcase for it. Stability, as explained by Li, is economic, political and social; and in the speech he stresses that this cannot be achieved before 'stabilising the mood of the masses'. Politics has a big role to play in stabilizing the public mood, says Li; and although people's difficulties need to be dealt with, cultural activities and entertainment could help 'enliven the atmosphere, sort out contradictions and dissolve negative sentiments'.[14] Neither should traditional culture be accepted uncritically. What is aimed at is a 'socialist culture with Chinese characteristics', where 'feudal' ideas and values have no place. Although these functions have always been emphasized in the CCP's cultural policies, the novelty of this policy is the increased significance it gives to traditional culture in patriotic education, which reflects a shift from revolutionizing traditional culture to carrying on traditional culture, even though a distinction is still made between outstanding elements and backward ones.

3.   Creating a Sense of Crisis: Scare Tactics and Its Politics

The past glory of the Chinese nation is supposed to encourage pride but not complacency. Accordingly, while refreshing memories of a glorious past, patriotic education also highlights China's historical tragedies since 1840, so as to drive home the message that the Opium War could happen again if China remains a technologically backward country. It is the duty of a patriot to prevent the nation from suffering more humiliations and restore to the nation its past glory. In addition, patriotic education is designed to create a sense of insecurity and danger. This is a trick well grounded in traditional Chinese wisdom: the adage is 'adversity and insecurity bring out the instinct to survive, and contentment and complacency lead to demise.' Not only does a sense of insecurity and danger 'impose duties and demand common effort',[15] it also helps set the national agenda to suit the Party. For, as Ying-shih Yu's insightful insightful observation tells us, 'in the face of a collective crisis, the main objective of our modernisation is invariably national prosperity and military strength (*fuguo qiangbin*).[16] But when the danger is removed, or perceived so, political reform, human rights and so forth might force their way onto the national agenda. Even China's national anthem purports to galvanize the nation into action by creating a sense of danger.[17] It is precisely this well-practicied art of rule which underlies the theory of 'peaceful evolution'.

While some academics have written on the origin, development and strategies of 'peaceful evolution', most articles on this subject are found in left-wing journals, especially *Banyue tan* (under the Department of Propaganda) and *Zhongliu* (co-edited by veteran cadre-writers Wei Wei and Lin Mohan). And, there are numerous reports, particularly in *Zhongliu*, about actual involvement by the CIA, VOA and agents from Hong Kong and Taiwan, which verge on fictional detective stories. The theory of 'peaceful evolution' systematically translates the notion of class struggle into a myth of actual conspiracy by the national and international bourgeoisie to subvert socialist systems through political, economic and cultural infiltration and influence. Many outside China dismiss it as a propaganda ploy, and therefore underrate its potency. A propaganda ploy it may well be, but nonetheless it serves the purpose of galvanizing the Party and nation into believing that imminent dangers threaten not only the CCP but the whole nation.

This conspiracy is said to have originated in the US in the late 1940s and been put on America's international agenda in the early 1960s, when President Kennedy, acknowledging the difficulty in eliminating socialist systems by force, opted for a policy of encouraging political changes in socialist countries through aid, trade, tourism, and personnel and cultural exchanges. It is said to have gone into full swing in the 1980s during the dramatic transformation of socialist systems across Eastern Europe, Vietnam and China. In early 1993, the Propaganda Department issued a document to warn the nation that the US had adjusted its political and military strategy and shifted its focus from the former Soviet Union to China, the last major socialist system in the world, and, that after its success in bringing down Communism in the Soviet Union, the US was now attempting to turn China into an eastern Russia within ten to fifteen years.[18]

The collapse of the Eastern bloc is widely represented in the media as a vindication of the 'peaceful evolution' theory. The Tiananmen events in 1989 brought the CCP, for the first time, face to face with such an 'evolution', and the danger of Chinese socialism collapsing looked more real than ever in the midst of the events and against the background of the developments in Eastern Europe. Western and overseas support for the students in Beijing, both moral and material, easily links into the myth of an international bourgeoisie collaborating to subvert socialism. Speeches and comments on socialism or new developments in Eastern Europe by American, EU and Japanese politicians and diplomats are cited as proof of a concerted and coordinated international offensive against socialist countries. The world-wide condemnation of the military crackdown of the students in 1989, and the subsequent sanctions against China by the US, Britain, Japan, Denmark, Sweden, Germany, Belgium, and Canada, were projected and perceived as further evidence of a coordinated plot.

Shortly after June 4th Deng claimed that 'The entire imperialist Western world plans to make all socialist countries discard the socialist road and then bring them under the control of international monopoly capital and onto the capitalist road'.[19] He went on to say that the cold war between the US and the Soviet Union 'may mean the end of one cold war, but it also marks the beginning of another two cold wars, one being directed at the entire South and the Third World countries, the other at socialism. Western countries are now engaged in a Third World War which displays no smoke of gunpowder'.[20] Jiang's speech, on the 70th anniversary of the CCP on July 1 1991, which clearly reflects conservative control over the overall ideological and policy agenda, stresses the link between domestic and international class struggle, actually endorsing the anti-peaceful-evolution campaign.

Between 1989 and 1992, the media were flooded with warnings against 'peaceful evolution'. Sino-Western, particularly Sino-American, reactions became quite tense during that period. In the summer of 1989, conservatives argued in the summer of 1989 that China should reorient foreign policy away from the West to build stronger ties with the remaining socialist states and the Third World.[21] A quick glance at newspaper headlines between 1989 and 1994 would give one the impression that the dangers of 'peaceful evolution' were to be taken seriously. A question often posed in newspapers and magazines is: Why are the Americans always making trouble over human rights, Taiwan, Tibet and other issues? And the typical answer given is: The US is out to get us! Not because we are a socialist country, but because the US is bent on dominating the world so a rising China is seen as a potential threat. As evidence, look at the former Soviet Union! Gorbachev got things wrong, of course, but the Soviet Union would not have disappeared had it not been for the American or Western conspiracy to destroy it under the disguise of promoting human rights and democracy. These type of scare tactics aimed at rallying the nation around the CCP are definitely more effective than resorting to a socialist ideology which has lost much of its credibility, or positively encouraging dreams of national revival.

It became apparent that Chinese leaders took on a siege mentality as a result of the concatenation of three series of events: the collapse of the Eastern bloc; the Tiananmen events; and international support for the students and condemnation of the Chinese government. These events, particularly the brutal suppression of the students, propelled the Chinese government and the Party into a deeper legitimacy crisis than it had experienced since the damaging examination of the Party's history and Maoism in the late 1970s and early 1980s. What newspapers described as a 'crisis of faith' among the populace, a loss of faith in Communism and disillusionment with politics, which had escalated between the late 1970s and 1989, continued to worsen. This is indicated by a number of surveys, on students and political workers, conducted after 4 June 1989. In this context, it was not surprising that the CCP took 'peaceful evolution' as 'a matter of life and death for the CCP'. The CCP's response to June 4th has to be interpreted, first of all, as an attempt to prevent the CCP from suffering the same fate as their counterparts in Eastern Europe and elsewhere.

A defeat of socialism by capitalism might not be a problem for many in China, but that of China by the West is to some, and national disintegration is to be dreaded by most. The CCP, therefore, has been at pains to convince the nation that the 'annihilation of the Party (*wang dang*) means annihilation of the nation (*wang guo*)', for without the CCP China would lose state sovereignty, national autonomy and national dignity.[22] This argument was far less convincing before the developments in Eastern Europe. Since then, however, the unanimous view in the Chinese media about the Soviet Union's fate is that it is a disaster, and one could befall China if the Party-state is weakened. This view is widely accepted among the populace. This is hardly surprising for a nation that attaches great importance to national unity. While the unity of China is more a myth than reality, today or in the past, as many in the West have correctly pointed out, national unity as a myth and ideal still holds enormous appeal in China. Even those who do not subscribe to the idea of national unity often feel compelled to refrain from voicing opinions in favour of taboo subjects such as ethnic separatists or Taiwan independence. This partially explains why the majority of people you talk to in China are more likely to agree with their government on such issues as Taiwan and Tibet. Even among political dissidents, including some in exile, few take exception to the CCP's position on territorial disputes, even though they might condemn it for its human rights abuses. The human rights issue has also been turned into a national issue: American and Western reaction is interpreted as a pretext under which to 'contain' China. Chinese nationalists, and many people who do not consider themselves as nationalists, can criticise the government for its human rights abuses amongst themselves, but when criticism comes from the US or the West, more often than not they slip into official rhetoric or get seriously enraged about the 'foreign interference' and its 'evil intentions'. In this respect, state nationalism enjoys considerable popular support.

In 1992, Deng, realising the negative implications of the 'theory of peaceful evolution' for his reforms, started to moderate the anti-peaceful-evolution rhetoric by saying: First, the threat was neither present nor imminent because 'hostile forces pin their hopes on the people of several generations following us...When we people of older generations are still around and have weight, hostile forces are aware no change can be effected'. Second, the threat was internal, not external: 'If something wrong occurs in China, it will come from within the Communist Party.'[23] In March 1992, the New China News Agency issued a six-page directive to instruct reporters to avoid harsh criticism of the US and to 'report well on bilateral relations and exchanges between China and the United States'. It also instructs that 'we should carry out a reasonable, beneficial, restrained struggle, and not use phrases such as "Western hostile forces headed by the United States"'.[24] In November 1992, Deng again urged the leadership to improve relations with the US by not raising the issues of 'peaceful evolution' so frequently and by compromising on human rights issues.

In a bid to take economic reforms back to the centre, Deng struck out against the conservatives through his southern tour. Following this, the left took active measures to resist the offensive. Deng Liqun said, during his trip to Wuhan and other cities, 'There is the core of economic work but also another core of fighting peaceful evolution and waging class struggle. And sometimes, the campaign against the peaceful evolution is more important'.[25] Chen Yun presided over a meeting of the Central Advisory Commission, on 17 February 1992, where he said that the only way for the CCP to avoid a Soviet-type collapse was to emphasise Communist ideology and strengthen Party building'.[26] It was only with military backing that in 1992 Deng finally won the day.[27] The hype over 'peaceful evolution' faded in 1992-3.

4.   Party-Centred Nationalism: Guo as a Package

It is evident that the anti-peaceful-evolution is primarily concerned with the position of the CCP as the ruling party, in spite of the strenuous equation of *wangdang* with *wangguo*. The same can be said about the patriotic campaigns and, indeed, about state nationalism itself. For serious as the CCP may be in its pursuit of national unity, national identity and national autonomy, its first and foremost consideration is the CCP itself rather than the Chinese nation. Of central importance in the CCP's version of patriotism is the desire to promote the 'country' or *guo* as a package by taking advantage of the ambiguity of the term, which can be translated into 'country', 'the land', 'nation' or 'state', and which, when combined with *jia*, as in *guojia*, is usually taken in every day parlance as the equivalent of 'the government', which, in turn, means the CCP. Packed into the term *guo*, therefore, is not only the notions of country, land, nation and state but also those of government and the CCP. Consequently, patriotism, or love of country, equates, in theory, with love for all these things.

As a matter of fact, Party propaganda takes pains to justify why the government and the CCP have to be included in *guo*. As Deng once said, 'Some say that it doesn't mean one is not patriotic if one doesn't love socialism. Is the motherland an abstract notion? What is patriotism without love for the socialist new China led by the Party?'.[28] Deng's argument is echoed in Jiang's speech 'Carry on and Develop the Tradition of Patriotism in New Historical Circumstances' and the CCP's 'Outline for the Implementation of Patriotic Education'. Both stress that patriotism is consistent with socialism, as 'only socialism can save China' and socialism represents 'the fundamental interest of the state, the nation and the people'.[29] These arguments are certainly not original; the CCP has been using the same line of argument ever since 1949. A remarkable difference is that, while socialism was very much promoted on its merit in the Mao era, it now feeds parasitically on patriotism, an unpalatable part of the patriotic package. As such socialism, or rather love of socialism, takes a back seat in the core virtues of spiritual civilisation: love of the motherland, love of the people, love of labour, love of science and love of socialism. The Party deserves love and loyalty because, to quote Jiang, 'the people have become masters of their country under the leadership of the Communist Party';[30] that 'our Party has carried on and developed the outstanding tradition of the Chinese nation, has sacrificed the most and made the most contribution in the struggle for national independence and in the defence of national autonomy'; and that 'the Chinese Communists are the most thorough patriots'.[31]

There is little doubt that the CCP's version of patriotism posits the Party as an embodiment of the nation's will, which naturally deserves the nation's loyalty, and which alone determines the content of patriotism and the connection between act and patriotic behaviour. In other words, it defines the nation by naming it.[32] The nation thus named, however, is more a means to an end than an end in itself. The end is first of all the security of the Party's rule, the achievement of the Party's goal and the mobilisation of the population for that purpose. This is best illustrated by the CCP's definitions of patriotism, which reflect the shifting focus of the CCP at different times. In 1951, for example, patriotism meant

> ... opposition to imperialist aggression and feudal oppression, it is upholding the fruits of the Chinese revolution, it is upholding the New Democracy, it is upholding progress and opposing backwardness; it is

upholding the working people, it is upholding the international alliance of China and Russia, the people's democracies, and the working peoples of the entire world; it is struggling for the future of socialism.[33]

Conversely, it was considered unpatriotic if, for instance, one spoke against the Sino-Russian alliance or refused to struggle for the future of socialism. Today, patriotism means

...pride in the country's outstanding contributions to the civilisation of humanity, its broad and profound traditional culture, to acknowledge the basic national conditions, to follow the political line of the Communist Party of China, to recognise the Party's achievements, to uphold socialist democracy and abide by the law, not to harm national defence, national security or national unity, and accept the principles of peaceful reunification, and one country two systems.[34]

It would be unpatriotic not to appreciate what the Party has done for the nation and take pride in the achievements as 'ours', or bring harm to the Party-state by demanding something that does not suit the 'national conditions', like human rights, liberty or democracy. Patriotism requires one to accept the Party's 'blueprint' for modernisation as the optimal model and work hard in order to achieve that goal instead of indulging in hedonism or idle talk about alternatives. It might even be considered unpatriotic if one suggested that Taiwan should be taken by force, given the CCP's preferred option is peaceful reunification; or Hong Kong should have the same political system as the mainland, which would contradict the 'one country two systems' formula. In short, at best patriotism includes loyalty to the Party and conformity to the Party and, at worst, allows for no opposition to its ideology and policies.

5. The CCP: An Organisation of and for the Industrial Proletariat?

It is fairly obvious that the CCP is keen to portray itself as the core of the nation. But what is this nation? Is it the 'Chinese people' - the pan-Chinese nation' (*Zhonghua minzhu*), the Han Chinese, the Chinese citizens (*guomin*), or 'the people'? The four overlap to some extent, but each has a recognisable boundary and they are not always compatible. A cultural and genealogical pan-Chinese nation could include the citizens of the P. R. C., the people of Hong Kong, Macao and Taiwan, and overseas Chinese. According to the Constitution, Chinese citizens include 'all persons holding the nationality of the People's Republic of China' regardless of ethnic, racial, religious, cultural or class differences.[35] Eager as the CCP may be to command the loyalty of all Chinese, its ideology determines that its 'nation' is basically 'the people' - the industrial proletariat, the peasantry, the petty-bourgeoisie and the national bourgeoisie. These are the four classes represented on the national flag, in the form of the four small stars surrounding a big star, which represents the CCP. Excluded from representation on the national flag, however, are not only un-revolutionary or counter-revolutionary classes, but also individuals of skin colours other than yellow, for while red stands for revolution, yellow indicates the racial and genealogical dimension of the CCP and the revolutionary classes.[36] It was taken for granted, by the designer of the national flag, that skin colour was the first criterion for defining the Chinese, for as he put it, when explaining the use of the yellow colour, the Chinese people are yellow.[37]

Thus, in the national flag and the state insignia lie huge contradictions. The revolutionary and racial overtones therein raise a number of very legitimate questions: Can black and white citizens of the P. R. C. qualify for 'the people'? Can they, as well as the un-revolutionary and counter-revolutionary classes, qualify as members of the pan-Chinese nation (*Zhonghua minzu*)? If so, on what conditions? And, if admitted, how do they respond to such national symbols that deny them representation and recognition? As the number of black and white Chinese is small, complaints about the privileged representation of the yellow race, are seldom, if ever, heard in public forums. But resentment over the privileged representation of classes has been growing since the late 1970s, and challenges to the class concept, since the early 1980s, have drastically reduced its potency.

The Leninist notion of the state was scaled down in both the 1954 and 1982 constitutions (more so in the former than in the latter). Both also emphasise citizenship, particularly in the articles on citizens' rights and duties. The 1982 Constitution declared that 'The exploiting classes as such have been eliminated in our country, although, bowing to the demands of the conservatives, the top leadership acceded to the left's claim that class struggle 'still exists'. Nevertheless, two significant caveats were added: It existed only 'within certain limits', and it no longer constituted the 'principal contradiction'.[38] After the landlords and the national bourgeoisie were declared extinct as classes, following the establishment of state ownership, the contradiction between the workers and peasants, on the one hand, and the landlords and bourgeoisie, on the other, became non-antagonistic so long as the latter did not exhibit their feudal or capitalist tendencies. In other words, they were theoretically included in the 'people'.

But they are still not represented on the national flag and state insignia. Neither are any social classes other than the proletariat, the peasantry, the petty-bourgeoisie and national bourgeoisie. As social transformation has rendered these political categories irrelevant, the national flag and state insignia are now truly out of date as national symbols. What is worse, they could even become sources of alienation to those who, aware of their symbolism, are eager to erase bad memories of the decades-long class struggle. In this sense, the constitutional anachronism is a political reality when national identity is at issue. Little wonder then that, unlike the 1954 Constitution, the 1982 Constitution, with all its subsequent amendments, the National Flag Act of 1990 and the State Insignia Act of 1991, are general and vague about what the five stars represent and, invariably refer to them as 'symbols of the People's Republic of China'. A recent youth study guide interprets the five stars as the CCP and 'the people of all nationalities around the country'.[39] All this suggests that the Party is aware of the inappropriateness of these symbols; but instead of revamping them, it is re-interpreting the class symbols in national terms.

The class concept was virtually dead by 1989. In the Hu and Zhao era, there was, as Song Ping pointed out in his speech at the Defence Academy in 1990, a trend of nationalising the CCP into an 'all-people party' (*quanmin dang*) or a 'national party' (*minzu dang*).[40] The concept of class struggle has been revived under Jiang Zemin as a result of enhanced leftist influence. In his speech, at the Party conference, convened by the Department of Propaganda, the Department of Organisation, the Central Policy Research Office, and the Central Academy of the CCP, in December 1989, Jiang affirmed the CCP traditional identity in terms of the Marxian class concept, as 'the class organisation of the Chinese working class (*gongren jieji*)' and 'the vanguard of the working class guided by Marxism, Leninism and Mao Zedong Thought'. He reiterated that 'the universal transformation of all class societies into classless ones can only be led by the industrial proletariat'; and 'the working class needs the Party and the Party cannot do without the working class'.[41]

Paradoxically, the post-Tiananmen leadership does not conceive of any advantage in broadening the CCP's constituency, but sees Hu and Zhao's nationalising strategy as a thinly veiled attempt to weaken the Party by removing it from its class base. Yet, on the other hand, the CCP portrays itself, or the Party-state, as the embodiment of the nation's will, representing the best interests of the whole nation, except the 'remnant elements of the exploiting classes'. But its affirmation today, as a party of and for the industrial proletariat, is much harder to reconcile with its self-portrayed image of the embodiment of national will than it was before 1978. Unlike in the Mao era, when it had some credibility, on account of the congruence between the Party's theory and practice, it is now challenged by the divergence between that theoretical formation and the changed social realities in China. The polarisation of rich and poor, uneven regional development, and ethnic tensions are only some of the fissiparous tendencies at work today. At the same time, changes in property ownership and relations of production that have resulted from economic reforms have led to the development of a distinct class society. If anything, interests are becoming increasingly differentiated and irreconcilable. The size of the exploiting and exploited classes, defined by Marxian criteria, is both increasing steadily as foreign companies, joint ventures and private companies, or businesses, continue to flourish. Furthermore, the partial privatisation of state enterprises has left an estimated 15 million 'masters of the country' jobless thus far, and that number is bound to grow as more state enterprises go to the wall.

Thus, class struggle looks like a solid reality instead of a theoretical construction. In a hard-hitting article in the People's Daily on 23 October 1992, leftist ideologue Deng Liqun declared that class struggle was more acute than it had been since 1949.[42] The irony is that by shifting towards a market economy, the CCP has not only created a fledgling domestic bourgeoisie and proletariat that well satisfy the Marxian definitions of these categories, but also brought the international capitalists into its own backyard. It has also endorsed a relationship of 'exploitation' - the extraction of surplus value. Marketisation evidently has a logic that runs counter to the CCP's class orientation. It is not easy for anybody to come to terms with the image of the CCP as an organisation of and for the proletariat, given that it is the Party who has set in motion and presided over the process of dismantling state ownership and creating exploitation, is itself even turning, to some extent, into a capitalist class, albeit 'red'. The contradiction is poised to destroy its own *raison d'être* and alienate its own constituency - the working class.

On the other hand, if state ownership and the planned economy levelled 'the people' in Maoist China, the market is doing the opposite in polarising, dividing and stratifying the society, thereby considerably reducing the membership of 'the people', or rather, the number of people who qualify for membership by Marxian standards. This is coupled with a widespread reluctance to identify with the proletariat and peasants as the progressive driving force of history, which have taken on a stigma as a result of the anti-revolution backlash in post-Mao China. Consequently, the concept of a class-based 'people' is of little credibility and relevance to anybody, except Party traditionalists who can make use of it in their attempt to frustrate or slow down the reforms. What is more, it is divisive and detrimental to the invention of a national identity, or a civic identity, that is more likely to bring about social cohesion and national unity in China.

It is too early to write off the class concept yet, as it is still institutionalised by the national flag, state insignia and Constitution. Since the imagining of nations is very much about their symbolisation and institutionalisation, one errs by underrating these national symbols. However, the point about the class concept should not be taken too far. For, after all, the CCP is pragmatic enough not to stick to it in practice at the expense of anything else that it can benefit from. In fact, it has often acted from expediency, diluting the concept of class, playing it down or even temporarily suspending it in order to win as much support as possible and achieve its tactical, strategic, short and long-term goals. The strategy it has perfected, in its 78-year history, is the united front, whose basis, in the 1990s, is nationalism.

6.   The United-Front Strategy: Political Dimensions of the Pan-Chinese Project

Such is the value of the united-front strategy that it is enshrined in the current constitution as of central importance to the Party:

> In building socialism it is imperative to rely on the workers, peasants and intellectuals and unite all the forces that can be united. In the long years of revolution and construction, there has been formed under the leadership of the Communist Party of China a broad patriotic united front that is composed of democratic parties and people's organisations and embraces all socialist working people, all patriots who support socialism and all patriots who stand for reunification of the motherland. This united front will continue to be consolidated and developed.[43]

The 1954 Constitution was even more frank about the function of this united front. It is, to quote the original words, 'mobilising and rallying the whole people in the common struggle to fulfil the fundamental task of the

State during the transition and to oppose the enemies within and without'.[44] This makes it fairly clear that the composition of a united front is determined by two things: the nature of the Party's enemy; and its fundamental task at a certain time. It is argued, on this basis, that members of the united front generally fall into the category of the 'Chinese people'.[45] Another way of putting this is that the 'Chinese people' is defined with reference to the Party-state's enemy and its fundamental task at a certain time. Support for the Party is demanded from members of this front; and they are put in a position where they can prove their love of country by their support for the CCP. On the other hand, the CCP has often been ready to put partisan loyalty and its ideology on the back seat when its enemy is outside of the Party or when its fundamental task requires more support than it can muster from Party members and supporters. The more difficult and urgent the task is, the lower the political requirement.

It is not hard to see, then, that the essential criterion for 'the Chinese people' here is an artificial one that serves a clear political purpose. This is one side of the coin: it only tells us the necessity of the united front to the Party-state and its terms for it. What is to be mobilised and rallied around the Party is, after all, 'the whole people', who have little reason or incentive to concern themselves with the enemy and the task of the Party-state. Of primary importance in enticing or morally compelling them to join in the front, is an identification between the Party's enemy and task and those of the nation, or, in the absence of such identification, the projection of the former in national terms. The theory of 'peaceful evolution' affords a good example of how 'hostile international forces' and anti-peaceful-evolution are projected as national enemies and a national objective.

It must be stressed, at this point, that the nation implied by 'national interest', in this case, is without doubt larger than the united front, even though the latter could be made so inclusive as to coincide with the former, should the nature of the Party's enemy and task make it necessary. To be more exact, the front is created out of a pre-existent community, with its shared historical memories and culture. In recruiting members from this community for the front, it is only common sense to advertise the benefit of membership from that community's point of instead of the front itself. For this reason, 'national interest' is brought in by the Party-state as a clarion call in its mass mobilisation, although what masquerades as 'national interest' is often nothing but Party-state interest, as is typified by a postulation in *Qiushi* that 'it is in the best national interest to safeguard the authority of the CCP and the government'.[46] Similarly, the Party-state encourages identification with itself by fostering a 'we' on the basis of common descent, as 'sons and grandsons of the Yellow Emperor' and 'descendants of the Dragon'. Needless to say, this type of cultural, as well as genealogical, Pan-Chinese identity, is a valuable resource for the Party-state to avail itself of in order to achieve a range of goals. But it is not an inexhaustible resource; it must be strengthened and rejuvenated. That can only be done by promoting what binds this identity - descent, shared memories, traditional culture, homeland, etc.; not the ideology of the Party, which more often than not proves counter-productive.

Since 1978 the fundamental task of the Party-state has not been a class struggle that would lead the people into a Communist utopia, but modernisation that primarily aims at national strength and national revival. A pressing task is reunification with Hong Kong, Macao and Taiwan. Another taxing task is to avoid national disintegration by quenching separatism in Tibet, Xinjiang, Inner Mogolia and elsewhere, and curbing centrifugal tendencies in the provinces. A no less urgent one is to counter the 'decadent ideas' and influence of the West that is seen to have resulted in a moral degeneration and generated a large amount of political dissent that could threaten the regime, or cause political instability. The enemy without refers to 'hostile forces' that challenge China's sovereignty or intend to contain China politically or economically. To fulfil all those tasks, and defeat this enemy, would certainly require more than just the 'people', and nationalism is without doubt more useful in this respect than a discredited Marxism.

A question is whether nationalism can or will replace Maxism as the CCP's official ideology. The simple answer is that the CCP is not yet ready to give Marxism up, not only because nationalism is no rose without a thorn, but because the CCP also has an enemy within to deal with. This enemy, for the time being, refers to those in the Party who are actively involved in 'bourgeois liberalisation'. The Party does not seem to have anything other than Marxism to rely on in its struggle against enemies within the Party, and in its attempt to rally the Party around the central leadership. Nationalism does not really take sides in factional politics. Both sides stand to gain from an image of genuine patriots, and just as conservatives and reformers can draw on nationalism in their attack on each other, so can dissidents within the Party mount challenges to Marxism and Party rule on nationalist grounds.

The post-Tiananmen leadership's attack on the Hu-Zhao factions has resulted in its shift towards the left and its reaffirmation of Marxism. It remains doubtful, however, how much substance there is to it. Moreover,

Marxism has lost ground as the Party is adopting two-track ideologies: Marxism for the Party and state nationalism for society. This is not to say that the CCP has actively taken it out of society; what it means, instead, is that it is not reinforcing it. That brings us back to the early observation that the CCP is taking a graded approach in its political requirements for Party and Youth League members, 'advanced elements', citizens and overseas Chinese. Party members are called upon to hold firmly to the Party's established ideals, moral values, and organisational discipline. This is the focus of 'emphasising politics'. It aims, in Jiang's own words, to ensure that 'Party and state leadership, at all levels, stay in the hands of people who are loyal to Marxism'.[47] It urges Party members and cadres to improve their understanding of Marxism and be aware of political developments instead of being engrossed in daily routines, so that they will follow the Party line more closely rather than drifting away from it under the influence of marketisation and economic decentralisation.

So far as citizens are concerned, unquestioned conformity is all the better, but what is emphasised are civic duties: 'to abide by the Constitution and law, uphold discipline at work, keep public order and respect social ethics, to protect public property, to pay taxes, to defend the homeland, and perform military service, to safeguard the unity of the country and the unity of all the nationalities, to keep state secrets, to safeguard the security, honour and interests of the motherland, and not to commit acts detrimental to the security, honour and interests of the motherland'.[48] And even less is expected of overseas Chinese: love of the motherland, which means first of all to support national reunification and not to oppose the CCP. Support for the CCP will certainly guarantee them the title of patriots; but they can still be regarded as patriots so long as they are not fundamentally against the CCP. For them patriotism is the essential requirement for membership in the CCP's Chinese nation. Admission into the nation means the admitted becomes a friend rather than an enemy, somebody to be educated, tolerated, united and used in its cause. As Mu Fu-sheng put it, 'Chinese Communists seem to count a genuine patriot half a comrade'.[49]

The graded approach in political requirements suggests at least two things to us: the CCP recognizes the fact that Marxism is not totally sufficient for all purposes; or it is resigned to the fact that it is no longer feasible to reinforce it. At any rate, nationalism can provide the CCP with a far broader basis of national authority than Marxism, as it appeals to the whole nation rather than simply the proletariat and peasantry. The question, however, is how effective the CCP's patriotic education can be. It has been very effective in so far as it has turned the tide around in the national debate over culture and tradition, from pessimistic introspection to confident assertion; and Westerners have lost discursive dominance to traditionalists. So far as the main target of patriotic education, the Chinese young, are concerned, there are research data to show it is not effective.[50] Neither is it effective with the intelligentsia who refuse to let the CCP dictate the terms for patriotism. What Mu wrote decades ago about Chinese intellectuals' response to the Party's demand still rings quite true today:

> For the intellectuals under the Communist regime the choice, if they have it, is between working for a Government with which they disagree but which is the only place where they can do some good for the country, and leaving or staying away from the country. ...This choice the Communists presents as one between patriotism and selfishness, because those who leave or stay away can neither change the Government nor serve the country...In China today many intellectuals serve patriotism under a penalty. The Communists want patriots for the sake of Communism, but these are patriots in spite of Communism.[51]

The only revision that needs to be made to this passage is that Chinese intellectuals today no longer need to choose between working for the government and leaving the country. Instead, as will be discussed in detail in later chapters, literary writers, historians and intellectuals are contesting, albeit often implicitly, both the CCP's definition of patriotism and arguing contrarily that love for the nation does not have to include love for the Party. Equally contested is the Party's monopoly on the right to name the nation. The point at issue is what is 'the Chinese nation' and what constitutes 'Chineseness'. At stake is not merely the nature of this nation, but the right and power to say who 'we' are as Chinese and how 'we' should carry on our collective life. And that has far-reaching implications in terms of the legitimacy of Party rule, as well as national goals and directions.

7.   State Nationalism in a Dilemma

While it remains to be seen to what extent state nationalism has strengthened nation-building, what is clear to us is that there are a number of theoretical and practical obstacles to the CCP's national identity project. The nation that the CCP is endeavouring to build appears to correspond to a 'state-nation', like the US or Switzerland, in so far as it is more or less multicultural and multinational.[52] According to Linz and Stepan, a 'state-nation' is not only desirable but also achievable, contingent upon 'the human capacity for multiple and complementary identities' and 'a common "roof" of state-protected rights for inclusive and equal citizenship'.[53] Needless to say, law-abiding citizens are easier to govern than individuals with little idea of citizenship. It is also apparent that the CCP does not fail to see the advantage of the idea of citizenship in forging a bond between the 50 odd ethnic groups in China, when its territorial unity is threatened by separatist demands based on cultural and religious grounds. In addition, the decay of Marxism has deprived the socialist identity of much of its attraction and tenability. It alienates more than it binds individuals and social groups when they feel compelled to re-define themselves on their own terms or claim 'We the people' instead of being passively named by the Party. Given these difficulties, the loss of prominence for socialist consciousness, the significant role given to civic culture in patriotic education is quite understandable.

This, however, does not imply in any way that the CCP is ready to go so far as to embrace 'civic nationalism', which boils down to 'the view that states should be composed of equal citizens whose ties to one another are purely "civic" in the sense that each acknowledges the authority of a common set of laws and political institutions'.[54] This is so for several reasons. For one thing, law-abiding citizens who fulfil their duties are certainly desirable, but not if they demand citizens' rights. It is in the interest of the Party-state to prevent national loyalty from shifting in any direction away from itself. Furthermore, civic identity in China is generally believed to be weak as the idea of citizenship has to break through the culturalism and people-rule *(renzhi)*, which have dominated the greater part of Chinese history and lingers on today. Despite its advocacy by liberal-minded intellectuals and politicians, since Liang Chichao, there are few signs to suggest that it has taken root in the Chinese society. To make it worse, owing to their lack of respectability and credibility, the political and legal institutions hold out little attraction as objects of identification, and thus have a limited role to play as cohesive agents. 'Constitutional patriotism', if possible at all in China, is without doubt contingent upon the integrity and authority of its laws and political institutions.

Even if China's legal and political institutions were perfect and authoritarianism gave way to democracy, it still remains a question whether 'constitutional patriotism' alone is thick enough to sustain a Chinese national identity. The same can be said for most other nations in the world, in the light of Anthony Smith's observation that nation-builders around the world invariably endeavour to forge, out of available cultural components, a coherent mythology and symbolism of a community of history and culture', as 'without some ethnic lineage the nation-to-be could fall apart'.[55] The CCP clearly concurs with Smith on the role of culture and history in nation-building, and does what most nation-builders do - foster a sense of belonging together by creating and drawing on the myth of a nation stretching back into the past as an organic body of poly-ethnic groups and multi-cultures (*yiti duoyuan*). Hence the promotion of traditional culture. What is more, the Party-state still holds dear what it sees as socialist consciousness or ethics, and is keen to salvage whatever might be palatable to be used in the new national project.

What the Party-state endeavours to forge is a mixture of national consciousness, socialist consciousness and civic awareness. It could be deduced from this that the CCP's version of Chinese identity combines both traditional and modern elements. The problem is that they simply cannot be combined into one, or even coexist peacefully, for the simple reason that they contradict each other in many ways, even though they do overlap here and there. The class concept, for instance, allows for no civic nation; indeed, even the nation has no place therein. The Leninist state, a 'nationless state',[56] is but an instrument of oppression of one class over another. It does not allow for a cultural nation either, because much of traditional Chinese culture, including its backbone, Confucianism, is stigmatised as either feudalistic or backward, or both, and therefore not acceptable until it is revolutionalized or modernised; and Chinese history is interpreted as 'the people's' history rather than national history. Moreover, revolutionary historiography is 'premised on a break between the present and the past', and it focuses on social and economic relations, rather than culture, thereby fundamentally invalidating cultural notions of the nation.[57] Neither can a civic identity and national identity accommodate the class concept. The successful construction of a civic identity almost certainly calls for a significant playing down of the Leninist state, if not its abandonment. That entails a re-writing of the constitution and revamping of the national flag and state insignia. It also requires a fair amount of 'thinning' of national identity based upon common history and culture, for it is often conflated with cultural Chineseness which is, in effect, more Han than Chinese and overlooks the existence of the ethnic minorities, therefore giving ethnic and other cultural identities sufficient reason to compete with it.

The challenge for the Party-state is how to balance or reconcile citizenship, cultural Chineseness and socialist consciousness. Despite its theoretical posturing, the CCP plays down the socialist identity in its nation-building practice so as to reduce tension between the socialist identity, on the one hand, and citizenship and cultural identities, on the other. Socialist consciousness does not present a real obstacle to national identity, so far as the Party-state is concerned, although it remains a central point of contestation for other identities. A compromise is thereby achieved at the expense of the socialist identity. Cultural Chineseness and citizenship are harder to reconcile because the former, as has been mentioned, bears the hallmarks of the dominant ethnic group - the Han. The approach that the CCP is taking appears to be an adaptive one, much as David Miller has proposed in *On Nationality*. Reconciliation is to be achieved, says Miller, not by 'thinning national identities to the point of where they cease to have any content that could compete with ethnic or other such cultural identities',[58] as radical multiculturalists propose; but 'by adapting inherited culture to make room for minority communities'.[59] What this approach entails is that

> ...existing national identities must be stripped of elements that are repugnant to the self-understanding of one or more component groups, while members of these groups must themselves be willing to embrace an inclusive nationality, and in the process to shed elements of *their* values which are at odds with its principles.[60]

Moreover, to achieve the latter goal, 'states may legitimately take steps to ensure that the members of different ethnic groups are inducted into national traditions and ways of thinking'. Clearly, these arguments for a 'state-nation' type of identity are more statist than nationalist. The Party-state's national project can be easily justified in this light, as a matter necessity - to maintain the state's existing territorial boundary and strengthen its internal unity. However, it is one thing to adapt inherited culture, in this case socialist Chinese culture, to make room for ethic minorities and other cultural identities; it is quite another matter of whether or not the latter are ready to be part of this game and take up that space. In more cases than one, ethnic minorities and other cultural identities have refused to identify, voluntarily and actively, with the dominant group or the existing nation-state, irrespective of efforts to make attractive the terms and conditions for inclusion and accommodation. In China, the Party-state faces challenges, not only from ethnic minorities, as a large body of literature demonstrates, but even from Han intellectuals, who are imagining their nation regardless of the CCP's dictates. Chapters 3 and 4 will explore how literary writers and historians, in particular, have taken the game of nationalism into their own hands and 'imagine' their own nation by taking advantage of the patriotic campaigns.

Notes

1   Jiang Zemin, 'Speech at the 40th Anniversary of the People's Republic of China', in *A Work Manual for the Construction of Socialist Spiritual Civilization*, the Office for the Construction of Spiritual Civilization, the Department of Propaganda, Zhonggong dangshi chubanshe, Beijing, 1997, p. 35.

2   *The People's Daily*, 23 Nov. 1989, p. 3.

3   Ibid., p. 4.

4   Ibid.

5   *Beijing Review*, Sept. 26-Oct. 2, 1994, p. 4.

6   *Liaowang*, No. 19, 1997, p. 16.

7   *Beijing Review*, Sept. 26-Oct. 2, 1994, p. 4.

8   Quoted in editorial in *Qiushi*, No. 9, 1990, p. 9.

9   Jiang Zemin, op. cit., p. 35.

10   Quoted in an editorial in *Qiushi*, No. 9, 1990, p. 9.

11   Li Ruihuan, 'Some Questions relevant to Enhancing the Outstanding Elements of National Culture', *The People's Daily*, 10 Jan. 1990, reprinted in *Qiushi*, No.10, 1990, pp. 13-14.

12   Ibid.

13   Yu Wong, 'Boy Wonder', *Far Eastern Economic Review*, 3 October 1996, p. 26.

14   Li Ruihuan, op. cit., p. 3.

15   E. Renan, 'What is a Nation?' in A. Zimmmern (ed.), *Modern Political Doctrines*, London: Oxford University Press, 1939, p. 203.

16   Ying-shih Yu, *On Modern Confucianism* [*Xiandai Ruxuelun*], Shanghai: Shanghai Renmin chubanshe, 1998, p. 240.

17   *Beijing Review*, Aug. 21-27, 1995, p. 4 . The national anthem: Arise, all ye who refuse to be slaves! With our flesh and blood, Let us build our new Great Wall. The Chinese nation faces its greatest danger. From each one the urgent call for action comes forth.   These original words date back to World War II. They were questioned during the Cultural Revolution and dropped during Hua Guofeng's brief

reign, but they were restored at the 5th Session of the 5th NPC on the grounds that 'the appropriateness of its call to patriotism was borne out in the people's persistent loyalty to them'. Although its words are not current, 'it enables the Chinese people to remain prepared for danger even in times of peace, ensure they will not forget the need to defend the nation's sovereignty, territorial integrity and national dignity. See Zhi Ye, 'Exercising Power on Behalf of the People', *Beijing Review*, No. 52, Dec. 27, 1982, p. 31.

18   *The Standard*, 4 June 1993, in *China Facts & Figures Annual* 1993, p. 72.

19   Deng Xiaoping, '*Disandai lingdao jiti de dangwu zhiji*', in *Deng Xiaoping wenxuan*, Beijing: Renmin chubanshe, 1993, vol. 3, p. 310.

20   Cited in Wang Zhengping, 'U.S. "Human Rights Diplomacy" Is Doomed to Fail', *The People's Daily*, 4 Mar., 1996, trans. in FBIS-CHI-96-054, 19 Mar. 1996, p. 10.

21   Harry Harding, *The fragile relationship: The United States and China since 1972*, Washington, D.C.: Brookings Institution, 1992, p. 236. Both Hu and Zhao have been criticized by hardliners as either 'pro-Japan' or 'pro-West'. It is argued that they attached so much importance to financial aid and technology that they were ready to make compromises in their foreign policy but showed no vigilance against the creeping influence of neo-imperialism. Jiang is more eager to be seen as standing up to the Americans and Japanese. In April 1995, for example, Beijing for the first time gave the green light to 'people's organizations' to seek wartime reparations from Japan. See *South China Morning Post*, 3 May 1995.

22   Jiang Zemin, 'Carry on and Develop the Tradition of Patriotism in New Historical Circumstances', *A Work Manual for the Construction of Socialist Spiritual Civilization*, the Office for the Construction of Spiritual Civilization, the Department of Propaganda, Zhonggong dangshi chubanshe, Beijing, 1997, p. 38.

23   Quoted by Allen Whiting, 'Chinese Nationalism and Foreign Policy after Deng', *The China Quarterly*, Number 142, June 1995, p. 299.

24   *South China Morning Post*, 28 Mar. 1992, p. 11.

25   *The People's Daily*, 11 May 1992, cited by Fewsmith, op. cit., p. 499.

26   Fewsmith, op. cit. pp. 499-500.

27   ibid., p. 501.

28   *Qiushi*, No. 9, 1990, p. 9.

29   Jiang Zemin, 'Carry on and Develop the Tradition of Patriotism in New Historical Circumstances', p. 37. See also 'Outline for the Implementation of Patriotic Education', p. 113. Note here that Jiang distinguishes between 'the nation' and 'the people'.

30   Ibid., p. 38.

31   Jiang Zemin, 'Speech at the closing session of the Sixth Plenum of the 14th Congress of the CCP', in *A Work Manual for the Construction of Socialist Spiritual Civilization*, the Office for the Construction of Spiritual Civilization, the Department of Propaganda, Zhonggong dangshi chubanshe, Beijing, 1997, pp. 66-7.

32   John Fitzgerald, 'The Nationless Sate: The Search for a Nation in Modern Chinese Nationalism', in Jonathan Unger (ed.), *Chinese Nationalism*, Armonk, New York: M.E. Sharpe, 1996, p. 80. As Fitzgerald has pointed correctly, the Communists are not the only ones that reserve the right to identify who makes up the nation. Sate-builders since the mid-nineteenth century have all presumed that the nation has no name of its own, whereas none has conceded that 'there might already have been a nation in existence capable of representing itself'.

33   Li Weihan, 'The Chinese Communist Party and the People's Democratic United Front', *People's China*, IV: 1, 1 July 1951, p. 38.

34   *Beijing Review*, Sept. 26-Oct. 2, 1994, p. 4.

35   Article 33 of the 1982 Constitution, Beijing: Zhongguo fazhi chubanshe, 1997, p. 10. For an English version, see *Beijing Review*, No. 52 Dec. 27, 1982, pp. 10 - 18.

36   Wang Zhanqui (ed.), *The National Flag, State Insignia, and National Anthem - Questions and Answers*, Beijing: University of Public Administration Press, 1997, p. 9.

37   Ibid.

38   See Preamble to the 1982 Constituion.

39   Wang Zhanqui (ed.), op. cit. , p. 12.

40   See Song Ping's speech at the National Defense University in Oct. 1990, quoted in *A New Work Manual for Party Affairs*, Beijing: Zhongguo yanshi chubanshe, 1995, p. 1673.

41   Jiang Zemin, quoted in *A New Work Manual for Party Affairs*, Beijing: Zhongguo yanshi chubanshe, 1995, p. 1673.

42   *The People's Daily*, 23 Oct. 1991, *Jingbao* (Monthly), 178 (5 May 1992, pp. 46-7, Hong Kong, trans. in FBIS-Chi, 18 May 1992, p. 22.

43   See Preamble to the 1982 Constitution.

44   See Preamble to the 1954 Constitution. For an English version see, e.g., S. B. Thomas, *Government and Administration in Communist China*, New York: Institute of Pacific Relations, 1955, pp. 181-96.

45   Lyman P. Van Slyke, *Enemies and Friends - The United Front in Chinese Communist History*, Stanford, California: Stanford University Press, 1967, p. 209, p.251.

46   Wang Jianwei, 'It is in the best interest of the people all over the country to safeguard the authority of the centre', *Qiushi*, No.8, 1995, p. 26.

47   *A New Work Manual for Party Affairs*, p. 1679.

48   See Articles 52 - 6 of the 1982 Constitution.

49   Mu Fu-sheng, *The Wilting of the Hundred Flowers: The Chinese Intelligentsia under Mao*, New York: Praeger, 1962, p. 234.

50   Stanley Rosen, 'The Effect of Post-4 June Re-education Campaigns on Chinese Students', *The China Quarterly*, No. 134, June 1993, pp. 311-34. We would like to thank Jonathan Unger for drawing our attention to Rosen's work.

51   Mu Fu-sheng, op. cit., p. 236.

52   Juan J. Linz and Alfred Stepan, *Problems of Democratic Transition and Consolidation*, Baltimore: The John Hopkins University Press, 1996, p. 34. Unfortunately, Linz and Stepan do not elaborate on the 'state-nation' other than to say that it is a multicultural or even multinational one that nonetheless still manages to 'engender strong identification and loyalty from their citizens, an identification and loyalty that proponents of homogeneous nation-states perveive that only nation-states can engender' (p. 35).

53   Ibid.

54   David Miller, *On Nationality*, Oxford: Clarendon Press, 1995, p. 189.

55   A. Smith, *National Identity*, Harmondsworth: Penguin, 1991, p. 42.

56   John Fitzgerald, op. cit., especially pp. 58-9.

57   Arif Dirlik, 'Reversals, Ironies, Hegemonies - Notes on the Contemporary Historiography of Modern China', *Modern China*, Vol. 22, No. 3, July 1996, p. 257.

58   David Miller, op. cit., p. 141.

59   Ibid., p. 189.

60   Ibid., p. 142.

3   Patriotic Villains and Patriotic Heroes: New trends in literary nationalism

The surge of nationalism in China in the 1990s, particularly state nationalism and its content, have been explored in the previous chapter. The aim of this chapter is to look at how the statist notion of the nation and patriotism are contested by literary writers, arguably the most articulate and creative group of Chinese intellectuals. In doing so, the chapter will also explore what role Chinese writers play in shaping nationalism; what sort of identity they are imagining; whether or not they have a hidden agenda; and what political implications this agenda might have.

The chapter comprises six sections. Section one outlines the general intellectual and political background to the rise of literary nationalism in the 1980s and 1990s. The second examines the 'search for roots' conducted by nativist writers and their endeavour to rediscover 'Chinese essence' in the ancient 'high culture' and, more significantly, in the preliterate 'low' cultural substratum, so that the Chinese nation could be rejuvenated by going back to its own roots. Section 3 sketches the making and re-making of patriotic national heroes in historical novels. Sections 4 and 5 focus on some influential literary works with anti-American and anti-Japanese themes. Finally, section 6 discusses the dual thrust of the imagining of the nation in Chinese literature in the 1990s.

Chinese writers have always been called on to serve the Party and to 'serve the people'. They have also carried on the tradition of serving the nation and state. During patriotic campaigns, many writers purport to inspire the nation with the tales of heroic Chinese soldiers and glorious victories during the Korean War, or simply assuming a more assertive stance towards the West; while a large number of officially endorsed writers have responded enthusiastically to the call of the Party, and the times, by turning once again to the Anti-Japanese War. The central theme of these works is, on the surface, the 'heroic spirit of the Chinese people'. This spirit is deemed by the CCP to be essential to nation-state building in China even today. Literary works with anti-American and anti-Japanese themes of reasonable quality usually have little difficulty finding a publisher even in the partially deregulated book market today. That is one reason for the large number of such works printed in the country, when academics find it increasingly difficult to publish without having to make financial contributions to publishers. China's archetypical enemies, as perpetuated in Chinese literature, are still Japan and the US. At a deeper level, the US in particular, or a West including Japan, loom large in the Chinese imagination as the distinct Other against which 'we Chinese' is defined. In many such novels, however, the war against Japan or the US is merely a camouflage or a background under which or against which a different war is waged - an anti-CCP war.

The preoccupation in literature with history and historical figures represents a different dimension of the 'search for roots', even though nativist writers and historical novelists are not often mentioned side by side. In this sense, 'the search for roots' in Chinese literature is really undertaken by two groups of writers - nativist writers and historical novelists, or seekers of roots in local traditions and customs, and seekers of roots in history. One thing they have in common is their past-orientation: Both rediscover 'our' collective self in the past. They share the conviction, to varying degrees, that there is something terribly wrong or undesirable about a revolutionary China and Westernising China, and the remedy for the ills of the present lies in the past, in the whole of China's cultural heritage. While one looks for this remedy in the folk, the other turns to outstanding Chinese of the past for embodiments of the best of the Chinese.

In the 1990s nativist writers continue to dig into local traditions and customs for 'outstanding elements of national culture' that could inject new life into today's weakened and demoralised nation. Many of these elements condemned in the Mao era as 'four olds' (*sijiu*), and many are not much less unsavoury to the post-Mao leadership. Historical novelists, on the other hand, use the past to serve the present by extolling patriotic strongmen like Wen Tianxiang, a popular patriotic national hero, and Zeng Guofan, a villain beyond redemption, according to the official historiography. Past heroes recast in a contemporary mould have easily found favour in the nation's eyes, whereas past customs and rituals, paradoxically, have satiated a sense of nostalgia and lost much of their aesthetic appeal. This is largely as a result of the initial success of nativist literature, particularly the international success of movies produced by fifth-generation directors, such as *the Yellow Earth, the Old Well, the Red Sorghum, Judou, Raise the Red Lantern,* and *Farewell My Concubine.*

As mentioned in chapter 2, the patriotic campaigns have created a much more favourable climate for Chinese writers to venture out and 'imagine' their own nation, which would be hard to do before 1978, when writers were enclosed in clearly marked boundaries and were given clear guidelines to follow. Nationalism is a new game with few ground rules to follow. Jonathan Unger puts it well: 'the content of Chinese nationalism has been up for grabs.'[1] This has increased the possibility for the writers to carry a hidden agenda in their patriotic rhetoric and open up the 'nation' as a site of contestation. Many of them have ventured further into forbidden territory, thus reducing the CCP's control over intellectual discussion. Others turn a blind eye to the Party line by creating a new species of patriotic heroes who are first of all Chinese rather than Communists, proletarians or even 'decent characters' by well-established 'Chinese' standards. In short, class consciousness is being edged out by national consciousness in the making of national heroes. Villains are not villains if they are patriotic, and more often than not, 'villains' like Zeng Guofan and Wang Qiming are more popular with writers and readers than national heroes like Wen Tianxiang and Lei Feng. Apparently the reason lies in a Chinese literary tradition that is obsessed with 'shady characters' of all descriptions, and the novelty such characters have today after decades of political control; but more importantly, it lies in the fact that they constitute a political statement which questions the myth of the CCP as the paramount leader of the nation. This subverts the CCP's patriotic heroes, and, in so doing, contests the CCP's definition of the Chinese nation.

An index of the impact of the works under discussion is the number of copies printed, which suggests that they are mostly produced for mass consumption. Although some books can still be subsidised or banned, writers have much to gain in terms of fame and income if their books appeal to a broad readership now that the market has started to operate. While rejecting any suggestion that creative writings like these are too much of a fantasy for any definite conclusions to be drawn from them, we nontheless concede, at the outset, the possibility of more than one interpretation of these stories. For instance, while many viewers love *A Beijing Man in New York* as a story of how a man made a fortune in the US, some young entrepreneurs, intellectuals and college students, including the director of the series, Jiang Wen, have relished its nationalist theme. Another point to be added is that different genres find their readers in different social or age groups. Generally speaking, however, anti-American and Anti-Japanese stories find most of their readers among high school students, young people, soldiers, and rural residents; nativist literature is particularly popular in rural areas and among the intelligentsia; and the historical novel, whilst enjoying enormous popularity across the social strata, is one of the most favoured genres in the countryside and finds a large number of fans among the intelligentsia.

It would be very satisfying to be able to pin-point what sort of impact these works have on different types of readers or viewers. Unfortunately, such information is extremely difficult to obtain. What this study attempts to do is to focus on what the writers are saying or implying in their works or in the mass media. All the works under discussion have been selected on account of their popularity and relevance to the study, and in judging their popularity and influence, the basic criteria are the number of copies printed and reviews and comments to be found in the mass media. In the absence of more accurate information about reader/viewer response, a substitute that can be proposed is the assumption that these are the voices of a group of the most influential people in China that are being heard by many people in the public arena, and their impact is likely to be in proportion to their profile. Besides, the audibility of these voices itself tells us a lot about what is happening in Chinese politics, and what is uttered and implied by a considerable number of influential writers in the nationalist enterprise can provide us with an insight into the true nature of the alternative 'Chinese nation' being imagined as well as its imagining, which might hardly be possible otherwise.

1. The Tide Changes in the 1980s and 1990s: From introspection to assertiveness

National revival (*minzu fuxing*) has been on the national agenda since the Fourth People's Congress in 1974, when Zhou Enlai launched China's four modernisations program. The hype died down quickly, however, with the political demise of Hua Guofeng and Deng Xiaoping's revaluation of the Cultural Revolution and reassessment of Mao's political legacy. 'Scar literature' (*shangheng wenxue*) in the late 1970s and early 1980s evolved into reflections on why all those disasters happened, which led, in turn, to a deeper cultural examination by the emerging Chinese *avant garde* who were eager to see the modernisation of China at a time when its cautious economic experiments were running into all sorts of problems. Increased media coverage of the outside world and lively debates about China's problems, which were encouraged by the relatively relaxed political environment under Hu Yaobang and Zhao Ziyang, quickly deflated the myth of national supremacy kept alive for many years through Communist propaganda and official control of information. And the collapse of Communism in Eastern Europe shattered any remaining national confidence based on the Communist ideology. As Jonathan Unger commented in *Chinese Nationalism*:

> With the demise of the Maoist ideology in the last two decades, a vacuum in commitment to public goals has become obvious among the people of China in what Chinese newspapers have called a 'crisis of faith'.[2]

This 'crisis of faith' was not simply confined to the realm of ideology; it became a crisis of faith in Chinese culture in general, which rekindled the century-old sense of national crisis that was briefly resolved by the CCP between 1949 and 1978. In the 1980s, there emerged again the perception that China was in deep trouble, economically, politically, socially and culturally. Striving to avert a national crisis, when confronted by Western economic or military might, the Chinese intelligentsia demonstrated the same sort of anxiety experienced by their forefathers in the Hundred Days Reform of 1898 and the Qing Reform of 1901-1907. In the 1980s, as at the end of the last century, China's intellectuals were grappling yet again with the issue of tradition versus modernity.

By upholding tradition 'nativist literature' became very popular in the mid-1980s but towards the end of the decade radical advocates of Westernisation got the upper hand. For the greater part of the decade, criticisms of Chinese culture and the national character, a trend that has been described by the establishment and nationalists as 'cultural nihilism' or 'national nihilism', predominated in political and cultural discourse.

The heated debate over the issue of tradition versus modernisation reached a flashpoint in 1988, following the screening on CCTV of the controversial series *River Elegy* (*Heshang*). It attracted enormous attention, through its sweeping generalisations about the nation's past and present ills, and national symbols, including the Yellow Emperor, the Yellow River, the Great Wall and the dragon. Some well-known academics commended the series for its vision and the sense of crisis that it conveyed. At a discussion in the *Literary Weekly* on 16 July 1988, He Xilai, deputy director of the Institute of Literature of the Chinese Academy of Social Sciences, spoke highly of 'the courage of the writers and their insight'. He believed it evoked in viewers a sense of crisis and frustration, and that these feelings would spur the nation on in its modernisation drive.[3] Chen Xuanliang, a PhD candidate from the People's University, thought *Heshang* was a slap in the face to the Chinese superiority complex. 'We indulge ourselves in nostalgia and reflect on our past, too,' he said. 'But we always say, we may be poor today but were much richer than yesterday. Who the hell do you think you are? This is an Ah-Q-type[4] of nostalgia or self-deception. People do not realize the imminent crisis. Now we are admitting at last that it is counter-productive to reflect on history like that'.[5]

Much has been written about *Heshang*, and there is no need to dwell on it here other than to highlight its radical anti-tradition thrust. We can get a fairly good idea about that from the sharp criticism of *Heshang* made by Yi Jiayan (widely believed to be a pen-name for Party conservative, Wang Zhen), in October 1988.[6] Yi Jiayan slashed the series on ten accounts, which basically summed up what all other critics had to say about it:

- *Heshang* was nihilistic and pessimistic in its total negation of 'the Yellow River civilisation' or the Chinese culture;
- It implied, through a geographical determinism, that the Chinese are born inferior;
- It insulted the Chinese people by satirising such national symbols as the Yellow River and the Great Wall;
- It ridiculed the attempts, made throughout Chinese history, at national unification and called for the dividing up of the country;
- It condemned the peasant uprisings and heroic struggles against imperialist invasions throughout Chinese history as destructive, and it sneered at Lin Zexu, Wei Yuan, Deng Shichang and other national heroes;
- It presented the socialist revolution in China and the international Communist movement as a failure;
- It advocated Eurocentrism and insisted that nothing could save China except capitalism and wholesale Westernisation;
- The writers of the series had their own agenda even though they appeared to be supportive of reforms and open door policies;
- The writers condemned Chinese intellectuals for dependence on the political establishment and projected themselves as

representatives of China's cultural elite and an independent leading force in the reforms; and

- *Heshang* was a hotchpotch of ideas, and, as such, certainly did not constitute an 'enlightenment movement' as its supporters claimed.[7]

Supporters and critics of *Heshang* shared feelings of frustration that China had failed to become a modern, trading nation. Opinions diverged, however, on whether Chinese culture had reduced the country to its present state. Conservatives and nationalists were infuriated to see Chinese tradition excoriated in favour of Westernisation.

In the 1990s, however, the tide changed: Pessimism began to give way to optimism, and introspection gave way to assertiveness. National confidence was boosted to unprecedented heights, not only by China's economic achievements, but also by speculations, in both the Chinese and Western media, that China would become a new superpower to be reckoned with in the next century. At the same time, Chinese nationalist sentiments were constantly stimulated, particularly by Sino-American friction and problems in Sino-Japanese relations, which intensified after the end of the cold war. Furthermore, as has been pointed out in the last chapter, the CCP's intensified patriotic indoctrination, after the Tiananmen events in 1989, did much to boost national confidence by condemning 'national nihilism'.

2. The Search for Roots: Rejuvenating the Nation with National Essence

'Search for roots' *(xungen)* remains popular in literature in the 1990s, although it has lost much of the prominence it had in the 1980s. It is parallelled in academic studies by the preoccupation with 'national essence' *(mincui)*, especially Confucianism. The 'search for roots' in Chinese literature in many ways typifies the defence of traditional Chinese culture by Chinese intellectuals as a whole. It is a new wave of 'culturalism' which permeates traditional thought in that it sees Chinese culture as the 'focus of loyalty' and the remedy for the country's present ills. According to this view, both Chinese tradition and national identity are challenged and eroded by modernisation. What is worse, China, as a late-developing country, is colonised economically, but more so culturally. 'As a third world country', to quote cultural critic Zhang Qinhua, 'China has been culturally colonised. A sense of loss stems from the fact that during China's transition from traditional to modern society, Chinese culture, either passively or through a rational choice, is bound to be assimilated by a foreign culture'.[8]

As Western culture burst onto the scene with a vengeance after China opened its doors to the world, many writers fell over each other to imitate Western writers or employ Western techniques, and critics by and large Westernised Chinese literary criticism, at least in terminology, by borrowing freely from the repertoire of modernism, post-modernism, structuralism, post-structuralism, Orientalism, post-colonialism. The 'search-for-roots-school' of writers treated this new fashion with disdain. According to Ah Cheng, the attempt at 'total Westernisation' during the May Fourth Movement has already caused a rupture in Chinese culture, and it is the writer's task today to close the gap rather than enlarge it.[9] In other words, Ah Cheng would like to see China resume its history from the point where it was interrupted, not only by Communism, but by the May Fourth Movement as well. Han Shaogong's advice to his generation was to search for the native Chinese roots, literary and cultural, so that Chinese literature would not simply follow the latest trends in the West. He cited a number of well-known foreigners who showed some interest in Chinese culture, as testimony to its superiority, and on his long list were, amongst others, Toynbee, Descartes, Einstein, Tolstoy, Sartre and Picaso. On the other hand, Han painted Western civilisation in rather gloomy colours:

> If Jesus saw the religious trials of the Middle Ages, if Einstein saw the desolation of Hiroshima, if Freud saw the red-lantern districts and x-rated movies, if Owen and Marx saw the gulags in the Soviet Union and the Cultural Revolution in China, they would be speechless with embarrassment.[10]

Pitting themselves against Western influence, these writers set out to bring out 'the Chinese essence' from local customs, rituals and folklores, and followed the style of Chinese literary classics in order to counteract the influence of the language of translated texts and restore the purity of the national language. The 'essence' was to be discovered not only in the language, motifs, symbols, and philosophy of ancient 'high culture', but also in the preliterate 'low' cultural substratum of religion, mores, songs, legends, material culture and 'ethos' of ancient Chu and Han.

Some writers, on the other hand, were more interested in recreating the uniqueness of China and the Chinese for Western readers. To open-minded writers and critics, this is a necessary attempt at cultural dialogue, without which Chinese literature would not make its way to the world, let alone win a Nobel Prize. Others argue, similarly, that local and national uniqueness is China's only ticket for entry into the global community; as the more local the more national, the more national the more universal. Nationalist writers and critics, on the other hand, find this projection of uniqueness repulsive, if not traitorous, for they believe it plays squarely into the hands of Orientalism and, what is worse, it is Orientalism internalised as it voluntarily endorses Orientalism at the expense of national dignity and national honour. This particular strand of literary nationalism is characterised by a virtual paranoia about the bad intentions that may underlie any representation, good or bad, of China or things Chinese, by Chinese writers as well as foreigners and overseas Chinese. This paranoia has led to a witch-hunt that has left few China scholars and nativist writers or directors unscathed. Under attack are not only directors like Zhang Yimou and Chen Kaige, who are said to have pandered to Western curiosity about the seamy side of China, but also Western scholars such as Joseph Needham and John Fairbank, who are generally believed to be friendly towards China, because they are said to be patronising. In terms of constructive alternatives as to how a native China can be represented to the world, these nationalists have nothing to offer at all.

Ironically, the 'search for roots' was inspired by an imported American TV series, *Roots,* and in spite of their differences, the writers of this group all drew their inspiration from a foreigner, Gabriel García Márquez, who won the Nobel Prize for literature in 1982. Very few foreign writers had attracted more attention and stimulated more discussion among Chinese writers than Márquez. In the words of critic Li Jiefei, 'There was hardly a literary conference or seminar where Márquez's name was not mentioned, and nearly every writer in China had a copy of *Hundred Years of Solitude*'.[11] Chinese writers saw in Márquez an example of a third world writer being recognised as world-class. For many years now, they have harboured grievances over the fact that the Nobel Prize in literature has never been awarded to a Chinese writer. So far as China is concerned, it has not had a fair go either because of ideological differences, unfamiliarity with Chinese works, or different tastes. Márquez's example now encouraged some of them, such as Ba Jin, to make a bid for the prize, whereas it was the endeavour of the intellectuals as a whole to make it a point of national honour to join the world as an equal and dignified member, through the creation of a national literature known to and accepted by the world.

Highlighted in this genre are such themes as the clash between tradition and modernity, between Chinese and Western values and nostalgic evocations of the past. But as David Der-wei Wang commented succinctly:

> (N)ative soil writings could not describe these themes without betraying certain of their limitations: To whom was native soil literature addressed (to the natives, who would not comprehend it or to the deracinated, whose belief might be imported and therefore unauthentic)? Where should the 'native' writer/narrator situate himself (or herself) in relation to all the 'insulted and injured' of history?[12]

David Wang correctly pointed out that the native writer/narrator vacillates 'between all-embracing humanitarianism and self-indulgence, between altruist commitment and elite escapism, between earthy 'soil' and imaginary utopia (or dystopia)'.[13] This genre has stimulated abundant curiosity about what the young man in *Shangzhou*[14] described as 'primitive' vitality missing in the modern Chinese, but has apparently failed to generate much enthusiasm about tradition or the traditional way of life. The search for roots in the past, or outside of the industrial cities, where the past is preserved through traditional ways of living, is more symbolic than substantive. An insurmountable difficulty for the nativist writer/narrator is that his/her romantic vision of the past cannot be sustained when reality intrudes, as best illustrated in *Shangzhou*, where 'the young man' embarks on his search for meaning in his birth place in northern China during his holidays, but feels compelled to return to the city at the end of his holidays.[15] What is discovered by the seekers of roots, and upheld as outstanding Chinese tradition, do not always come out clearly in the nativist literature but are often vaguely referred to in terms of certain qualities or values, such as 'primitive vitality'. These qualities and values are more presentable in the abstract than in the concrete, as manifested in action or a 'slice of life'. It is ironic but not accidental that some of the most enduring images in nativist literature are of bandits, bound feet, red lanterns, concubines, drinking sprees, adultery and incest. As a consequence, the upholding of a better alternative to Western culture by nativist writers amounts to little more than a weak ego-defensive response to the challenge from the West. Its nationalist appeal lies chiefly in its defensive rhetoric of traditional culture, its argument for a national literature and its insistence on the purity of the national language.

3.   Historical Novels: The Making and Re-making of National Heroes

Traditionally, the historical novel has not only been popular but also very influential. The reasons for this are at least threefold: its 'historicism';[16] its role as the single most important source of knowledge about history for a large proportion of the population; and its leading role in a tradition where history is manipulated so as to comment on contemporary political and social realities.[17] The dramatic increase, in recent years, in the publication of historical novels and the production of historical drama in the theatre, in the cinema and on TV, is without doubt a result of the 'national essence heat'. A second contributing factor is the animated rediscovery of local culture. The heat is then turned up by commercial exploitation.

Two historical novels have been particularly influential in recent years: *Wen Tianxiang*, by Yang Youjin; and *Zeng Guofan*, by Tang Haoming, both of which were first published in Hunan Province. *Wen Tianxiang* was encouraged and supported by Hunan provincial leaders, while *Zeng Guofan* enjoyed enormous popularity throughout the country, especially in Hunan and among the country's intelligentsia. This reflects the pride that Hunan people take in two of their most prominent local heroes, and these novels can be seen as an effort to rediscover their local culture and reconstruct their local identity. At the same time, Wen and Zeng are two of the most well known historical figures throughout the country, and both works have been well received all over China. As Zeng Guofan will be discussed at length in the next chapter, we will focus on Wen here.

Like the *New War and Peace*, *Wen Tianxiang* was promoted as a textbook for patriotism. As a patriotic national hero, Wen has been glorified for more than 700 years. While his nationalist appeal is still current, his example has suffered from overuse. Besides, his immaculate image has been so established over the centuries that the author is not left with much room for manoeuvre in his characterisation. This praiseworthy image without blemish, as one critic, Wu Xiwen, put it, is monotonous. Of particular interest in *Wen Tianxiang* is Yang's handling of the awkward issue of Wen's patriotic national hero status. The dilemma is that Wen's enemies were the Mongols. Historically, the Mongols did not belong to the Song Dynasty, but they are citizens of the PRC today. If Wen is regarded as a Chinese national hero, then what are the Mongols? This dilemma is not only faced by Yang but also by other writers and historians in general, not only in the case of Wen

Tianxiang but also of Yue Fei and many other historical figures. In his short speech at a discussion on traditional culture and patriotism, which took place shortly after the Tiananmen events of 1989, influential critic and academic Ji Xianlin commented:

> Some people in history studies circles were stuck with rigid concepts for a long time in the past. They were shy of speaking of the resistance against the Mongols in history as patriotic, because the Mongols are now an ethnic group of the Chinese nation. That may be true today, but the war was between two separate nations. How can we look at history as if it is today's reality?[18]

Ji's comments obviously do not solve the problem, but they highlight two things that are of particular interest to us here. One is that Yang's dilemma is shared by others; at the same time, it must be pointed out that Ji speaks of the Han resistance against the Mongols as patriotic, not the Mongol expansion, even though he acknowledges that the Mongols belonged to a different nation. This view is certainly not uncommon in history books published in the PRC. There is sufficient reason to say that Chinese literature and historiography have basically been a Han affair. While Yang's novel does not significantly deviate from the views of Wen held by PRC writers in general, it is worth noting that it offers a modified version of the Han-Mongol conflict in the Song period. Kublai Khan, and some of his generals, are not shown in a bad light, and their ambition to unify China, in particular, is treated not without respect and admiration. In fact, what Yang does in the novel is to depict the Mongols as competitors rather than 'bad guys', and the real battle is between Wen Tianxiang and the corrupt elements in the Song Court. This treatment reveals an enhanced national consciousness in the place of Han identity on the part of the author, and accords with a literary trend, in recent years, of recreating not only Han emperors but an unprecedented number of non-Han emperors, such as Ghingis Khan, Kangxi, Qianlong and Guangxu. It is worth noting, too, that Yang emphasises Confucianism as a an important part of Wen's making. One can attribute Yang's emphasis to being truthful to history and dismiss any suggestion that it has something to do with the revival of Confucianism since the late 1980s. It cannot be denied, however, that it would have been inconceivable before 1978 for any writer to uphold Confucianism as Yang does. Yang's novel confirms the renewed interest in Confucianism since the 1980s as the heart and soul of Chinese culture.

4.   The Anti-American War: An Assertion of Chinese Values

On the anti-American front, the Korean War continues to be the main source of ammunition. But anti-American sentiment is nowhere more eloquently articulated than in *A Beijing Man in New York*, a TV series screened in 1993. In fact, the central theme of the show, can be summed up according to well-known writer and critic Zha Xiduo, in a single line: 'Screw you America'.[19] Wang Qiming, a hooligan by Maoist standards, made a fortune in the US against incredible odds. One day, he hired a white American prostitute. Before having his way with her, he scattered a bundle of greenbacks over her, and forced her to say repeatedly, 'I love you.' She did and he was satisfied. Another popular scene occurs when Ah Chun, Wang's lover, said, 'They (the Americans) can quite easily imagine a world without China, but could never conceive of a world without themselves'. Wang responded angrily, 'Fuck them! They were still monkeys up in the trees while we were already human beings. Look how hairy they are, they're not as evolved as us. Just 'cause they have a bit of money!'.

Reportedly, Chinese viewers, including bureaucrats and young intellectuals, were full of praise for the series.[20] Anti-American or anti-foreign sentiments are also common in the peculiar genre of reportage (*baogao wenxue*) published in 'low-brow' magazines, whose massive readership ranges from factory workers to villagers. It often abounds with stories of how Chinese have out-manoeuvred foreigners or how many foreign girls have married Chinese men. One reportage in *Literature and Life* (*Wenxue yu rensheng*) laments the fact that thousands of Chinese women married foreigners in the 1980s, and lists a set of exciting new figures: in the 1990s, thousands of foreign women have married Chinese men; in Guangdong Province alone, foreign brides reached a total of 40,000 by 1992, and the number is on the rise.[21]

Surprisingly, even Sha Yexin, a renowned playwright and former director of the Shanghai People's Artistic Theatre, has joined in this nationalist enterprise. His recent reportage in *Four Corners* (*Dongxi nanbei*), later adapted into a play, tells the story of a Chinese student, Qu Xiaoxue, studying in the US. While working as a part-time housekeeper for a rich American banker, Qu was subjected to all sorts of insults: She was summoned with a bell by the banker's mother because she could not remember Qu's name; and she was given left-over food. When she told them she was quitting, the banker flew into a rage. 'I've despised Negroes all my life,' he shouted, 'but you Chinese are worse!'.[22] Qu tried to explain and demanded her pay. The banker insisted that his mother had paid her, and when Qu pointed out that he was lying, he slapped her across the face, grabbed her by the hair and pushed her head against the wall until she lost consciousness.

Qu took on the American legal system and won. She won single-handedly, through determination and cleverness. She made the banker repeat his apology loudly three times in court, and tore up the cheque she was given as compensation, shouting,

> Go to hell, American dollars! What I want is dignity! Dignity! ...Some people think if they have money they can have everything; if they have money they can discriminate against other peoples; they can do anything they like; they can hurt the innocent; they can win court cases. But let me tell you, money can't buy the dignity of a Chinese girl. ...Let me also tell you, while going though this court case in the last four years, I've completed my Master's in sociology and PhD in information technology. I can proudly say: I haven't done badly at all! [23]

Qu Xiaoxue's victory is nothing compared with that of Li Han in *Doomsday* (*Mori zhi men*), a Chinese hero on the world stage. In fact, his name Han literally means 'Han Chinese' or 'man'. The story starts in Hong Kong on the Chinese New Year's Eve in the year 2000. Li Han, a PLA officer, came across a young woman named Chan, who was endowed with the power to foresee future events. The story unfolds as a world-wide war escalated: Presidents were assassinated; heads of states were held hostage; and terrorists attempted to annihilate mankind by using a computer virus. As expected, Li Han saved the world in the end. The first of its kind, *Mori zhi men* was extremely popular. The first edition of 200,000 copies were sold out quickly. For the first time, a Chinese man, instead of the James Bond type, was playing the role of a hero who saves mankind, and for the first time Hong Kong, instead of London, Paris, New York, or Washington, was the centre of events. In the words of critic Zhu Xiangqian, '*Mori zhi Men* is an assertion of orientalism over Eurocentrism'.[24]

These stories confirm that the well-known Chinese inclination to distinguish sharply between foreigners and themselves is alive and well. They also reveal some typical nationalist responses to the disgrace that China has suffered since the Opium War. Commenting on *The Beijing Man in New York*, Barmé wrote that 'It could be argued that by having his way with an American whore while buying her endearments with a shower of greenbacks, Wang Qiming's action is the most eloquent recent statement (in inversion) of the century-old Chinese-foreign dilemma'.[25] According to Linda Jaivin, 'the series represents the coming of age of Chinese narcissism, and it bespeaks a desire for revenge for all the real and perceived slights of the past century'.[26] Both their comments can be applied without much modification to Qu Xiaoxue's victory.

A point to be added here is that, what Linda Jaivin called 'all the real and perceived slights', have been made to look very real in Chinese literature and mass media. Given the large number of stories like these, and reports about Sino-US friction, it becomes easier to comprehend the enmity towards America in China. Another point to be stressed is that in both stories money assumes great significance in generating pride and confidence, whereas 'Chinese' values hold the key to success. Qu's academic success, amidst all the distractions of her court case, resulted from the fact that she was more intelligent, determined, persistent, hard-working, mentally tough and dedicated than her American counterparts. Wang demonstrated the same sort of 'Chinese' attributes, and it is these attributes that led to his triumph over David, his American rival in love and in business, who is romantic but immature, frivolous, emotionally unstable, fragile, capricious and unscrupulous. Wang's conquest of an American prostitute (symbolising America?) is made possible by his possession of bundles of money; whereas Qu's triumph is first of all a triumph over it, without which, according to Qu, discrimination, injustice, and hegemony would not be possible. This new emphasis on money contrasts sharply with culturalism's emphasis on culture alone, let alone the socialist pride in the great motherland, even though the acquisition of money is facilitated in the stories by unique 'Chinese' values. Undoubtedly, this reflects the importance attached to money as Chinese society becomes commercialised. The unprecedented assertiveness of Chinese nationalists, like Song Qiang, Zhang Zangzang, Qiao Bian, Wang Shan and Jiang Wen, could at least be partially attributed to China's increased economic strength.

A still more significant point to be added to Jaivin's comments on 'Chinese narcissism' is that its 'coming of age' is little more than an Ah-Q-typical declaration of victory, and it boils down to little more than a mere gesture - Wang Qiming showing a middle finger in defiance of America at the end of the series. Still, it is only one side of the story. The other side of it is that the nationalistic gestures of defiance, and symbols of conquest, are remarkably undercut by the beautified imagery of New York, and thinly veiled attempts to flaunt to Chinese viewers, who cannot see with their own eyes, a modern paradise of luxurious houses, cars and living standards. To satisfy the curiosity about foreign lands, particularly of advanced Western countries, has been a major commercial consideration for some publishers and TV and film makers in recent years. The paradise-like New York in *A Beijing Man in New York* might also be explained in commercial terms, but the demand for it by viewers and the recreation of it on TV, bespeaks something other than revenge, and that is admiration, although it is not unqualified admiration, or unqualified admiration for all. The collective Chinese response to the US can even be said to mix admiration with resentment, and these sentiments jar with each other in *The Beijing Man in New York*. Thus the nationalistic assertiveness is accompanied by a sense of inferiority in the series, and this, as has been pointed out by many, is a typical characteristic of insecure nationalism.

5.   The Anti-Japanese War: Re-claiming Victory on Behalf of Nation

The Anti-Japanese War has been the subject matter for many thousands of novels and poems since the 1930s. It has always been a powerful generator of nationalism and the number of works in this genre has increased since the late 1980s. Their publication is usually accompanied by official fanfare, this was particularly so during the celebrations of the 50th anniversary of the Chinese victory over Japan. It would be quite wrong, however, to suggest that official encouragement alone accounts for the increase of works in this genre, and their new popularity. There is reason to believe that it reflects the anti-Japanese sentiment that has been growing in China since the anti-Japanese demonstrations by Chinese students in 1984 and which reached new heights during the *Diaoyu* Islands (Senkaku) disputes in 1996.

Resentment against Japan stems from a perception, shared by many, that Japan is still unrepentant of its atrocities in China, and other countries, during World War II; that militarism is deep-rooted in Japan; that Japan is not grateful to China for giving up its right to reparations, when it threatens to suspend aid to China over nuclear tests and other issues, while the aid should really be regarded by Japan as another form of compensation that the Chinese people deserve; that Japan rips China off through 'cunning' trade practices and tries to slow down China's modernisation by blocking technology transfer, while it should be helping China to catch up, because Japanese invasion is largely responsible for China's backwardness today; and that Japan sees China as its chief enemy and is eager to collaborate with the Americans in containing it.²⁷ State nationalism has added substantive fuel to the flames of popular nationalism. The 1990s, as a result, witnessed a nationalist movement without parallel in the last few decades. According to eminent dissident Liu Xiaobao, the 'ultra-nationalist' movement in the 1990s has surpassed all others since 1949.²⁸

It should be pointed out that, unlike novels with an anti-American thrust, anti-Japanese works are invariably set in World War II, which betrays a dilemma that the Chinese government has on its hands. On the one hand, the Chinese government has always used the war for the purpose of patriotic education, and at times used public resentment against Japan to pressure Japan into a compromise on bilateral relations. On the other hand, it is eager to build a friendly relationship with Japan, and, for that reason, has usually discouraged or suppressed any formal expressions of anti-Japanese sentiments directed at the current Japanese government. As a matter of fact, anti-Japanese protests over the *Diaoyu* Islands were discouraged; as were petitions for compensation from the Japanese by war victims in the late 1980s, and petitions in 1996 to have Japanese chemical weapons deactivated and disposed of in Japan rather than China. Anti-Japanese sentiments are not always easy for the Chinese government to handle, as for tactical reasons the Chinese government has openly admitted to the Japanese government. It is under enormous pressure to act uncompromisingly on such issues as the *Diaoyu* dispute and the disposing of chemical weapons left in China by Japan, but the Chinese government cannot do so without damaging Sino-Japanese relations which it is eager to improve. Compromises by the Chinese government have often caused resentment among nationalists, and even the general public. In all those cases, just as in giving up the right to reparations, the Chinese government has been widely seen to have sacrificed national interest for the sake of some Japanese good will which has never materialised. In that sense, anti-Japanese sentiments can easily backfire on the government.

Among all the works about the Anti-Japanese War the one that has won the hearts of prominent conservative leaders is the eight-volume *New War and Peace (Xin zhanzheng yu heping)* written by the 82-year-old veteran cadre-writer, Li Erzhong. Adhering to the class point of view, the novel emphasises the Party's paramount leading role in the war. A seminar on Li's lengthy work was organised in Beijing even before it was completed. Li Ruihuan commented, 'I believe this novel will have a good impact in the patriotism and revolutionary tradition education'.²⁹ Sun Renqiong described *New War and Peace* as 'a textbook for patriotism'. Bo Yibo, and Wang Renzhong also, emphasised the novel's patriotic theme.[30] A second seminar took place in 1994 and present were Sun Ping, Ma Wenrui, Deng Liqun, Lin Mohan and other Party veterans and cadre-writers. A 'Special Committee for the Study of *New War and Peace*' was set up to maximise the patriotic impact of the novel.

The special treatment of the novel must be attributed to the fact that it fits in well with the official brand of nationalism. But even a veteran cadre-writer like Li has broken new ground by decorating his works with a few Nationalists, namely Feng Yuxiang, Zhang Xueliang, and Zhang Zizhong, who figure prominently because of their dedication to the national cause. In fact, in the first four volumes of the novel, the central hero is Zhang Xueliang. In this respect, this work differs from traditional anti-Japanese novels written before 1978. This is, however, more an attempt to create the impression of objectivity and make the work more novel rather than anything else. Besides, Feng Yuxiang, Zhang Xueliang and Zhang Zizhong have appeared frequently in movies and literary works in recent years. As compared with younger writers, Li is very conservative in his portrayal of patriotic Nationalists. War novels by Wang Huo, You Fengwei, Zhou Meiseng and Shang Kaiwen, divert much further from the Maoist orthodoxy.

The contribution of the KMT to the Chinese victory over Japan was not even mentioned for a long time by mainland historians or writers. It was not mentioned in school textbooks, either. For decades, the official line was that the CCP alone led the nation in the war while the Nationalists were more eager to fight the Communists than the Japanese. It was probably not until the movie the *Bloody Battle of Taierzhuang (Xuezhan Taierzhuang)* was released in 1988 that the general public became aware of the KMT's participation in the resistance. Since then, a number of young writers, particularly Wang Huo, Zhou Meiseng, Zhang Tingzhu, and Jiang Jianwen, have produced some popular works about patriotic KMT soldiers and generals fighting the Japanese as members of the Chinese nation. A good example is Wang Huo's *War and Man (Zhanzheng yu ren)*. Wang's hero, Tong Shuangwei, is a high-ranking KMT official and legal expert. In spite of his political convictions and affiliations, however, he saw himself first of all as a Chinese and responded to the CCP's call for national resistance: his partisan loyalty was overridden by the sense of duty to the nation. He also put the nation before his own interests by refusing to be part of the Wang Jingwei puppet regime propped up by the Japanese, despite being offered a coveted position.

Ye Zhaoyan and Shang Kaiwen detach themselves from the Communist-Nationalist politics to the extent that political beliefs are irrelevant in their novels, as is social background. The single most potent driving force behind their heroes is a nationalistic sentiment. Mr Ding in Ye Zhaoyan's *The Moon Tower* (*Zhuiyue lou*), was a member of the Qing Imperial Academy, now leading a life of fortune in Nanjing. After the city fell to the Japanese, he put up a personal fight by refusing to leave his Moon Tower and he instructed his family to bury him in the tower when he died so that he would not be subjected to the indignity of seeing, or being seen, in life or in death by the Japanese. So far as Ye is concerned, Mr Ding was no less heroic than soldiers fighting at the front, and by virtue of his unyielding integrity, he becomes another one in a long line of Confucian scholars in history and literature, who would rather die than live under the same sky with invaders. Unlike Mr Ding, Shang Kaiweng's hero in *A Legend in the Grandpa Mountains* (*Laoyeling chuanqi*), Guan Pengfei, was an untouchable - a fierce-looking bandit who used to make a living by stealing horses. After the Japanese invasion of Heilongjian, he formed a small army and dealt the Japanese one blow after another by dint of courage and clever tactics.

This trend of depoliticising the Chinese resistance was probably started by Mo Yan in *Red Sorghum*, which was first published in 1986. Mo Yan's hero, Yu Zhanao, had no affiliations to the CCP, nor to the KMT. A bunch of poorly armed and poorly organised bandits, Yu Zhanao and his men did not seem to have anything to do with any 'isms' except a rough and ready nationalism: China was invaded by the Japanese; and as Chinese, it was their duty to fight the invaders. 'They murdered and robbed; they served the nation loyally,' declares the narrator matter-of-factly at the very beginning of the novel.[31] This seemingly illogical description appears to be intended to defy logic, especially the logic that Chinese readers are accustomed to. The point that Mo Yan is apparently making is that being murderers and robbers does not prevent Yu Zhanao and his men from serving the country loyally. Another way of putting this is that murderers and robbers can also be patriots. Little attempt is made to explain their motives in the novel, still less in the film version. One is left with the impression that it was the most natural thing for them to have done.

There is hardly any doubt that the creation of heroes like Yu Zhanao, Guan Pengfei, Mr Ding and Tong Shuangwei is an attempt to subvert the perfect Communist hero in Maoist literature. It is also a challenge to official historiography and CCP propaganda. Collectively, the creators of the above heroes have contradicted the myth created by the CCP; perpetuated by Chinese literature from the 1950s to the 1970s; and subscribed to by many well into the 1980s. The message that comes through clearly is that patriotism is no longer the sole province of the CCP, nor is class a valid criterion of patriotism; the Anti-Japanese War was a spontaneous act of the Chinese nation rather than one motivated by political beliefs; and patriotism is primordial rather than instilled through socialist education. In other words, these works do not simply recreate the heroic resistance of the nation; they deal a blow to the CCP in the process by leaving it out of the picture or cutting it down to size, and by bringing into the limelight enemies of the CCP or elements that it considers not worthy to be members of the Chinese nation.

6. The Dual Thrust of Literary Nationalism

Official endorsement of *New War and Peace* and *Wen Tianxiang* are understandable, but silence about the rest of the works discussed above is quite extraordinary, although no longer surprising. On the one hand, the relaxation of political control is well documented, and it is a well-known fact that local authorities and publishers now enjoy more autonomy as a result of limited decentralisation and marketisation. In the last few years, in particular, the CCP and the central government have been following the strategy of concentrating on macro control and refraining from micro control (*zhuada fangxiao*). On the other hand, the Maoist ideology has decayed, with the rapid social changes, to such an extent that it has no more than nominal significance. The CCP does not appear to have the strength or even the intention to defend it so long as it is not openly attacked. Moreover, local CCP organisations and local governments are more interested in economics than politics, in spite of Jiang Zemin's call to emphasise politics. Besides, as government officials and PLA officers get involved in business deals they might be more eager to protect their own vested interest than to stand on Party principles so long as they do not get into trouble. Consequently, the book market is flooded with everything ranging from superstition to pornography. But it is absolutely wrong to suggest that it is now a free market. For the authorities can and do ban anything that they want to, as evidenced by the large number of books banned and publishers closed since 1978.

The deviation of the above works from the Party line precludes any possibility of official endorsement, even though their patriotic impact is something that CCP propagandists dream of. But neither are they censured, as many literary works were in the past. This is a clear indication of the increased freedom that writers now enjoy. So long as the CCP does not effectively stop them, Chinese writers and academics will continue to test its tolerance and win every bit of territory in an war of attrition, as they have been doing ever since 1978. The result will be increasing freedom of expression, political tolerance and uncontrolled public space.

For want of a better alternative, the reliance on patriotism, as a unifying ideology, is most likely to continue in the future. But the patriotism expressed is hardly reliable. For, as has been discussed, it by no means complies with the CCP's terms, if it has any. On the contrary, the nationalist rhetoric turns out to be a double-edged sword: It attacks the West and Japan, on the one hand, by arousing anti-American and anti-Japanese sentiments, and the CCP, on the other, even though it benefits from it. While it has an enormous patriotic impact, it is often accompanied by a hidden agenda that targets the Maoist ideology and the Party-state. There appears to be a deliberate insistence, on the part of the writers, on making 'our nation', instead of the Party-state, the focus of loyalty; and there seems to be a disguised attempt to exclude the CCP from the 'Chinese nation' that is being imagined.

To Ah Cheng and Han Shaogong, for example, the Communist movement in China is foreign intrusion; and their call to the nation is to return to the real Chinese tradition, stigmatised by the Communists. Nativist literature's return to the roots represents a rejection of the socialist heritage, together with the modern or Western influence, and its embracing of the tradition and culture stigmatised by the Communists is nothing but an act of defiance. The novels set in the anti-Japanese War seek to deflate the myth that the CCP led the nation to victory and the myth that socialist consciousness and Marxism are the prerequisites for bravery. The anti-American stories take place outside the CCP's sphere of influence. The heroes' success results from their being Chinese rather than having a socialist consciousness or pride in the socialist motherland, as was invariably the case in literature before 1978 and sometimes in the 1980s and 1990s. The historical novels, especially *Zeng Guofan*, contradicts Marxist historiography and presents readers with a new species of national heroes, nourished by Chinese tradition and Chinese culture rather than recast in the Marxist mould.

The CCP's reliance on nationalism is clearly an attempt to reconstruct a broader basis of national authority as rapid social changes are rendering the Maoist ideology irrelevant day by day. Its value will continue to decrease in the face of the new challenges, such as the integration of Hong Kong and unification with Taiwan. However, the CCP's traditional role, as guardian of patriotism, diminishes as patriotism ceases to be its sole province, as the ambit of what is seen to be patriotic becomes expanded to include what is unacceptable or even abominable to its fundamental ideology, and as the content of patriotism is no longer dictated by the Party, but modified and redefined by writers and intellectuals. By creating a new species of national heroes, out of bandits, hooligans, landlords, KMT officers and officials, and traitors, the writers are including in the new nation that is being imagined those who have previously been excluded by the CCP. By leaving the CCP virtually out of the picture, they are certainly not keen to include it in this nation. In doing so, they give one a fairly good idea as to who and what is included in 'their' nation. And by recasting them in the 'Chinese' mould, rather than the Marxist or CCP ones, highlighting their 'Chineseness' and firmly planting them in the Chinese tradition and culture rather than class consciousness or partisan loyalty, they make the nature of 'their' nation quite clear. It is probably not too far-fetched to see this as a struggle to break free from the shackles of Communism; a struggle motivated by the deep conviction that China has been led astray by the CCP, that China is better off returning to its own roots, and that 'their' new Chinese nation will not be able to emerge without ridding itself of the un-Chinese influence of the CCP. Neither is it too far-fetched to see it as an endeavour by the intellectual elite to assume a leading role in the invention of a new nation.

This nation is referred to as 'their' nation because they are doing the 'imagining'. The CCP version of the Chinese nation, while parts of it might have strong appeal to popular nationalism and overlap with that of the intelligentsia, is not received with much enthusiasm in the media except by a handful of Party mouthpieces, such as the *People's Daily*, *Qiushi*, and *Banyue tan*. It is the writers and intellectuals, particularly a number of prominent ones, who are playing a leading role and swaying the debate. The 'national essence' heat itself and the revival of Confucianism speak volumes for the influence that Chinese intellectuals have on the society, when they are allowed to make themselves heard. It is, thus, fair to say that they, more than anybody else, are doing the 'imagining', and it looks as though the newly imagined Chinese nation will be shaped by them more than by any other social group.

This sheds some light on just who is imagining the nation, who are included or excluded, what the new nation is like and where the nation is going. Many signs point to a diminished role for the CCP and an expanded one for the intellectual elite in this national project. As it is, the CCP has already lost effective control over all significant intellectual debates on cultural and national issues, whereas the intellectuals are now exerting increasingly greater influence on the society than before 1978, and their leading role in intellectual and political debates of national significance, since the late 1980s, are nothing short of remarkable. The traditional respect for knowledge and for intellectuals as individuals may be disappearing as the Chinese society becomes commercialised, but their position as the guardian of 'national essence' and 'engineers for the soul' has not been challenged. Their opinions are well regarded by a population that is rightly sceptical of official channels of information. Furthermore, the conservative intellectuals of the 1990s have the added advantage over their radical colleagues of the late 1980s that, unlike the latter, they are embracing the Chinese tradition rather than condemning it, therefore facing far less resistance from the conservatives within the CCP and large proportions of the population; and that they are tolerated by the new, more conservative leadership because their return to the Chinese roots cannot be said to be unpatriotic, notwithstanding its adverse impact on the CCP.

With the decrease of political control and increase in the freedom of expression, their influence is bound to grow further, although it could be undermined, to some extent, by commercialisation; and before other social groups develop in strength and influence, the intelligentsia will continue to lead in intellectual, cultural or social debates. It will be surprising if that position is not translated into the power to generate and shape public opinion. If the CCP is no longer able to dictate public opinion, it will be forced to respond to it with still greater flexibility than it has already demonstrated. There is even the likelihood that a highly autonomous civil society will fill in the gap that results from the receding presence of the CCP in the public arena as it further withdraws from micro control and is forced out of other areas. There is no denying that this process is already well under way, even though the changes might not seem obvious at first glance.

These implications, however, do not seem to matter to the CCP yet, either because they have not dawned on its leadership, or because there is little it can do to contain the intellectuals. So, for the time being, the hundred flowers of nationalism are encouraged to blossom. And for the first time in the literary history of the PRC, villains and heroes are marching together under the same banner, the banner of patriotism.

Notes

1   Jonathan Unger (ed.), *Chinese Nationalism*, Armonk, New York: M.E. Sharpe, 1996, p. xvi.

2   Ibid., p. xi.

3   *Wenyi bao (Literary Weekly)*, 16 July 1988, p. 3.

4   Ah Q is the protagonist of *The True Story of Ah Q* by Lu Xun. Ah Q has a way of deceiving himself into believing that he has won every time he has lost. In China today, it has become a synonym of 'self-deception' - a trick used to maintain one's peace of mind or complacency in the face of humiliation.

5   See report in the *Literary Weekly*, 16 July 1988, p. 3.

6   *The People's Daily*, 17 July 1989. The editorial revealed that Yi Jiayan's article was withheld on Zhao Ziyang's instructions, and that Zhao showed the series to visiting foreign dignitaries. It stands to good reason that Zhao did not want to see the reforms damped by another campaign against 'bourgeois liberalism' which could result from a drawn-out attack on *Heshang*. Besides, it could sway public opinion in favour of his struggle with the conservatives on the issue of expanding the reforms.

7   Ibid.

8   Zhang Qinghua, *'Fanguan yu dingwei: ershi shiji zhongguo wenxue de wenhua jingyu'* ('Retrospection and Relocation: The Cultural Environment of Chinese Literature in the 20th Century'), *Wenyi pinglun (Literary Reviews)*, Jan 1996, p. 42.

9   Ah Cheng, 'Mankind Bound by Culture' (*Wenhua zhiyue zhe renlei*), *Wenyi bao (Literary Weekly)*, 6 July 1985, cited by Wang Lin in 'On the Mythical Quality of the Search for Roots in Literature', *Shehui kexue yanjiu* 4, 1994, p. 108.

10   Han Shaogong, 'Yexingzhe mengyu' ('Dream Talk of a Night Walker'), in Lin Jianfa (ed.), *Zhongguo zuojia mianmian guan (Modern Chinese Writers)*, Shidai wenyi chubanshe, 1994, p.139.

11   Li Jiefei, '*Xungen wenxue: gengxin de kaishi*' ('The Search for Roots in Literature: A New Beginning'), *Wenxue pinglun*, Aug. 199, pp. 102-3.

12   David Wang, Introduction, *From May Fourth to June Fourth - Fiction and Film in Twentieth-Century China*, Cambridge: Harvard University Press, 1993, p. 3.

13   Ibid.

14   Jia Pingao, *Shangzhou: Endless Tales*, Beijing: Huaxia chubanshe, 1995, vol. 3, p. 7.

15   Ibid., p. 214.

16   Andrew H. Plaks wrote in 'Towards a Critical Theory of Chinese Narrative', in *Chinese Narrative: Critical and Theoretical Essays* (Princeton: Princeton University Press, 1997), that 'Any theoretical inquiry into the nature of Chinese narrative must take its starting point in the acknowledgment of the immense importance of historiography and, in a certain sense, 'historicism' in the total aggregate of the culture. In fact, the question of how to define the narrative category in Chinese literature eventually boils down to whether or not there did exist within the traditional civilization a sense of the inherent commensurability of its two major forms: historiography and fiction'. p. 311.

17   This tradition is extensively studied in Jonathan Unger (ed.), *Using the Past to Serve the Present: historiography and politics in contemporary China*, Armonk, New York: M.E. Sharpe, 1993.

18   Ji Xianlin, '*Zhongguo zhishifenzi de aiguo chuβantong*' ('The Patriotic Tradition among Chinese Intellectuals'), *Xinhua Wenzhai*, May 1989, p. 164.

19   Zha Jianying, *China Pop: How Soap Operas, Tabloids, and Bestsellers Are Transforming a Culture*, New York: The New Press, 1995, p.17.

20   See Sang Ye, 'Zhunbei haole ma?' ('Are You Ready?'), translated by Barmé with Jaivin, in *The Year the Dragon Came*, Brisbane: Queensland University Press, 1996, cited by Barmé in 'To Screw Foreigners Is Patriotic: China's Avant-Garde

Nationalists', in Jonathan Unger (ed.), *Chinese Nationalism*, Armonk, New York: M.E. Sharpe, 1996, p. 183.

21   Mu Fu, 'Yangniuer Zhongguo ze xu' ('Foreign Girls Find Husbands in China'), in *Wenxue yu rensheng (Literature and Life)*, No. 138, April 1996, p. 16.

22   Sha Yexin, 'Zhongguore de zunyan buke ru' ('Chinese Dignity Is Not for Sale'), in *Dongxi nanbei (Four Corners)*, Mar. 1997, pp. 4-5.

23   Ibid. p. 5.

24   Zhu Xiangqian, 'Jiushi niandai: changpian junlu xiaoshuo de chaodong' ('The 90s: Novels with Military Themes'), *Wenxue pinglun (Literary Reviews)*, Jan. 1996, p. 58.

25   Geremie Barmé, op. cit., p. 210.

26   Linda Jaivin, 'Life in a Battlefield', *Asian Wall Street Journal*, 24-25 Dec. 1993, cited by Barmé, op. cit., p.184.

27   These views are expressed by Song Qian, Zhang Zangzang, and Qiao Bian in *China Can Say No*, Beijing: *Zhonghua gongshang lianhe chubanshe*, 1996.

28   Liu Xiaobo, 'Chinese Ultra-Nationalism in the 1990s', Internet:http://bjs.org/bjs/44/31.

29   Quoted by Wen Liping in a report on the seminar, *Wenyi lilun yu pinglun (Literary Theory and Criticism)*, Mar. 1993, p. 132.

30   Ibid.

31   Mo Yan, *Hong lao liang*, Hong Kong: Xueshu chubanshe, 1986, p. 1.

4 Reimagining the Nation: The 'Zeng Guofan phenomenon'

Following the discussion of state nationalism and its construction of national identity in chapter 2, and the examination of the Chinese intellectuals' competing notions of nation in chapter 3, this chapter will focus on the Chinese intellectual search for a civic and territorial notion of national identity. As early as the last century, Liang Qichao entertained the vision of a pan-Chinese nationalism (*da minzuzhuyi*), extending automatic membership of the Chinese nation to the Manchus, Mongols, Uighur, and Tibetans. Today's Chinese intellectuals continue this tradition by inventing a pan-Chinese identity, as is well demonstrated by the case of the 'Zeng Guofan phenomenon'.

Zeng Guofan (1811-1872) has been one of the most controversial figures in modern Chinese history. He has been variously judged a 'saint' as well as a 'lackey of the Manchus', a 'cold-blooded killer', and a 'traitor'. Since the mid-1980s, interest in Zeng in China has escalated into a virtual frenzy. Between January 1981 and March 1997, publications on Zeng have included *The Complete Writings of Zeng Guofan*, *The Letters of Zeng Guofan*, two biographies, a script for a 50-episode television series entitled *Zeng Guofan*, a play with the same title, 433 articles, and half a dozen book-length studies.[1] The debate broke out of the ivory tower of academia with the publication, in 1993, of Tang Haoming's popular three-volume historical novel *Zeng Guofan*, which caused a sensation throughout the country as well as in the Chinese diaspora in Asia: it was printed 19 times between October 1993 and May 1996, and over a million copies were sold in the first two years alone. And there is still no sign of a slackening of interest. Such is the obsession with Zeng in China that it warrants the label 'the Zeng Guofan phenomenon'.

What is the fuss over Zeng Guofan all about? One explanation is that it has to do with the renaissance of Hunan regional culture that took place in 1993-94. Another view emphasizes that readers today can find in Zeng's career a 'textbook' of classic Chinese power politics. Still another explanation holds that it is a reflection of the popular yearning, in the 1990s, for national heroes.[2] Zeng's newly-found popularity can also be attributed, in part, to the fact that he was taboo between 1949 and 1978. This has made it all the more tempting for scholars to set the record straight, although it has to be admitted that not all Chinese historians and scholars are in this debate for the same reason. Contributors to the 'phenomenon' include aspiring young historians and undergraduate students who are eager to make a name for themselves, and even business people who are keen to capitalize on the Zeng frenzy. What is most striking is that Zeng appears to provide writers and readers with all sorts of opportunities and possibilities, and such seems his significance that an answer to questions about him can appear to be the key to many problems that confront Chinese society.

What is most important to us is the ideological and political dimension of the phenomenon, something which has scarcely been touched upon so far. Regardless of their seeming preoccupation with historicity, the arguments and counter-arguments are evidently not just about the past. Neither are they simply about Zeng Guofan. They reach far beyond Zeng to traverse at least three overlapping areas: academic, political, and cultural. The most fundamental questions raised in the debate are not only about historical studies but also about class analysis and historical materialism; revolution versus evolution; and tradition and culture. Above all, the debate raises a fundamental underlying issue, that is, the issue of national identity, or the reimagination of a Chinese nation through the rewriting of 'Chinese' history. The real site of contestation in this debate is the nation, and the central theme is 'Chineseness'.

1. The Ups and Downs of Zeng Guofan Since the Late Qing

The current 'Zeng Guofan phenomenon' may be a product of the 1990s, but it is certainly not the first revival of Zeng since the late Qing. Zeng has been 'rediscovered' at major critical junctures when competing ideologies or value systems clashed and Chinese political and intellectual elites sought a new historical consciousness, or wished to enlist new energies for a difficult task on a national scale.

From the Late Qing to the 1980s

Zeng Guofan's place in history was secured when Xue Fucheng, at the request of Li Hongzhang, wrote a report to the emperor to commend Zeng's virtues and achievements. In his report, Xue compared Zeng to

China's outstanding ministers of all time, Zhu Geliang, Lu Zhi, and Si Maguang. Leading Qing reformer Liang Qichao believed that Zeng would have been the salvation of China at the end of the nineteenth century had he been alive and well. Liang argued that the *Collected Essays of Zeng Guofan* (*Zeng Wenzheng gong quanji*) provided valuable answers to restoring order to China. The nationalist project of Confucian modernizer, Zhang Zhidong, - 'preserving our race, our religion, and our state' - arguably owed more to Zeng's influence than anything else in placing 'our religion', or Confucianism, squarely in the center of the triad, to be preserved above all else and used to guide the preservation of 'our race' and 'our state'.

Sun Yat-sen's republicans attacked Zeng because of his identification with the Manchus, although on this point they were quite moderate compared with the Marxists, and even more so after their anti-Manchu revolution succeeded. Zeng was back in favor during the brief restoration of Yuan Shikai, who backed his cause against the republican revolutionaries, with Confucianism and claims to religious and cultural orthodoxy. Chiang Kai-shek's promotion of Confucianism, and Zeng, as 'a model for national salvation and nation building' might have been part of a scheme to secure some certainty during the first tumultuous decades of the century, but it was first and foremost aimed at the Communists. Chiang even commissioned a booklet, *Zeng Guofan and Hu Linyi on Military Affairs*, for which he personally wrote a preface, so that his generals, with this manual in hand, could defeat the Communists, just as Zeng's army had routed the Taipings.

Under Chiang's sponsorship, the study of Zeng reached its first climax in the 1930s and 1940s. Half a dozen book-length studies on Zeng were published, all of which portrayed him as the first man in the last five hundred years to have put his learning to good practical use in his political and military career; as one of the 'perfect' men of the past and present; as a brilliant example to be emulated by China's youth for self-education and self-perfection; and as a statesman who made an enormous contribution to the nation and state. That image, like his image in the 1990s, is quintessentially 'Chinese'.

The young Mao Zedong, before he realized it could not bear up under the scrutiny of Marxian historiography, professed that the only man in modern China whom he admired was Zeng Guofan.[3] But such sentiments were not repeated by anyone until the 1980s. There was considerable interest in Zeng before 1957 and, even then, some historians raised objections to branding Zeng a traitor on the grounds that he remained loyal to the Qing. Until 1974, Zeng was mentioned from time to time, but only as a target for criticism, during the Criticizing Lin Biao and Criticizing Confucius Campaign, because of his Confucian credentials.

Zeng Guofan in the 1990s

Interest in Zeng reemerged gradually between 1979 and 1988 - only 65 out of the 433 articles were published during those ten years - but started to soar after 1989. The skyrocketing attention paid to Zeng apparently parallels the spread of the 'national essence fever' that emerged in 1989, and, in terms of content, the 'Zeng Guofan phenomenon' is really part and parcel of the latter. It is not easy to find satisfactory answers as to the causes of these complex social trends, but it can be generally argued that the fever arose in the 1990s to meet the need of a new historical consciousness or a feeling of continuity projected backward and forward amidst the massive uncertainties of the time.[4]

More specifically, China in the 1980s and 1990s was caught up in two major sociopolitical processes: accelerated modernization and the abrupt ending of the Cold War. That 1989 marks significant changes in China is not at all surprising, given the Tiananmen events and their far-reaching consequences. Post-Tiananmen China not only saw a change of guard in the Chinese Communist Party (CCP) leadership, but also the resurgence of cultural nationalists and the rise in national confidence, as the economy improved. The brutal suppression of the students did much to intensify a 'crisis of faith' which had already become manifest before the June events. It was not merely a loss of faith in Communism but a loss of faith in Chinese culture and tradition in general. The combined effect of the collapse of Communism in Eastern Europe; serious problems that plagued China's trial-and-error reforms; the influx of Western ideas and concepts; and the loss of faith in Chinese tradition and culture, reduced national confidence to such a low ebb that the 'correct' view of the 1980s was that nothing except wholesale Westernization could save China.

In the 1990s the backlash against the 1980s Westernization discourse took the form of a 'national essence fever', as intellectual elites began to reevaluate and rediscover tradition. A perception of ethical degeneration, as a result of the heady commercialization of the 1990s, created an urgent demand for moral regeneration. This has gathered additional strength by feeding on the CCP's Patriotic Campaigns which promote 'relevant elements of national culture'.

Moreover, calls for a strong primordial Chinese cultural unity have become more strident in the face of a number of new challenges in the 1990s - growing regionalism and secessionist movements in Tibet and Xinjiang, the integration of Hong Kong and Macao; the drive for reunification with Taiwan; and the vision of a 'Cultural China' - where a stigmatized Marxist ideology is a liability rather than an asset.

The 'national essence fever', in both form and content, is highly reminiscent of 'the search for roots' in Chinese literature in the 1980s. Returning to the spirit of the past means a historical perspective that reads the appropriate trends into events, accompanied by a revaluation of historical figures to identify instruments of national destiny or obstacles to it.[5] Nationalist historians not only need to re-create an authentic past but, in order to rally the community behind them, create new heroes to personify the cultural tradition of China. Thus Zeng has been rediscovered precisely because he is now widely seen as a national hero who saved China from chaos and who, as reputedly 'the last Confucian', best represents the Confucian tradition and should thus be emulated.

The Pros and Cons in the Current Debate

In the official CCP historiography, Zeng stands condemned as a 'traitor to the Han' (*Hanjian*), a 'traitor to his country' (*maiguozei*), and a 'cold-blooded killer' (*guizishou*). This verdict was sanctified by authoritative philosopher Feng Youlan. For over three decades, Feng's judgments were accepted as the CCP's official position and were not openly challenged until the beginning of the 1980s. Although Chinese historians are still not unanimous about Zeng, his rehabilitation is now becoming a solid reality, regardless of the opposition from Marxist historians, who are certainly not dead and buried, even though they are steadily losing ground. There is now something approaching a consensus that Zeng was an exemplary Confucian man of literary and professional achievements and moral excellence, and that the prominence of his role in modern Chinese history has been surpassed by few. The main battle, of course, is fought over his characterization as a 'traitor to the Han', a 'traitor to his country', and a 'cold-blooded killer'. Table 4.1 summarizes the major points of contention based on the 43 articles found in *Fuyin baokan ziliao* and quantitatively compares the arguments and counter-arguments.

Table 4.1   Major Points of Contention in the Debate on Zeng Guofan

Contention	yes	no	mainly affirmative	mainly negative	NA
1. Was Zeng a traitor to the Han?	2 (4.7%)	26 (60%)	0	0	15 (35%)
2. Was he a traitor to his country?	4 (9.3%)	21 (49%)	0	4 (9.3%)	14 (33%)
3. Was his suppression of the rebels justified ?	4 (9.3%)	5 (12%)	10 (23%)	3 (7%)	21 (49%)
4. Was his handling of the riots justified?	1 (2.3%)	3 (7%)	9 (21%)	8 (19%)	22 (51%)
5. Did he play a positive role in *yangwu?*	23 (53%)	1 (2%)	8 (19%)	2 (4.7%)	9 (21%)
6. Was *yangwu* positive ?	28 (65%)	8 (19%)	2 (5%)	1 (2.3%)	4 (9.3%)
7. Should Zeng, the Confucian man, be denounced?	1 (2.3%)	6 (14%)	5 (12%)	21 (49%)	10 (23%)
8. Was he an exemplary man of virtue ?	25 (58%)	1 (2%)	7 (16%)	4 (9.3%)	6 (14%)

Source: Based on 43 articles published between Jan. 1981 and June 1997 and extracted in *Fuyin baokan ziliao, Zhongguo jindai shi.*

The first four points of contention in Table 4.1 revolve around the question of whether Zeng was a 'traitor to the Han', a 'traitor to his country', and a 'cold-blooded killer'; the last four go well beyond Zeng's historical role and his character and bring into focus such issues as China's modernization and Confucianism. In the answers to these questions lies a large range of important issues in China's intellectual and political life. For the sake of clarity, let us now look at each of the first three questions individually before discussing the political implications of the debate.

2. Han-centric Conceptions of National Identity Under Challenge

The labels 'traitor to his country' and 'cold-blooded killer' are primarily based on Zeng's suppression of anti-French riots in Tianjin in 1870, and his crushing of the Taiping rebellion. But the official historiography is necessarily vague about the epithet 'traitor to the Han' because of the CCP's declared opposition to Han chauvinism and its fear of inciting ethnic division. It is nonetheless fairly clear that the only reason that Zeng was labeled a 'traitor to the Han' was his loyalty to the Manchu Qing dynasty, despite the fact that he was of the Han nationality himself. Some historians, who apparently do not distinguish between the 'Han' and the 'Chinese', but take it for granted that the former equals the latter, even go so far as to condemn him as a 'traitor to his country' for the very same reason. Many others insist that an evaluation of Zeng, from Han and Marxist perspectives, falls short of being 'objective', and is unacceptable to many Chinese people, including those Han who regard the Qing dynasty as a Chinese state.

Was Zeng Guofan a 'traitor to the Han'? Feng Youlan's answer was definitely affirmative, the reason being that 'Zeng Guofan and a bunch of followers had no national loyalty but willingly turned themselves into obedient slaves of the Manchus and slaughtered Han people'.[6] Of course, the Han people that they 'slaughtered' included Taiping rebels, and thus a question about ethnic loyalty becomes intertwined with ideology. From a Marxist point of view, the rebels were on the right side of history whereas Zeng was not. But to condemn Zeng as a 'traitor to the Han' on that score is hardly tenable. The accusation is not much more tenable if it is based upon his loyalty to the Manchu dynasty. For those reasons, the first label is not seriously defended today by anyone.

A few historians have vaguely referred to Zeng as a 'traitor to the Han', in their discussions of his ruthless campaigns against the rebels, and his identification with the Manchus. However, not a single article that we have read makes any attempt to justify the label. A common argument is that it is not fair to accuse Zeng of betraying the Han people because, first, 'both the Han and the Manchus belonged to the same Chinese nation, which had been fostered for over two centuries when Zeng came onto the scene'; and second, 'the Manchu dynasty was a legitimate Chinese state' and loyalty to the state, which encompassed the Han, was not a betrayal of the Han.'[7] If Zeng was a traitor to the Han, they argue, then Lin Zexu, Wei Yuan, Zuo Zongtang and many others, who served the Qing dynasty, cannot possibly be patriotic national heroes. To perpetuate the label, they further argue, runs counter to the interest of the whole nation by dividing the Han and the Manchu peoples.[8]

Was Zeng a 'traitor to his country'? Here the debate centers on Zeng's dealings with Westerners, particularly his handling of the Tianjin riots. His critics believe he sacrificed national dignity and the interests of the people.[9] His defenders, on the other hand, contend that he did the best he could under the circumstances, and that he did not give in wherever he could stand firm, in order to minimize damage to the Chinese government and to the local community in Tianjin. In any case, he was by no means a 'traitor to his country', even though he was not entirely blameless.[10] Much of the argument over labeling Zeng a 'traitor to his country' revolves around his role in the modernization movement (*yangwu yundong*). Critics of Zeng Guofan in this regard, and they are not many, fall into two main categories: those who are skeptical of his role rather than of the movement itself, and those who are critical of both. The former take exception to his moderate foreign policy, which was built on, in Zeng's words, 'sincerity, credibility, honesty, and respect'. To his sharpest critics, these Confucian principles meant nothing under the treaty system but appeasement of the invaders at the cost of state sovereignty and national dignity. These critics charge that Zeng's policies of 'appeasement' are responsible for China's humiliations from the late Qing to 1949.[11] The historian Zhu Andong suggests that the modernization program was futile because of Zeng's appeasement policies, as the more China gave in to the West, the weaker it became, thus launching it on a vicious circle that rendered any advance in technology insignificant. In this regard, some historians have contrasted Zeng's moderate, pragmatic foreign policies with the belligerent stance of Lin Zexu and Zuo Zongtang; these critics conclude that there is no comparison between 'Zeng's cowardice' and the 'patriotic heroism of Lin and Zuo'.[12]

Those who find nothing positive, either in Zeng's modernization program or in the modernization movement itself, consciously or unconsciously start from a Marxist point of view and continue to use the pre-1978 revolutionary language. Their conclusion is that Zeng had gunboats built for no other reason than to protect Western interests and facilitate foreign invasion;[13] that the whole program was an effort on the part of the ruling landed class, of which Zeng was a representative, to wipe out the Taiping rebels and salvage the crumbling reactionary

Manchu Qing dynasty; and that in order to achieve that objective, Zeng and his associates had to collaborate with the imperialists.[14]

Most historians, however, recognize Zeng's contribution to China's first steps toward modernization and the positive historical impact of the movement. It is frequently pointed out that it was under his aegis that China's first steamship, first arsenal, and first machine-tool manufacturer were born. It was also with his support that education developed quickly in China; the first Chinese students were sent to the West to study modern science and technology; and the first translation service was set up to take control of the flow of information from the West, which had theretofore been monopolized by foreign missionaries. In short, thanks to Zeng, China began to open its doors to the outside world.

Many authors also agree that, while Zeng's foreign policy may have been imperfect, its moderation, realism, and rationality ensured peace and facilitated national self-strengthening.[15] To some, Zeng's major contribution was that he translated the idea of *shi yizhi* (acquiring the wisdom of the foreigners) into a social reality, and started a process of industrialization that has had a most profoundly positive impact on modern China.[16] On that basis, some even claim that not only was Zeng not a 'traitor to the Han' but he was actually a national hero.[17] At any rate, Zeng's belief that China could improve its lot through systematic application of science, technology, and social organization appears to fit better with the Chinese idea of modernization today than Sun Yat-sen's ethnocentric nationalism and Mao's Marxist alternative.

Zeng is not the only influential historical figure to have been recently revalued. Under review have also been Guo Songtao, Li Hongzhang, and Lin Zexu, and even Wen Tianxiang and Yue Fei, archetypal Chinese national heroes, and Qin Hui, the archetypal traitor. Guo Songtao and Li Hongzhang, in particular, were both closely associated with Zeng. Guo, China's first ambassador to Britain, could be described as a pillar in Zeng's think-tank, which consisted of a large group of intellectuals who operated outside the establishment but nevertheless were committed to safeguarding a centuries-old tradition of orthodoxy. It was Guo who overcame Zeng's reluctance and talked him into leading the anti-Taiping campaign. And it was also Guo, as is often pointed out, who was responsible for Zeng's moderate foreign policies. Thus, if Zeng is a traitor, Guo cannot possibly be a patriot, as he is portrayed; and if Zeng is to be condemned for his role in the defeat of the Taipings, then Guo is certainly not blameless.

In recent years, historians have questioned the juxtaposition of Yue Fei as national hero and Qin Hui as traitor, because, for one thing, Yue's enemies and Qin's allies were the Mongols, many of whose descendants are today citizens of China. Since Yue Fei was fighting for the Han, and since the Chinese nation now includes Mongols, it then becomes problematic to continue to promote him as a patriotic Chinese national hero, just as it is questionable to label Zeng a traitor to his country because of his loyalty to the Chinese state created by the Manchus. The use of history to promote nationalism, in a polyethnic nation like China, has caused no small amount of confusion and resentment among ethnic minorities. Underlying Yue's glorification and Zeng's condemnation is a tacit assumption that 'Han' equals 'China'. That assumption has now been brought into question in the debates on Zeng Guofan, Guo Songtao, Yue Fei, Wen Tianxiang, and Qin Hui.

There is insufficient evidence to enable us to say with any certainty, that Lin Zexu is being replaced by Zeng Guofan, Guo Songtao, and Li Hongzhang in the 'hit parade' among Chinese historians - indeed, Lin is and will continue to be regarded as a hero by Chinese nationalists, due to his integrity, well-established image, and popular appeal. But growing skepticism about Lin Zexu, coupled with a trend toward positive evaluations of Zeng, Guo, and Li, reflects shifting attitudes with respect to the 'Other'. A patriotic national hero, though Lin may be in the eyes of ultra nationalists today, the distinction between belligerence and rational diplomacy is no longer one of patriotism versus treason. To speak for the rational/moderate model of Zeng, Guo, and Li calls for a vision of the world as comprising nations that are more or less equal rather than as one consisting of a civilized 'us' and a barbaric 'them'; it is a vision that recognizes that conflicts are best resolved through negotiations and compromise.

3. Pan-Chinese Identity Superseding Revolutionary Identity

A Cold-Blooded Killer?

The epithet 'cold-blooded killer' is by far the thorniest question in the entire debate because of its political entanglements. Some historians - Jiang Duo, Liu Leyang, Dong Caishi, and Dong Qing among others - condemn Zeng for crushing the Taiping rebellion. They start from the premise that the Taipings were progressive, whereas Zeng represented the reactionary feudal landed class. Jiang Duo's argument is, in many ways, representative of the interpretations - as well as the political inclinations, methodology, and emotivity - of these historians. He is therefore worth quoting at some length:

> It seems impossible to justify Zeng Guofan's crime of suppressing the Taiping Heavenly Kingdom. Reversal of the verdict will not be easy. In any case, the fervent Taiping movement was the first national democratic movement in the nature of a bourgeois revolution led by peasants. It was mainly a progressive and just movement. The Qing dynasty supported by Zeng Guofan, on the other hand, represented the decadent forces of the feudal aristocratic and landed classes. As the last feudal regime, it was an embodiment of corruption and violence at their worst. It also surrendered national dignity in exchange for peace with foreign invaders. It was a reactionary and unjust regime on the whole. . . I do not think any more needs to be said as to where a progressive Marxist historian should stand.[18]

But Marxist historians are few in this debate. Some defend Zeng within the framework of class analysis and conclude that it was only natural for Zeng, a representative of the landed class, to oppose a peasant rebellion that threatened its rule.[19] Others defend Zeng on the grounds that the rebels, who became corrupt and went astray at the later stages, ceased to be a progressive force, and therefore their eradication was justified.[20] One author cleverly attacks the rebels by quoting the negative comments - which have been conveniently forgotten by Marxist historians - of Karl Marx on the rebels.[21]

Others simply ignore class distinctions and represent the conflict as one between state and rebels, or one over tradition and culture. The Taiping rebels, they argue, were not only out to destroy the legitimate state but Chinese culture and tradition as well. Peng Qian, for instance, argues that Hong Xiuquan posed a greater threat than any other rebel in history because he declared war on both the state and Chinese culture. In the eyes of Zeng Guofan, Peng suggests, at stake were 'the mores, morality, literary classics, and laws of several thousand years'.[22] What motivated Zeng in his ruthless campaign against the rebels was a determination to safeguard Chinese tradition; Zeng was thus an embodiment of the Chinese state (*wangchao*), Chinese tradition (*shendao*), and Confucianism.[23]

Some historians directly question the assumption that held sway for decades that peasant rebels are necessarily a progressive force. They even liken the 'cultural genocide' committed by the rebels, to the leftist excesses of the Gang of Four during the Cultural Revolution. Peng Qian, for instance, writes:

> A comprehensive study of the documents will enable us to see that the former [Zeng's suppression the Taiping rebels] has to do with their erroneous policy of liquidating or even randomly destroying the national culture. Imagine this: If . . . the works of Confucius, Mencius, and other Chinese philosophers are all banned and no one is allowed to read *Shijing* without the approval of Hong Xiuquan, would it be possible for our traditional national culture to survive? Is not that the same as what the Gang of Four did during the Cultural Revolution? For this reason, some scholars say that Zeng Guofan's Hunan Army was not really about defending the emperor but about accepting responsibility to safeguard the national culture.[24]

Peng goes on to question the progressiveness of peasant rebels:

> Did peasant movements throughout history play a positive role in the process of historical development? Did they have a negative impact while making some positive contribution? These questions are worth studying scientifically. The Taiping movement is no exception. . . . Historical evaluation should be able to stand the rigorous test of time.[25]

Revolution versus Evolution

The debate on Zeng Guofan versus Hong Xiuquan involves a clash of two remarkably different paradigms, namely evolution versus revolution. The revolutionary paradigm held sway over the writing of Chinese history for more than three decades. It guided the construction of a revolutionary identity on the foundation of a worker-peasant alliance. In the process, much of the past, that did not accord with this revolutionary vision, was erased. Modern Chinese history, under this paradigm, became a narrative of 'two processes' and 'three climaxes'. One of the processes was 'the colonization and semi-colonization of China by imperialists and Chinese feudalists'; the other was 'the struggle against imperialists and their running dogs by the Chinese people'. The three climaxes are 'the Taiping Revolution', the *Yihetuan* (Boxer) movement and the Revolution of 1911.

The challenge to this narrative has been surprisingly bold in recent years. Hu Bing, for instance, commented, in a speech published in the prominent journal *Wenshizhe* (*Literature, History and Philosophy*), that 'ultra-leftism in historiography is manifested in the belief that only revolutionary violence is just and in the failure to see the progressiveness of innovation and reform'.[26] Kong Linren's opinion was that both the peasants and the bourgeoisie fall within the category of 'the people'.[27] Renowned scholar Li Zehou wrote an article in 1994 entitled, 'Revolution Is Not Necessarily a Good Thing in China.' His target was not merely all the revolutions from 1911 to 1978, but also what he identified as the source of these revolutions, namely, intellectual and political radicalism, pioneered by Tan Sitong. After pointing out that Chinese Marxist historians have habitually taken a negative view of reform, he declared it is now time to abandon that type of revolutionary language and mentality.[28] Some Chinese scholars in exile in Hong Kong, enjoying the luxury of freedom of speech, excoriated revolution in a book entitled *Farewell to Revolution*.[29] Their definition of revolution is so comprehensive as to cover the French Revolution. In the same vein, they go far beyond the Qing reforms led by Kang Youwei and Liang Qichao to applaud the English Reformation. Their message is simple: turn away from the radical revolutionary social/political discourse and toward cultural conservatism.

Such a stance, not only rejects revolution as undesirable both as a concept and a practice, but denies the Chinese revolution its historicity by describing it as a historical aberration. Consequently, the Taiping and Boxer movements are almost 'forgotten', and the peasants and proletariat, cornerstones of a progressive revolutionary identity, are sidelined. Modern Chinese history is thus being rewritten as a natural, continuous process of evolution, led by the bourgeoisie instead of the peasants, wherein the progressive force is Confucianism. The focus has shifted back from certain economic aspects - the material means of production and ownership - to the realm of culture.[30] In its repudiation of the Marxists' conscious break with Chinese tradition, the new historiography gravitates toward 'new history' (*xin shixue*), which highlights the continuity of history and focuses on the evolution of China as a nation, the communal identity shared by the Chinese people, and the unique characteristics of the Chinese nation.

This anti-revolutionary trend developed steadily through the 1980s and 1990s. An excellent summary of this trend can be found in eminent Marxist historian Gong Shuduo's criticism of 'reversing the verdict' on Yuan Shikai:

> Reversals of judgments on historical figures and events are not unheard of in history, but they have become a fashion today. Speeches and writings

intended to reverse judgments on people and events in modern Chinese history are very common, and reversals take place as easily as pancakes are turned over in the pan. . . . The Taiping peasant rebellion led by Hong Xiuquan is now described as a 'historical regression' whereas Zeng Guofan's suppression of the rebellion is said to have made 'an enormous contribution to the prevention of a regression'. The Revolution of 1911 and the May 4th Movement are viewed as 'radical' [movements which] . . . not only disrupted the natural development of modern Chinese history, but had an adverse impact on the natural development of Chinese history today. The list of reversals goes on.[31]

It is worth emphasizing that this trend has developed regardless of counterattacks from CCP propagandists in *Seeking Truth* (*Qiushi*), the mouthpiece of the CCP's Ministry of Propaganda, the left-wing *Popular Forum* (*Qunyan*), and *Midstream* (*Zhongliu*), most of which are directed at what is described as the 'ideological thrust' of the trend. An article in *Zhongliu*, for example, put it simply, and correctly: 'farewell to revolution means farewell to Marxism, to socialism, and to the whole revolutionary tradition of the Chinese people'.[32] But its argument against the anti-revolutionary discourse is less than convincing, as it calls for the defense of all things under attack, a daunting task in China's current political and intellectual climate.

4. Reconstructing National Identity on a Confucian Foundation

At the cultural level, the debate on Zeng Guofan is primarily about Confucianism - the culture of the intellectual elite and of the general populace - and traditional Chinese values, or in short Chineseness. As a descendent of Zeng Zi, one of the main disciples of Confucius, and as an erudite Confucian (*tongru*), Zeng Guofan has impeccable Confucian credentials. Most critics attack Zeng from a class standpoint, clearly distinguishing between the progressive culture and values of the revolutionary classes and the reactionary values of the landed class. Zeng's defenders apparently refuse to engage in a debate on values in terms of class analysis and simply get on with the business of 'rediscovering' the values of Chinese nationalism, as if they were axiomatic.

In this, as in many other things, Zeng is the antithesis of the Taipings, who adopted Christianity and attacked Confucianism.

Therefore, some historians portray the Taipings not only as rebels against the Chinese state but as rebels against Chineseness itself. Here, the anti-revolution thesis parallels the argument against Westernization: both revolution and Westernization are historical aberrations. In fact, the call to 'return to the roots' results from a popular perception of ethical degeneration. In this common view, Chinese history deviated from its own natural path during the decades of revolution between 1911 and 1978 and it is now time that China returned to its 'true' historical path. A similar suggestion is that the remedy for the ills of a revolutionary China and a Westernizing China lies in the past, in the whole of China's cultural heritage, and in Confucianism in particular. When historians represent Zeng Guofan as an embodiment of tradition and Hong Xiuquan as a destroyer of tradition we perhaps learn less about Zeng and Hong than we do about the historians' own identification.

The rediscovered Zeng was an outstanding statesman who saved China from chaos. He was an accomplished man of letters, an influential educator, a trustworthy friend, and an exemplary man who led a simple life, attached great importance to learning, and upheld the four principal ideals of the Confucian man (achieving self-perfection, managing the family, governing the empire, and bringing order to all under heaven). Praise of Zeng as a statesman highlights his loyalty to the state and responsibility to the nation, which, among other things, compelled him to take on a job, against his own judgment that there was little he could do to avert the crisis at hand, prevented him from contemplating a coup urged by Zuo Zongtang and his own brother, Zeng Guoquan, and motivated his passion for modernization.

But nowhere is Zeng the Confucian better portrayed than in the setting of the family, valorized in Chinese culture as the embodiment of the nation's morality and the nurturer of the young. Zeng's image as a 'perfect' family man puts him well ahead of Mao Zedong, who is generally believed to have failed in that role. In fact, Zeng, as a strict but loving father, is often said to find no parallel in modern China. Evidence of Zeng's success as a father is contained in reports on the achievements of his descendants, among whom are some of China's most eminent diplomats, poets, scientists, educators, and scholars.[33]

Zeng's new image is, in short, one of the *junzi,* or gentleman. Yet in spite of his association with the establishment, he was a commoner of humble origins, not a member of the aristocracy. He, nevertheless, qualifies as a member of the Confucian moral elite. Indeed, inherent in his portrayal is an ethical quality that comes, not with birth, but is achieved through education and the practice of virtue. Therein lies part of his appeal. Zeng's image as a quintessential 'Chinese man', transcends ethnicity and class to offer a Pan-Chinese national consensus predicated on a presumed universal Chinese ethical quality.

The rediscovery of Zeng, 'the last Confucian', is linked with the revival of Confucianism in the past decade. It can be seen, at the same time, as a result of and contributor to its revival. It was perhaps not accidental that the subject of the first international cultural conference to take place in China, after the 1989 Tiananmen events, was Confucian thought.[34] Widely regarded as the heart and soul of Chinese culture, Confucianism is now at the core of the 'national essence' that is being rediscovered, reinvented, and reembraced today. In a word, Confucianism is again an essential criterion for defining the community. To quote from an article in *People's Daily*, Confucianism has reemerged as a progressive force 'advancing toward the twenty-first century with a smile on its lips'.[35]

The rehabilitation of Zeng Guofan and the revival of Confucianism are further complemented by the renewed interest in the myth of the Yellow Emperor, the supposed ancestor of the Chinese people. Confucius and the Yellow Emperor even enjoy a large measure of official recognition and support from the CCP: the Confucius Association of China and the Yellow Emperor Association of China are headed by former vice-premier Gu Mu and retired general Xiao Ke respectively.

Behind the Zeng Guofan phenomenon, the revival of Confucianism, and the 'national essence fever' is an endeavor by Chinese intellectual elites to redefine who 'we' are in a new era of modernization and ideological transformation. While some may dismiss this out of hand as merely a 'psychological search for symbols of confidence' and 'historical comforts',[36] others may see it as a recognition of their nation as a high civilization with a unique place in the world. It is a fallacy to dismiss one or the other, given the complexity of the psychology of the responses and their mutability. It is not easy to prove that the 'return to the roots' in China is not a psychological search for symbols of confidence and historical comforts, but it is equally difficult to deny that the objective of the Chinese intellectual elites is 'to recreate this nation which, integrating the traditional and the modern on a higher level, will again rise to the forefront of world progress'.[37]

5. The Politics of History and National Identity

It is apparent, in the ideological transformation and shifting perceptions of Chineseness and the Chinese nation, that history has become a branch of ideology and a component of the new Chinese national identity. The systematic rewriting of history is part of the attempt by Chinese intellectual elites to re-create 'our' authentic past and redefine who 'we' are as Chinese. And therein lies the contestation over Marxism and the Chinese nation in the debate on Zeng Guofan.

The common representation of the debate, as merely a historiographical logomachy, obscures significant implications of the Zeng phenomenon. Particularly questionable is the professed motive of many of those involved in the debate. As in academic and intellectual discourse in China, in general, partisans in this case claim no other goal than 'to be objective and faithful to history' - a quasi-religious catchphrase that is accepted virtually without question. The question of objectivity is far too complicated to be dealt with here; suffice it say that what constitutes a 'fact' in history is highly problematic. For one thing, Chinese historians are rewriting the past, and in doing so have adopted a point of view about the Chinese nation that contrasts sharply with Marxist and traditional Han notions. Second, the rewriting of history has been based not so much on new facts that have come to light as new value judgments that have ensued from the ideological transformation and reimagination of the Chinese nation. For these reasons alone, the subjective and ideological nature of the debate on Zeng Guofan cannot be concealed by claims of objectivity or autonomy.

Furthermore, Chinese history, like much of nationalist historiography elsewhere, can be said to belong to a type of history that Croce called 'rhetorical' or 'practicistical'. Rhetorical history becomes a question of politics, religion, or morality as it is closely linked with them.[38] It is well known that nationalist historians are not only 'creators' of history but also myth-makers who combine a romantic search for meaning with a scientific zeal to establish mythic and authentic purpose on authoritative foundations.[39] Their history can be easily dismissed as pseudo-history, but it is surely harder to disentangle it from 'true history'.

In any case, the distinction between 'true history' and pseudo-history is irrelevant to us here for the simple reason that what we are interested in is the politics of the writing and rewriting of Chinese history, and how national identity is reconstructed through the rewriting of history. Insofar as national identity is concerned, it is the sense of common history that forms its core no matter whether that history is rediscovered or invented and no matter how garbled and mythical it may be. And it is stating the obvious to say that selective forgetting or deliberately 'getting the history wrong' is sometimes essential in nation-making. There is no denying that these are often constructed histories in which a society validates and mythologizes what it considers to be its essential characteristics.

The politics of history and national identity involved in the debate over Zeng Guofan has unfolded at several levels. The foremost concern of most academics may be to set Chinese history right. This felt need arises from the fact that, for most of the past half century, narratives of Chinese history have been shaped by the class viewpoint and historical materialism, that is to say the revolutionary paradigm. The rewriting of history requires a new paradigm to replace the old; in the debate on Zeng it is a counterrevolutionary paradigm that is driving out the revolutionary paradigm. This shift implies a redefinition of 'the people' that make up the political community: they are now identified on the basis of a shared history and culture rather than on the basis of 'class' in the Marxist sense.

The case against Marxism is not only that socialist revolution is an undesirable alternative, but that it is an un-Chinese concept that has led China astray from its natural path. China was led astray because it lost touch with its own tradition and cultural roots in Confucianism, the foundation of the Chinese nation. Rewriting Chinese history as a process of natural cultural continuation is not simply a subversion of Marxist historiography and repossession of our history but a redefinition of the nation. Another feature of the new paradigm is that it embraces a much expanded Chinese nation. Mongols, Manchus, and other ethnic groups are now thought to have made great contributions to the Chinese nation, and are no longer treated simply as foreign invaders. Chinese civilization and Chineseness is thus depicted as a melting-pot containing a rich ethnic soup. To identify oneself as Chinese, therefore, is not necessarily to identify with the Han or to renounce one's ethnicity.

While the Party-state has much to gain from the primordial attachment to Chinese history and culture, it also has much to lose. The revaluation of Zeng Guofan and the rewriting of history, as we have said, contradicts Marxist ideology. Yet, contrary to a common impression and belief, Marxist ideology has not vanished. It remains one of the CCP's so-called four cardinal principles. Moreover, although Marxism may have lost credibility as an ideology, Marxist theories dominate pre-1978 Chinese literature on history, politics, economics, and influence no small proportion of what is written today. Finally, the attitudes and habits that developed in the Mao era linger on.

What this means to many Chinese historians is that Chinese history, or the national biography, is still very much Marxist and therefore not 'ours'. As 'our' history shows who 'we' are, it has to be set right in the light of 'our' new vision of ourselves and our identity. But that cannot be done unless we break out of the Marxist framework, for it is the Marxist framework that has produced unauthentic narratives. Of course, the reverse is also true: as 'our' view of ourselves today has changed, the new identity has to be projected back into 'our' past, and history must be rewritten to validate and institutionalize the new identity. The past is of such paramount importance to national identity that to rewrite the nation's history is to reimagine the nation.[40]

In rewriting history in a nationalist mode, Chinese scholars inevitably find themselves on a collision course with Marxist historiography. As open and explicit challenges to Marxism and the CCP are not allowed, what is done, as in the debate on Zeng Guofan, is to challenge the content of Marxism and the authority of the CCP without naming what is being challenged. In this sense, the debate on Zeng contains a roundabout challenge to Marxist historiography, and the Marxist class notion of nation, and constitutes a negation of both. Insofar as the relationship between paradigms is one of power, what is to be dislodged from supremacy and deprived of legitimacy, political and intellectual, is not just revolution, socialism, and Marxism but also Marxist historians and Communists whose claim to dominance rests upon them.[41]

It can be argued further, that the re-narration of history is in itself an act of political empowerment. This is a demand for the right and freedom to say who 'we' are and who 'we' have been, as well as the exercising of that right and freedom. It goes without saying that the subversion of the existing narrative is a challenge to the polity upon which that narrative bestows legitimacy. More directly, given John Stuart Mill's ideal of nationality (nation) that government 'should be government by themselves [i.e., a nationality] or a portion of themselves, exclusively',[42] the inclusion in and exclusion from 'we' has significant implications with regard to legitimacy, even for an authoritarian regime like China's.

6.   From Ethnocentric to Pan-Chinese Notions of the Nation

The conviction that Zeng Guofan was neither a 'traitor to the Han' nor a 'a traitor to his country' reflects a conceptual transformation from an ethnocentric to Pan-Chinese notion of the nation. It departs from the traditional ethnocentric notion of China as a Han nation, where 'faithfulness and righteousness are ways of human discourse and are not to be extended to alien kinds',[43] as well as from the republican revolutionary version, reformulated by Zhang Taiyan, by combining Wang Fuzhi's notions of evolutionism and elements of Social Darwinism.[44] It also departs from the Marxist notion of the nation-state as a territorial-political unit with a class-based 'people', from which individuals and groups could be excluded as class enemies by application of arbitrary and constantly shifting political criteria.

It is perhaps not coincidental that Zeng's sharpest critics are either Marxists or Han historians - or both - who are still influenced by the Han-centric ethos of Chineseness. Such individuals seem more or less committed to the status quo. By contrast, those who have recast Zeng in the role of national hero are constructing a new national identity. In other words, behind the debate on Zeng is a pair of vastly different notions of the nation: the ethnocentric notion that refuses to accept anyone not born into the community, versus a 'modern' Pan-Chinese notion, that extends membership in the community to all ethnic groups. Nevertheless, the latter is still very much Han-centric. For, after all, the criterion with which the community is defined is Han culture, and the past that this nation supposes is the Han past. Furthermore, even the rewriting of history today is still a Han affair, because it is a Han history by Han historians. The cultural conception of the nation has not gone far beyond the vision of such Confucian modernizers as Kang Youwei and Zhang Zhidong, who imagined a Chinese nation based on Confucian principles, that included ethnic minorities provided they accepted those principles.

Underlying the view that Zeng Guogan was a traitor is clearly the old Chinese-barbarian or Han-barbarian mentality - with the 'barbarians' including ethnic minorities and foreigners. The vision of the world as one of parallel nations, each with its own characteristics and destiny, has been slow to take root in China owing to deeply held ways of thought. The vision of China as the center of the world persisted even after China's defeat in the Opium Wars. Eventual recognition of the economic and military superiority of the Western Other, all the more traumatic because of that defeat, was accompanied by fear, resentment, and hatred. To this day, having to borrow from a superior antagonist has remained a constant source of bitterness for radical Chinese nationalists. Thus, denying that Zeng Guofan was a traitor testifies to a new vision of the 'Chinese nation' and a new outlook on Han-ethnic and Chinese-foreign relations in the 1990s. This new concept of the nation, at least in theory, includes all citizens of the People's Republic of China (PRC), irrespective of racial, religious, or cultural backgrounds, although in practice what is often consciously or unconsciously promoted as 'Chinese' culture is actually Han culture or 'progressive' culture. To the extent this notion includes all ethnic groups in the PRC, it is Pan-Chinese.

The transformation of a Han-centric China into a 'modern' Chinese nation, and the casting off of a revolutionary identity in favor of a Pan-Chinese national identity, accords with international trends in constructing national identities, and encourages cohesion among ethnic groups by playing down ethnicity. There is a clear awareness in China that the reconstruction of Chinese national identity is vital to the survival and well being of the nation-state in the face of all sorts of centrifugal and fragmenting tendencies. It is also obvious that underlying the Pan-Chinese project is the assumption that a national identity is compatible with all ethnic identities, not only Han but non-Han as well. The idea of multiple and compatible identities is perhaps more useful than assimilation in encouraging national identification among ethnic groups; it is a step forward from both ethnocentric and Marxist notions of the Chinese nation in that it no longer hinges on biological descent or class. Moreover, Pan-Chinese nationalism has grouped people in a large scale; it is perhaps in part preparing for a way towards regionalism and globalism. And the civic identity, that pan-Chinese nationalism advocates, may also help to reduce the ethnic tensions. However, it is difficult to achieve a Pan-Chinese national identity, for the ultimate question is whether there is a sense that the 'Pan-Chinese' belong together on the basis of a set of characteristics that was often referred to in the past as 'national character'.[45]

Equally problematic is the intellectual articulation of a cultural conception of the nation as 'a group of people who differentiate themselves from others on the basis of a set of perceived cultural differences'.[46] It is Pan-Chinese insofar as membership is not determined by racial or ethnic criteria, but by knowledge and practice of 'Chinese' principles. It can, thus, be taken up if these principles are learned or yielded if they are renounced. Membership is open; but whether it is totally free is doubtful, as it might incur the obligation to conform, to some extent, to what is regarded as 'Chineseness', which is in reality largely monolithic and certainly more Han than, say, Tibetan, Mongolian, or Uighur.

The cultural conception of a Chinese nation seems to be a double-edged sword. It lends some legitimacy to Beijing's claim of sovereignty over Taiwan,[47] as the idea of 'Cultural China' emphasizes the common cultural heritage shared by China and Taiwan, and underlines the cultural bond between them. However, 'Cultural China' - as the name implies - is predominantly premised on cultural rather than political bonds and interactions. The basic assumption at its heart is that the nation is a cultural community, or a tangible spiritual domain; that it is a cultural entity embracing all in a common framework that can be founded on a living language and culture; and that Chinese culture is above political and social divisions, whereas the state is an instrument to secure peace, justice, material existence, and cultural survival and revival.

The emphasis on culture, to the extent that it is above politics or the state(s), is perhaps not as helpful to the CCPs cause of political unification, as some might believe. For one thing, it implies a neutrality about the political bickering across the Taiwan Strait. This rejection of partianship, in turn, implies that whoever protects and promotes Chinese culture and tradition will enjoy moral support. Conversely, a government or state that fails in its duty to Chinese culture can lose support and legitimacy; sentimetns of attachment would shift according to whichever government or state is perceived to be the guardian of Chinese culture and tradition. What is more, it might even be argued that there are advantages in having a multitude of political states striving for excellence in the wider cultural nation, although some people decry as artificial the political divisions among the Chinese. In any case, there seems to be space within the framework of a 'Cultural China' for competing political entities.

Moreover, the anti-revolution and anti-Marxism discourse in China is not surprising after the three traumatic decades from 1949 and 1978. Whether Marxism can be erased from the Chinese consciousness is quite another question. Having been translated into specific ways of doing things and ways of thinking, it has thus become part of Chinese identity, just as Buddhism did long ago. To reject Marxism as alien culture is to reject a component of contemporary Chinese national identity. At any rate, it is easier to renounce Marxism than to exclude and eradicate it from Chinese culture. Neither does it look likely that Chinese nationalism, with its many weaknesses, will replace Marxism as the dominant ideology.

Finally, the conceptualization of Pan-Chineseness will throw into question a large range of issues, from history to affirmative action policy.[48] That, of course, is well beyond the scope of this chapter and remains the subject of future research. In addition, it is conceivable that the Pan-Chinese national identity will be confronted with two challenges: the first, from post-modernism, which plays down the importance of national identities; and the second, from ethnic minorities within China, and independence activists in Taiwan, who do not share the Pan-Chinese identity. The first challenge may not manifest itself in China in the near future, but the second is close at hand. It is evident that ethnic nationalism and Taiwan's nationalism have been on the rise in the last decade and pose a threat to the project of Pan-Chinese nationalism.

Notes

1   These statistics, for the period between Jan. 1981 and 15 June 1997, were obtained through the China Social Sciences Data Base at the Shanghai Library.

2   Yang Nianqun, 'Wo kan "Zeng Guofan xianxiang"' (My views on the 'Zeng Guofan phenomenon') *Ershiyi shiji* (*Twenty-First Century Bimonthly*) Oct. 1994, p. 135.

3   Li Rui, 'Wei shenme "dufu Zeng Wenzheng"' (Why did Mao admire Zeng Guofan?), *Dushu* 2, 1992, p. 8.

4   According to Rustow, late modernizing societies generally share an ambivalence towards modernity and their own traditions. As massive uncertainties arise under the impact of modernization, 'a feeling of continuity much be projected backward as well as forward'. See Dankwart A. Rustow, *A World of Nations: Problems of Political Modernization*, Washington, D.C.: the Brookings Institute, 1967, p. 42.

5   John Breuilly, 'The sources of nationalist ideology,' in Hutchinson and Smith (ed.), *Nationalism*, Oxford: Oxford University Press, 1994, p. 109.

6   Cited by Ma Yongshan, 'Zeng Guofan "Hanjian" shuo zhi yi' (Questioning Zeng Guofan's label of 'a traitor to the Han'), *Nei Menggu minzu shiyuan xuebao* 1, 1987, p. 82.

7   Xu Shanhe, 'Zeng Guofan shi aiguozhe' (Zeng Guofan was a patriot), *Xiangtan daxue xuebao* (sheke ban) 1, 1989, p. 86.

8   See, for example, Peng Qian, 'Tantan Zeng Guofan yanjiu wenti' (On the study of Zeng Guofan), *Qunyan* 1, 1986, pp. 34-35; Ma Yongshan, op. cit., p. 83; Deng Yunsheng, 'Zeng Guofan Hanjian maiguozei bian' (A challenge to labeling Zeng Guofan a 'traitor to the Han' and 'a traitor to his country'), *Qiusuo* 1, 1988, p. 123; Shen Jiarong, 'Zeng Guofan "maiguozei an" xintan' (A revaluation of the Zeng Guofan 'case of treason'), *Shixue yuekan* 1, 1990, p. 45; Xu Shanhe, op. cit., p. 86.

9   See Jiang Duo, 'Lüelun Zeng Guofan qi ren' (A brief evaluation of Zeng Guofan), *Shehui kexue* 2, 1989, p. 76; Yi Mengchun, 'Zeng Guofan zai banli Tianjin jiaoan zhong de xinli maodun' (Zeng Guofan's psychological conflicts in handling the Tianjin riots), *Jindaishi yanjiu* 1, 1990, p. 91; Wang Linmao, 'Rujia lunli guannian zhidao xia de Zeng Guofan Hua yang jiaoshe sixiang' (Zeng Guofan's thought on Sino-foreign negotiations guided by Confucian ethics), *Jindaishi yanjiu* 3, 1996, p. 185; Dai Xueji and Xu Ru, 'Zeng Guofan de "yuyi" sixiang lunlüe' (Zeng Guofan's strategies to defend China against invasion), *Fujian luntan* 2, 1984, p. 40.

10   See, for example, Xu Shanhe, op. cit., p. 86; Deng Yunsheng, op. cit., p. 124; Ma Yongshan, op. cit., pp. 82-84; Shen Jiarong, op. cit., pp. 49-50.

11   Liu Leyang, 'Lüetan Zeng Guofan de lishi gongzui yu xueshu diwei' (A brief evaluation of Zeng Guofan's merits and demerits and his intellectual influence), *Jianghai xuekan* 4, 1987, p. 84.

12   See, for example, Zhu Andong, 'Ping Zeng Guofan zai jindaishi shang de zuoyong he yingxiang' (Zeng Guofan's role and influence in modern Chinese history), *Qiusuo* 1, 1988, p. 115.

13   Zhu Zhenhua, 'Zeng Guofan he jindai keji' (Zeng Guofan and modern science and technology), *Jianghuai luntan* 1, 1984, p. 117.

14   Dong Qing, 'Zeng Guofan de yisheng' (A sketch of the life of Zeng Guofan), *Shandong daxue xuebao* 1, 1983, p. 35; Wang Shaopu, 'Zeng Guofan yangwu sixiang de xingcheng, xingzhi he zuoyong' (The formation, nature, and role of

Zeng Guofan's ideas on modernization), *Lishi yanjiu* 2, 1983, p. 176; Dai Xueji and Xu Ru, op. cit., p. 40.

15   Deng Yibing, Wang Jiping, Cheng Xiaojun, cited by Rao Huaimin and Wang Xiaotian, 'Zeng Guofan yanjiu shuping' (An overview of Zeng Guofan studies), *Hunan shifan daxue shehui kexue xuebao* 5, 1986, p. 8.

16   Yang Guoqiang, 'Zeng Guofan jianlun' (A brief evaluation of Zeng Guofan), *Lishi yanjiu* 6, 1987, pp. 97-100.

17   Xu Shanhe, op. cit., pp. 86-90.

18   Jiang Duo, 'Lüelun Zeng Guofan qi ren', op. cit., p. 75.

19   Ma Yongshan, op. cit., p. 83.

20   Shi Xingzhou, 'Dui Zeng Guofan pingjia de zhenglun' (Contending evaluations of Zeng Guofan), *Jiefang ribao*, 25 Jan., 1987, p. 4.

21   Zi Zhongjun, 'Aiguo de zuobiao' (The criteria for patriotism), *Dushu* 6, 1996, p. 62.

22   Peng Qian, op. cit., p. 35.

23   Ibid., p. 35; Ma Yongshan, op. cit., p. 83; also see Shen Jiazhuang, 'Zeng Guofan yu Hong Xiuquan bijiao' (A comparison of Zeng Guofan and Hong Xiuquan), *Guangming ribao*, 5 Aug. 1987, p. 3; and Yang Guoqiang, 'Zeng Guofan he chuantong wenhua' (Zeng Guofan and traditional culture), *Jindaishi yanjiu* 1, 1989, pp. 58-83.

24   Peng Qian, op. cit., p. 35.

25   Ibid., p. 36.

26   Hu Ping, Kong Linren, Qi Qizhang, and Chen Yueqing, 'Guanyu Zhongguo jindaishi jiben xiansuo wenti' (A few questions about the basic framework of modern Chinese history), *Wenshizhe* 3, 1983, p. 50.

27   Ibid., p. 51.

28   Li Zehou, 'Guanyu wenhua xianzhuang daode congjian de duihua' (A dialogue about moral reconstruction in contemporary culture), *Dongfang* 5, extracted in *Zhongliu*, Oct., 1994, p. 29.

29 Li Zehou and Liu Zaifu (eds.), *Gaobie geming: Huiwang ershi shiji Zhongguo* (*Farewell to revolution: Looking back upon twentieth-century China*), Hong Kong: Tiandi tushu youxian gongsi, 1995.

30 Arif Dirlik, 'Reversals, Ironies, Hegemonies: Notes on the Contemporary Historiography of Modern China', *Modern China* 22, 3 July 1996, pp. 256-7.

31 Gong Shuduo, 'Yuan Shikai zhi an fan bu de' (The verdict on Yuan Shikai must not be reversed), *Zhongliu* 11, 1995, p. 36.

32 Zhang Haipeng, 'Bochi "gaobie geming" de miushuo' (Refuting the absurd slogan of 'farewell to revolution'), *Zhongliu* 2, 1997, pp. 29-31.

33 Cheng Xiaojun, *Zeng Guofan yu xiandai Zhongguo wenhua* (*Zeng Guofan and Modern Chinese Culture*), Changsha: Hunan renmin chubanshe, 1991, pp. 9-10.

34 Chen Xi, op. cit., p. 10.

35 *The People's Daily,* (overseas edition), 8 Sept. 1994, p. 1.

36 The words are those of Rustow, *op.cit.*, pp. 41-42; Kohn, *The Idea of Nationalism.* New York: Macmillan, 1944, pp. 429-30; and Gellner, similarly, sees the return to the past and the folk as a typical defensive response to exogenous modernization, *Nations and Nationalism*, Oxford, Eng.: Oxford University Press, 1983, pp. 57-61.

37 Hutchinson, 'Cultural nationalism and moral regeneration', in Hutchinson and Smith (ed.), *Nationalism*, 1994, p. 128.

38 Benedetto Croce, *History: Its Theory and Practice.* New York: Russell and Russell, 1960, p. 42.

39 Hutchinson, op. cit., p. 123.

40 As John Stuart Mill wrote, 'The strongest cause for the feeling of nationality ... is identity of political antecedents; the possession of a national history, and subsequent community of recollections; collective pride and humiliation, pleasure and regret, connected with the same incidents in the past' (Mill, *Representative Government*, 1861, quoted in Alfred Zimmern, *Modern Political Doctrines*, London: Oxford University Press, 1939, p. 206). To Ernest Renan, one of the two essential elements that make up the 'soul or

spiritual principle' of a nation is the 'possession in common of a rich heritage of memories' (*What Is a Nation?*, 1862, in Zimmern, op. cit., p. 203). Even such cultural dimensions as language, religion, customs and institutions 'remain secondary (though still of great importance to the sense of common origins and history of the group)', according to A. D. Smith (*The Ethnic Revival.* Cambridge, Eng.: Cambridge Univ. Press, 1981, p. 67).

41   The clear relationship between paradigms and power is delineated by Arif Dirlik: 'The supremacy of one paradigm over others does not rest merely on a superior ability to explain available "facts"; it is also an ideological supremacy that expresses power relations within a context of social relations and ideologies. Paradigms do not just guide inquiry; they control it, excluding alternative explanations and, therefore, those who favor or promote alternative explanations' (Dirlik, 'Reversals, ironies, hegemonies: Notes on the contemporary historiography of modern China'. *Modern China* 22, 3 July, 1996, p. 244).

42   Mill, *Representative Government*, 1861, quoted in Zimmern, op. cit., p. 20.

43   P. Dura, 'De-constructing the Chinese nation', in Unger (ed.), *Chinese Nationalism, op. cit.*, p. 35.

44   Ibid., p. 42.

45   David Miller points out that as members of a nation are not thrown together to share a common fate, 'a national identity requires that people who share it should have something in common', that there 'must be a sense that the people belong together by virtue of the characteristics that they share' (Miller, *On Nationality*, Oxford: Clarendon Press, 1995, p. 25).

46   Townsend, 'Chinese nationalism', in Unger (ed.), *Chinese Nationalism, op. cit.*, p. 6.

47   For a discussion of the legitimacy question, see He Baogang, *The Democratisation of China, op.cit.*, chap. 10.

48   He Baogang, 'Can W. Kymlicka's liberal theory of minority rights be applied in East Asia?', in Paul van der Velde and Alex McKay (eds.), *New Developments in Asian Studies*, London: Kegan Paul, 1998, pp. 20-44.

5 The National Identity Question, Nationalism, and Democratization in China and Taiwan

In the last three chapters, we have reviewed in detail the development of Chinese neo-nationalism and its role in the construction of new Chinese identities. As shown before, Chinese pan-nationalists play up the fact that the Taiwanese are Han Chinese, and that China and Taiwan share a Confucian legacy. At the same time, they make a concession in that socialist elements of Chinese national identity should not be imposed upon Taiwan. It seems that pan-Chinese national identity constitutes a source of reunification. However, the rise of Taiwan nationalism, assisted by the democratization process, challenges the basic assumptions of Pan-Chinese nationalism.

This chapter aims to compare nationalism and democratization in Taiwan and China, and, in particular seeks to develop an understanding of the rise of Taiwanese nationalism and its impact on democratization; as well as the impact democratization has on the politics associated with national identity question. It will examine the effects of democratization and nationalism identifying two crucial structural factors which continue to contribute to the outcome in managing the national identity conflicts across the Taiwan Strait.

The chapter begins with a comparison of the national identity question and the rise of nationalism in Taiwan and China. It then investigates the impact of the national identity question and nationalism on democratization in Taiwan, and the impact of democratization on the Taiwan national identity question, going on to contrast the relationship between democratization and nationalism in China and Taiwan. The idea of federalism, as a super-national arrangement which could manage national identity conflicts, its limits and resistance to it, are also discussed. The chapter concludes with hypotheses concerning the impact of Chinese democratization on the resolution of the Taiwan question.

1.   The National Identity Question

The question of Taiwan's independence did not arise during the Chiang regimes because both sides shared an imaginative community and reunification was taken for granted. Despite holding different ideological positions, both Mao Zedong and Chiang Kai-shek held the same view about the future of the Chinese nation-state: that it should include Mainland China and Taiwan. In this sense, both were Chinese nationalists beyond ideological differences.

Under Chiang's regime, there was no national identity question except the 'provinces problem'. People in Taiwan were classified into two groups: 'benshengren', the people from the province of Taiwan; and 'waishengren', the people from other provinces of China. The 'provinces problem' referred to the sensitive relations between Taiwanese and Mainlanders. It involved, for example, the issue concerning the fair distribution of public office positions among the two groups.

Since the beginning of democratization, in 1978, the unification forces have gradually eroded, while the pro-independence forces have increasingly grown in Taiwan. The Democratic Progress Party (the DPP) challenges the virtually unquestionable assumption of reunification, held by officials and peoples in Taiwan, on Mainland China and overseas. Huang Xinjie (Huang Hsin-chieh), former chairperson of the DPP, for example, asserts that the presumption of reunification is due to Chinese psychology.[1] The DPP has challenged the assumption that Taiwan is simply one province of China, and has refused to use the concepts of 'bengshengren' and 'waishengren', so that the so-called 'provinces problem' has now disappeared, at least for Taiwanese nationalists. It has now transformed into Taiwan's national identity question; that is, Taiwan is one unique nation and is entitled to have its own independent state. Today, Taipei is ruling out the very issue of Taiwan's unification with China, and reunification ceased to be an electoral issue in the 1996 presidential election in Taiwan. Meanwhile, independence, from *de facto* independence to formal recognition by the international community, has become an important issue.

It is difficult to categorize Taiwan's national identity question in terms of ethnicity. Arguably, most people are perceived to belong to the same race and use the same written language while speaking different dialects (however, this view is now challenged by the DPP). Mainlanders and the Taiwanese are best regarded as sub-'ethnic' groups. The group who came to the island prior to or during the 1895-1945 period of Japanese rule, and speak Hokkien or Hakka, are usually referred to as the 'Taiwanese', who make up the majority of the population. The remainder are Mainlanders who fled to Taiwan, after 1945, and their descendants. The focal point in the national identity issue in Taiwan is the relationship between Taiwan and China. While those deeply attached to Chinese culture and tradition tend to identify themselves as Chinese, pro-independence Taiwanese are more inclined to take an active part in the construction of a new Taiwanese national identity. Independence has far more supporters among the Taiwanese than among the Mainlanders. According to a 1992 survey, 39.5 percent of Taiwanese respondents supported independence, compared to only 18.5 percent of Mainlander respondents.[2] However, sub-ethnic conflicts in Taiwan's politics have been successfully contained as a result of the intermingling of Mainlanders and Taiwanese; the Taiwanization of the KMT; the abolition of register systems, which has eradicated the official categories of 'Mainlanders' and 'Taiwanese'; cross-political support (Taiwanese support for the KMT, and Mainlander support for the DPP); and the cooperation between the DPP and the New Party in the legislative *Yuan*.

The national identity question of Taiwan is a political question, rather than a cultural or ethnic one. One Taiwanese scholar acknowledges that, culturally and ethnically, the Taiwanese may be considered Chinese, or more properly Hans. But the issue is that people sharing the same cultural heritage do not have to accept the same political entity as shown by the case of Australia and England.[3]

China and Taiwan face different forms of the national identity question. Taiwan has only the straightforward question of independence, while China confronts not only secession movements within China, but also the question of reunification with Taiwan. Surely, for Taiwanese nationalism, Taiwan's independence means an internal 'unification' process. That is, a new project of nation-state building must incorporate all conflicting social forces into a political entity and develop a new sense of that common entity for all peoples living on the island, regardless of where they originally came from. This is a key process for Taiwan's independence. Nevertheless, Taiwan must confront the question of the redistribution of political resources and positions among different sub-ethnic groups. In the current political climate, the Taiwanese are likely to be winners and the Mainland Chinese losers in the process of democratization, a trend which is likely to continue in the battle for Taiwan's new national identity.

China's national boundary, or identity, question involves not only maintaining the existing national unity but also reunifying with Taiwan. China, therefore, has a more complex national identity question than Taiwan. Unlike Taiwan, Beijing will likely face a chain reaction in which Taiwan's independence encourages secessionism in other parts of China. In the eyes of Beijing, an independent Taiwan will provide political leverage to the separatists of Tibet and Xinjiang. From Beijing's standpoint, preventing Taiwan's independence and achieving reunification is a key to containing other secessionist movements in China. Moreover, Taiwan's national identity question involves no race dimension, because both Chinese and Taiwanese are perceived to belong to the same race. In contrast, China confronts the challenge from Xinjiang where there is a race question, that is, secessionists there are seen to belong to other races.[4]

2.   Inventing a New Nation: Nationalism in Taiwan

It should be acknowledged that Taiwan's nationalism is still in the making and there are different versions and evaluations of it. Here we only outline the main elements and the ways in which it facilitates the construction of a new nation. Reinterpretations of people, history, culture and language are the main methods used to construct a neo-Taiwanese nationalism.

The rise of Taiwanese neo-nationalism has been associated with the DPP, which has invented and promoted Taiwan's identity as distinct from Chinese identity.[5] A distinctive Taiwan identity is also expected by other countries in the international system: if Taiwan wants to be a member of the international community, it must give up its claim as a genuine represent of China. The rise of Taiwan's nationalism can be understood with reference to the international system. Taiwan lost its seat in the UN in 1971; and as at end of January 1999, it is only recognized by 28 countries.[6] China remains firmly opposed to Taiwan's admittance to the UN, on the grounds that this would constitute dual membership for a region which is already a member by virtue of being a Chinese province. Beijing has been trying to force Taipei into accepting China's terms for reunification by marginalizing it internationally through diplomatic maneuvering. Ironically, such efforts have prompted Taiwan's endless and bold search for international status. Taiwan is compelled to expand its international status in a world order divided into states, lest it should be pushed out of the international community, into isolation. Taiwan, therefore, has much to gain from *de facto* or formal independence, and international recognition for its separate political entity, but little to lose except an increasingly ludicrous dream by some to retake the Mainland.

History also provides some clues to the issue of Taiwan's emerging nationalism. Taiwanese nationalism has been developing since the process of anti-alien resistance in the 17th century.[7] Taiwan was first a colony of Holland, then was under Zheng's rule between 1662-1683; Qing's rule between 1683-1893; Japanese rule between 1895-1945; and the KMT's rule from 1945 until today. As the first colony of Japan, it was deemed a symbol of Japanese imperialist power and was thus elevated as an example of cooperation with the New Order in East Asia. The Japanese ruled the island with due consideration to its socio-political traditions. Taiwan had civil government, while Korea had a Japanese military government.[8] Further, the KMT's killing and suppression of indigenous Taiwanese, in the wake of its occupation in the 1940s, sparked hatred towards the KMT and created an impetus for self-rule by the Taiwanese.

The history of Taiwan has also been reinterpreted by Taiwanese nationalists. They reject the view that Taiwan shares a 5000-year history with China, and assert that Taiwan is no more than 400 years old, beginning with Holland's colonization. To some degree, Taiwanese nationalism is pro-Japan and considers Japan's colonization as positive and constructive for Taiwan's economic development. At the same, time it regards the KMT's rule as ruthless, negative and exploitative.[9] Cheng-Feng Shih argues that Chinese influence on the Taiwanese nationalist movement was 'negligible', while Japanese liberal impacts were surprisingly more crucial.[10] It is argued further, that after fifty years of Japanese colonization, the Taiwanese must have, unintentionally or intentionally, gained certain Japanese cultural characteristics, ranging from custom, to housing, food, clothing and language. The Taiwanese were even proud to join the Japanese imperial armed forces. As supporting evidence, Shih cites the example of Li Yuan-che, a Taiwanese-American and a 1986 Nobel Prize winner, who recalled one time that he had never felt he was Chinese, even when Taiwan was returned to China in the wake of the Second World War.[11] Shih, however, notes that Han culture had been used as a symbolic weapon to rally nationalist support in order to counter alien Dutch, Manchu, and Japanese culture in Taiwan.[12]

An excellent example of rewriting history is a new series of textbooks for some 350, 000 junior high school students that has caused heated debate in Taiwan. On June 22 1997, new Party Legislator, Lee Ching-hua charged that the volumes on history and society promoted Taiwan independence and are loaded with pro-Japanese and anti-Chinese sentiments. According to Lee, of the two volumes seem to glorify Japan's 1895-1945 colonization of Taiwan, and two textbooks do not use the terms 'Chinese' or 'the Chinese people' at all. Instead, the term 'Taiwanese' is used.[13] Moreover, the reference to Sun Yat-sen as the 'founding father' has been removed.

The Democratic Progressive Party with its nationalist reconstruction efforts, has resisted the use of Mandarin, a cultural symbol of Chinese identity. Instead Taiwanese nationalists have used a distinctive Min-Nan dialect. Cheng-Feng Shih argues that the term 'dialect' blurs the exact extent of the linguistic differences and is somewhat misleading, since 'dialect' may only suggest differences in pronunciation and tone for the same word. Shih asserts that the differences between Hoklo/Hakka and Mandarin are even more marked, including not only different pronunciation and tone, but also distinctive grammar features and different lexical items.[14] The prevalence of Hoklo and Hakka-Taiwanese is noticeable during election campaigns, when Hoklo and Hakka are deemed imperative to attract native Taiwanese voters.[15] The revival of Taiwanese folk literature is basically a movement to translate spoken Taiwanese into a written form in the hopes of consolidating a Taiwanese national identity against a Chinese one.[16]

The promotion of Taiwanese language is not only concerned with the construction of a new Taiwanese national identity, but also with the distribution of power and cultural resources. In the past, and even today, some Taiwanese have perceived that speaking 'right' (e.g., speaking Mandarin) is the only way to become upwardly mobile, and therefore they have consciously adopted Mandarin exclusively at home. However, for the Taiwanese masses, entangled in the structure of the vertical division of labor, Hoklo or Hakka-Taiwanese is their main media of daily communication, as long as they do not seek a job in governmental institutions.[17] To demand Hoklo or Hakka as the official and national language is to empower Hoklo or Hakka speakers and to diminish the domination of Mandarin, and its associated elite class.

Taiwan nationalism is criticized by scholars and writers from China, Taiwan and overseas. One author claims that Taiwan's native consciousness is not an open one based on a modern sense of human rights. It is not mutually respecting, but excluding. He cites historian Professor Xu Zhuoyun, who criticizes Taiwanese nationalists for mixing up four different concepts of culture, nation, state and political power.[18] As another example, Yin Wan-Lee argues against the view that Taiwan, as a nation, is based on its unique language, by pointing out that Fujianese (Fukienese) originates from the southern region of Fujian (Fukien)

Province in China, and continues to be a dialect in that region. It is also identical to Mandarin in writing, in grammatical structure and most of the vocabulary. As spoken dialects, there is no greater difference between Fukienese and Mandarin than, for example, between Cantonese and Mandarin.[19]

One may contend that Taiwanese nationalism is not strong enough and is still in an early stage of development. In an affluent and plural society like Taiwan, the rich Taiwanese have immigrated to other countries, such as Australia, to escape a possible war with China. Some surveys indicate that less than 50 percent of the respondents support Taiwan's independence. On the other hand, many people in Taiwan still think of themselves as both Chinese and Taiwanese. One survey finds that 630 persons, constituting 45.1 percent of the respondents, think of themselves as both Taiwanese and Chinese.[20] This constitutes a challenge to *exclusive* Taiwanese nationalism which focuses on difference: for example, 'We are Taiwanese, and you are Chinese!'. A radical proposal by exclusive Taiwan nationalists is that national treasures, displayed in Taiwan, should be returned to Beijing in order to cut off the cultural link with China.

3. Comparing Neo-Nationalism in Taiwan and China

The Nature of nationalism

Chinese neo-nationalism has various forms, including state nationalism, popular nationalism, pan-Chinese nationalism, and primitive and limited civic nationalism. State nationalism, however, stands out as the most influential. Official state nationalism centers on the Party-state and encourages the development of loyalty to the state through an idea of a 'Pan-Chinese' identity. This pan-Chinese nationalism is a product of the state and is imposed from above. It is designed to permit the gigantic Chinese super-state to appear attractive under the banner of nationalism. It is a means for legitimating the massive body of the nation-state. Moreover, it attempts to woo the Taiwanese people and win support for the unification cause. Arguably, this Pan-Chinese nationalism enjoys some support from intellectuals and the populace at large (chapters 2-4).

In contrast, Taiwanese neo-nationalism is a popular phenomenon, coming from below, originating in the 'local' and the public, and building on a genuine sense of Taiwanese identity. A quantitative indicator of the 'popularity' of Taiwanese nationalism can be found in results of six surveys conducted in 1998, which found that around 38 percent of the respondents saw themselves as Taiwanese.[21] For Taiwanese nationalists, Chinese state nationalism, whether the Mainland Chinese or orthodox KMT version, is not genuine; only the sentiments of the Taiwanese people can provide the foundations of an authentic nationalism. Contemporary Taiwanese nationalism criticizes the Republic of China, and its state nationalism, for suppressing Taiwanese nationalism and the discourse of independence.[22] Taiwan's nationalists have challenged the official nationalism, envisioning the Taiwan of the future as an independent state, built on an indigenous (pre-Japanese, pre-KMT) history.

The relations between state and popular nationalism

State nationalism in China has used popular nationalism and anti-America slogans to provide legitimacy for its regime. The Party-state has co-opted popular nationalism to sell the official definition of patriotism, and has even granted freedom of expression and increased the level of political tolerance for popular nationalists who can write and publish their works (chapter 3).

Nevertheless, some intellectuals hesitate to recognize the current Chinese state as a legitimate representation of the Chinese nation. Chinese cultural nationalists have their own largely hidden agenda that targets Maoist ideology and the Party-state. They are making their own vision of 'nation', even excluding, or rejecting, socialist national identity as defined by the Party-state. Chinese popular nationalism may constitute a threat to the CCP and ultimately undermine the dominance of the CCP (chapter 3).

Similarly, Taiwanese popular nationalism has undermined the old state nationalism of the KMT. The KMT's old state nationalism in Taiwan, linked to the project of unification, has become weaker, and its anti-Communist identity has faded into history. Moreover, the KMT cultivates an indigenous image, with its indigenous wing seeking the recognition of Taiwan as a sovereign entity. The Taiwanization of the KMT regime, an increasingly free and assertive mass media, and an awakening electorate, all have challenged the assumption that the Mainlander-KMT elite can impose its vision of unification on the remaining segments of Taiwan's relevant political strata.[23]

The concept of the 'New Taiwanese', advocated by President Lee in December 1998 (or earlier in 1995), indicates that Taiwanese nationalism has already developed into a kind of neo-state nationalism. Over the years, steps have been taken to instill, within the younger generation of

Mainlanders, the notion that they too are Taiwanese. In his later years, Chiang Ching-kuo frequently remarked that, having lived in Taiwan for so long, he considered himself to be both Chinese and Taiwanese.[24] There is considerable evidence that Mainlanders, living in Taiwan, will increasingly consider themselves Taiwanese. As Yu-tzung Chang reports, in a 1992 survey, 19.8 percent of the respondents regarded themselves as 'Taiwanese', 29 percent as 'Chinese', and 45 percent as both. In 1995, however, the above figures changed to 30.1 percent, 18 percent, and 47.3 percent, respectively. The percentage of those who regarded themselves as 'Taiwanese' had increased by 10.3 percentage points, while those who considered themselves 'Chinese' decreased by 11 percentage points.[25]

The notion of the New Taiwanese was used by the opposition Democratic Progressive Party, several years ago, in calling upon Mainlanders living in Taiwan to relinquish what it called their 'greater China' mentality.[26] It was not adopted as official ideology until President Lee Teng-hui presented the idea of the New Taiwanese as a means of promoting national harmony, during campaigning for the December 5 1998 legislative, mayoral and city council elections.[27] Lee appealed to voters to support his party's candidate for the Taipei mayorship,. describing the candidate, Ma Ying-jeou, as a 'New Taiwanese'. The concept of New Taiwanese aims to nurture a common identity among the various sub-ethnic groups and unite all citizens in the pursuit of political reforms. Ma's subsequent victory, and the victory of the KMT in a solid majority of seats in the Legislature, indicate that the New Taiwanese identity had taken shape.[28] A survey of Taipei city citizens, conducted by the *United Daily News* in the wake of the December 1998 election, found that 68 percent of the respondents agree with the New Taiwanese concept promoted by the ruling party.[29] Now, even the New Party recognizes the concept of New Taiwanese. The consensus on the new Taiwanese, reached by main political parties, albeit with different interpretations, indicates the formation of a civic and territorial notion of Taiwan's identity.

Although a discourse of New Taiwanese has become an element of state nationalism, there are at least two differences between this neo-state nationalism and radical popular nationalism.[30] First, radical Taiwanese nationalists emphasize the exclusive nature of Taiwanese nationalism; from this perspective, Taiwanese are not Chinese. By contrast, Lee's understanding of New Taiwanese does not exclude the notion of a Chinese identity, for he envisions that New Taiwanese will become 'New Chinese' once a free and democratic system is established in Mainland China.[31] Eminent dissident, Wei Jingsheng, supports the use of the term, 'New Taiwanese', although he insists that Taiwanese people are also Chinese people. As he put it, 'A white horse is still a horse'.[32] Second, the concept of New Taiwanese implies a civic and territorial definition of Taiwan's identity; that is, people living in Taiwan should identify with the Taiwan Island as their home. By contrast, radical nationalists advocate a cultural or ethnic notion of Taiwanese identity; that is, Taiwanese are seen as a nationality with a unique culture, history and ethnicity.

The political implications of nationalism

While pan-Chinese nationalism is expansionist, in the sense that it aims to reclaim lost territories such as Taiwan, Taiwanese nationalism is imagined to be confined to the island, because Taiwanese aspirations for independence, are by their very nature, not expansionist. Taiwanese nationalists argue that the government of Taiwan should not concern itself with the suffering of overseas Chinese in Indonesia because they are not Taiwanese; and that the government of Taiwan should not encourage the teaching of Chinese overseas. Taiwanese nationalism challenges the fundamental assumptions of overseas or borderless Chinese nationalism mentioned in chapter 1. For example, they think the description of Taiwanese democratization as 'the Chinese first democratization'[33] is inappropriate. Taiwanese nationalism demands a new constitution, which is, above all, a question of the political community, its territoriality and people, and its political structure. Taiwanese nationalists perceive the idea of popular sovereignty as the foundation for a new independent state. In 1994 the DPP convened a 'people's constitution conference' calling for a new national flag.[34] In the 1996 election, there was a consensus that Taiwan's President must be Taiwanese. And, moreover, the DPP aims to solve the national identity problem through a referendum on gaining formal independence from Mainland China.

One of the fundamental political goals of Pan-Chinese nationalism, on the other hand, is the reunification of Taiwan and China. For example, in May 1998, Jiang Zemin started a new initiative by calling for 'political negotiations' with Taiwan, and shifting attention from the KMT to the opposition party and the 'patriotic Taiwan compatriots'. His suggestion, that hopes for reunification should lie with the Taiwanese people, betrays the general despair over Lee Teng-hui, who is seen to have no interest in reunification at all.

Pan-Chinese nationalism attempts to hold China's territories together. In the framework of pan-Chinese nationalism, patriotic education should not emphasize Han nationality, and 'Chinese' is not defined as 'Han'. Instead, the 'Chinese' are defined as all peoples living in the current territories of the PRC. For pan-Chinese nationalists, the biggest threat comes from the Han themselves, when they do not recognize this modern notion of 'the Chinese'. One scholar argues, 'If Chinese amounts to Han, then questions of secession and independence arise. If we adopt a broad view of Chinese, the conflict between the Han and Tibet is only one between two nationalities'. Such conflict, according to this understanding, does not challenge the unity of China, because it is not a question of separation.[35] Pan-nationalists thus search for a new Chinese identity, one which transcends narrow nationalities.

The influences on the resolution of the Taiwan question

Pan-Chinese nationalism in China shares the basic assumption of the old official nationalism, under the Chiangs, that reunification is an essential element for a modern notion of the Chinese nation-state. This unification framework, however, was eroded when Taiwan's state nationalism moved away from the unification goal. As a result, pan-Chinese nationalism clashes with today's Taiwanese nationalism over this fundamental goal. Friedman asserts, 'The new, post-Mao nationalism in China not only challenges Taiwan's autonomy, it also could endanger peace in the Pacific-Asia region'.[36]

Although holding different visions of Taiwan's future, Chinese pan-nationalists and Taiwanese nationalists share the view that the independence of Taiwan means the failure of China's reunification project, and China's reunification with Taiwan implies the failure of the DPP's independence project. This kind of nationalist thinking leads people across the Taiwan Strait to think that this is a zero sum game in which one side must lose so that the other can win, and consequently compromise over the national identity question is thought to be difficult, if not impossible. However, it is worthwhile drawing attention to another way of thinking whereby we can see the old boundary/identity problem in a new light. The idea of 'ambiguity about boundaries' suggests that some boundary questions can be pursued in an ambiguous way so that boundaries are not clearly demarcated, and exclusive authority over boundaries is not established. A contemporary example is the 1998 referendum in Northern Ireland, which was not clear about whether to pursue reunification with Ireland or maintain unity with the UK. This may be positive and beneficial in that it helps to avoid conflicts and clashes. Such ambiguity is a key component of the tolerance of liberal-democracy. If Chinese nationalists do not make any compromise on the unification question, and Taiwanese nationalists continue to push their independence cause, the clash between these two and nationalisms is inevitable.

4. The Impact of the National Identity Question and Nationalism on Democratization

Nationalism affects not only the resolution of the Taiwan question, as discussed above, but also the democratization process. Taiwanese and Chinese democratization share similar origins, yet have dramatically different outcomes. First, let us look at the democracy/autocracy index for China and Taiwan. The autocracy index of China was 8 between 1975-1976, and dropped to 7 between 1977-1994. By contrast, the autocracy index of Taiwan was 7 between 1975-1986, which dropped slightly to 6 between 1987-1990, and fell to zero between 1991-1994. China's democracy score was zero from 1975-1994, while the democracy score of Taiwan was zero between 1975-1990, but rose to 6 between 1991-1994.[37]

Let us also look at the waves of democratization. Since the high point of Gengshen reform in 1980, China has had two democratic movements. The first mini wave of democratization was the democratic wall movement between 1978-1981; the second was the student protest and democratic movement, which began in 1986, and reached its zenith in 1989. Moreover, since 1982, there has been an undercurrent of small, quiet and local democratization in the form of village elections.

In Taiwan, mass demonstrations against the KMT in Kaohsiung, in December 1979, can be seen as the first wave of democratization, which was ruthlessly suppressed by the KMT. The second wave began with the formation of a quasi-opposition party in May 1984, followed by mediated talks between the KMT and Tangwei, in May 1986, and the formation of the DPP in September 1986.

The similarity lies in the fact that both the CCP and the KMT suppressed the first wave of democratization in China and Taiwan. However, the greatest difference occurred when the leadership in Taipei was changed. General Wang Sheng was removed in May 1983, signifying the displacement of hardliners. Lee Teng-hui was nominated as Vice President in March 1984, which accelerated Taiwanization. Most importantly, President Chiang Ching-kuo decided on liberalization in October 1986, and rescinded martial law in 1987. The passing of Chiang Ching-kuo, the succession of Lee Teng-hui, in January 1988, and the reelection of Lee Teng-hui, in March 1990, have resulted in the ascent of reformists. In 1991, Lee Teng-hui terminated the period of national mobilization for the suppression of the Communist rebellion. The Mainland-elected parliamentarians were forced to retire in 1991. The DDP won 31 percent of the vote in the parliamentary elections of 1992, 41.03 percent of the vote in local government elections in 1993, and 43.67 percent of the vote in the Taipei Mayoral election in 1994. It lost the 1996 Presidential election, won the local election in 1997, and faced a small setback in the December Legislative and mayoral elections of 1998.

Needless to say to explain these different trajectories, various factors, such as the level of economic development, income, growth of the middle of class, education, international relations and the return of overseas students, have contributed to different outcomes. However, we would like to stress the role of the national identity question and nationalism. As we discussed earlier, China has faced a more complex and difficult national identity problem than Taiwan. The CCP has faced monumental internal and external pressures: student protest movements in 1986-7 and 1989, the breakdown of the Soviet Union, unrest at the peripheries of China, and conflict with the UK over the Hong Kong question since the Anglo-Chinese agreement on Hong Kong in 1984. Particular attention should be paid to secessionist movements. 1990 saw popular demonstrations of support for Greater Mogolian nationalism on both sides of the border. In March 1992, a group of 500 Buddhist demonstrators marched in Lhasa in support of independence. In mid-May of that year, 69 people were reportedly arrested in a series of street demonstrations, led by monks and nuns carrying Tibetan flags. In February 1992, Muslim separatists in Urumqi blew up a Chinese bus, killing six and wounding more than 20. All these events have cetainly not lessened the CCP's fear of the disintegration of China.

By contrast, Taiwan lost its seat in the UN, and was further humiliated by the USA's recognition of the PRC in the 1970s. This had great implications for the politics of national identity. When the KMT could not represent China in the UN, it no longer had a legitimate claim over the whole of China. As a result, Chinese national identity, which constituted a legitimate basis for the regime, was fundamentally eroded. While relying on the success of economic development as the basis for legitimacy, the KMT also supported liberalization and democratization in Taiwan in order to regain legitimacy, win international sympathy and overcome Taiwan's isolation. In short, the KMT promoted democratization as a strategy to regain legitimacy, while the CCP resisted democratization as a strategy to avoid disintegration.

There is a huge difference with regard to the forces of democratization in China and Taiwan. Students and liberal intellectuals were driving forces in Chinese democratization, and they have established a weak coalition with workers.[38] Nevertheless, they did not, and could not establish coalitions with ethno-nationalists who demanded secession. Moreover, Chinese neo-nationalists are not driving forces for democratization, rather they have been hostile to democracy. It is not surprising that Chinese writings on nationalism seldom mention the term 'democracy', while Taiwanese writings on nationalism discuss some aspects of democracy and democratization.[39] Taiwanese independence activists have been pushing for democratization and have successfully established coalitions with liberal intellectuals. Indeed, the Dangwan movement was a product of liberal and independence movements.[40]

Taiwan's democracy is now widely seen as valuable, because democratization helps Taiwan win international support and gain legitimacy against its rivals. Taiwan's creative path toward democracy is also a source of pride for Taiwanese nationalists. In contrast, Chinese nationalists see democracy as a foreign product and alien to the Chinese people.

While Taiwanese nationalism has contributed to the initiation of democratization, according to Professor Hu Fu, it will hinder the consolidation of Taiwan's democratization.[41] This is because the nationalist independence movement has raised questions concerning the political community and the constitution, and is likely to provoke intervention from China to end the democratic cause in Taiwan. While the nature of this argument is hypothetical, it indeed raises issues concerning the impact of Taiwanese nationalism and the national identity question on the process and pace of democratization. It appears that the threat of Mainland China is working in favor of the KMT, in electoral terms, thus arguably delaying the progress of habituation to democracy. It is observed that the DPP's attempt to promote Taiwanese independence has created some distance between the DPP and a considerable number of Taiwanese voters who are in favor of the status quo and do not want to see adverse reactions from China. This view is supported by the fact that the DPP faced a setback in the 1991 National Assembly election, and in the 1996 Presidential election, when it pushed the independence agenda.

Taiwan's democracy will run into a critical crisis if it fails to deal with the independence issue appropriately. This is evidenced by the fact that Taiwan's bid to return to the international community, and Lee's visit to Cornel University in 1995, prompted China's missile tests in the Taiwan Strait in 1996. China's intervention would be a key factor influencing the future of democracy in Taiwan. Taiwanese nationalist votes cannot stop

Chinese bullets if they come. The survival of Taiwan's democracy finally depends on the resolution of the identity issue with China. The influence of the identity issue on Taiwan's democratization is clearly outlined by Yun-Han Chu, Hu Fu and Chung-in Moon:

> This historic condition [a legacy of divided nationhood] suggests a special role for the communist rival regime, whose desire for unification--by hostile means, if necessary--may become a new democracy's most menacing destabilizing factor. Also, this structural condition accentuates the international component of regime legitimization by exposing a sitting regime to loss of international recognition. Finally, a legacy of divided nationhood may activate a legitimacy crisis of the state structure in the course of regime transition....In Taiwan, a deep-seated national-identity crisis obstructs the lasting compromise on constitutional design necessary to democracy's consolidation.[42]

5.   The Impact of Democratization on the National Identity Question

While section four discussed the impact of nationalism and the national identity question on the democratization process, this section will reverse the question and examine the impact of democratization on the national identity question. The effects of democratization on Taiwan's national identity question are various and complex. People have different notions of 'positive' or 'negative' effects depending on their political positions. One may argue that the democratization of Taiwan has facilitated unification, and made exchanges across the Taiwan Strait possible. The business sector has made use of the opportunity provided by democratization to transfer its surplus capital and technology to Mainland China, despite restrictions imposed by Taiwan's government. Such increasing exchanges and economic interdependence could facilitate unification. Nevertheless, the democratization of Taiwan has strengthened forces for independence more than those for unification. Democratization, combined with other factors, such as a growing native nationalism in Taiwan, a history of Japanese colonial rule and the KMT's suppression of the Taiwanese, the isolation of Taiwan in international relations, and the Mainland's blockade policy, has contributed to the independence movement.[43]

The effects of democratization on the independence movement can be analyzed through the themes of protection of political and civil liberties, political competition among parties, and political elections, and their impact on the strategies of political parties over Taiwan's national identity question.

Taiwan's democratization has made it possible to discuss and construct Taiwan's national identity. The democratization of Taiwan has provided the protection of political and civil liberties, and the relaxation of political controls on mass media and individual expression. Under Chiang's regime, those who openly discussed the independence of Taiwan were heavily punished. Today, people can openly speak about independence without fear. Furthermore, since democratization, opposition parties have been allowed to exist and expand.

Democratization has redistributed political powers and resources between Mainlanders and Taiwanese in favor of the latter. The influence and power of pro-unification groups have decreased, while pro-independence forces have gained increasing influence and power. The legislative and political changes in Taiwan in 1991, the DPP's influential seats in the National Assembly, and its successful demand for transparency in Mainland policy, have made any secret deal with Beijing out of question. It was rumored that secret negotiations across the Taiwan Strait were undertaken under Chiang Ching-kuo's instruction. After Chiang's death, in January 1988, Beijing hoped that Lee Teng-hui would continue the process and send a five-man group for a secret visit to negotiate for reunification. Such a thing did not happen because of dramatic political changes in Taiwan.[44]

Under democratic conditions, political parties have used the national identity issue to shore up political power. To preempt the DPP's ability to exploit sub-ethnic cleavages and the identity issue, President Lee introduced the Taiwanization of the KMT. This has changed the image of the party from an externally imposed Mainlander institution to a Taiwanese-controlled party. The Taiwanese component of the party has risen steadily from 15 percent, in 1976, to 35 percent in 1988, and again to 54 percent in 1993. At the same time, the Central Standing Committee's Taiwanese membership rose from 19 percent, in 1976, to over 60 percent, in 1993.[45] The KMT is now portraying itself with an indigenous image. Its anti-Communist identity has faded into history. The indigenous wing of the KMT is also seeking the recognition of Taiwan as a sovereign entity separate from China. The KMT is using the unification process to create conditions for greater autonomy, or eventual independence.[46] Taiwanese KMT elites and some second-generation Mainlanders do not share the vision of unification with Mainland China. As a result, Taiwan has decided to abandon the idea of conquering the Mainland; its idea of nationalism has much less to do with unification than with independence. In the July 1997 fourth round of Constitutional revision, the KMT and DPP worked together to freeze the Taiwan provincial government which was seen as a symbol of Taiwan's subordination to China.

The electoral results between 1995-1998 in Taiwan revealed opposition to both unification and independence. The majority of voters did not take an extreme position, but favored the middle ground, namely, maintaining the status quo. Arguably, this result is due to a lack of consensus on basic security questions regarding the threat from China, and to the growth of the middle class and its calculation of strategies and choices. In the 1995 parliamentary election, Zhang Shijie, who urged voters to 'Use "One Nation Two Systems" to Save Taiwan', received only 855 votes. The other candidates of the pro-China Labour Party received only 498 and 510 votes respectively.[47] The New Party, a pro-unification party, failed to gain even one post in the 1997 November election for city mayors and county magistrates. In the 1996 Presidential election, the pro-independence DPP won only 21.3 percent of the vote, and the newly formed Taiwan Independence Party failed to win a single post. As an editor of *The Free China Journal* put it: 'The fact that it only garnered 0.19 percent of the total vote is an unmistakable indication that its secessionist campaign platform has little appeal to Taiwan's increasingly sophisticated voters'.[48]

Moreover, the outcomes of elections have had an impact on the strategies of the DPP with regard to the independence question. Since electoral support for the DPP decreased partially, due to its independence position, in 1996, a major faction of the DPP has become pragmatic, adjusted its radical independence policy, and moved towards the middle ground. During the campaign period for city mayors and county magistrates, in November 1997, the DPP reoriented its objective. Stepping back slightly from the independence platform, the party channeled its campaign energies towards social welfare issues in Taiwan.[49] Hsu Hsin-liang, the DPP's chairperson, and his Formosa Faction, also advocated negotiations with Mainland China on trade, postal and transportation ties, the so-called 'three direct links'. The strategy paid off at the polls for the DPP, which won an unprecedented victory by taking 12 out of the 23 county magistrate and city mayor posts, while the KMT only gained 8. Significantly, at the DPP's symposium in 1998, a pragmatic and progressive consensus was reached. Despite the division within the DDP,[50] it was agreed that Taiwan should be viewed as enjoying independent sovereignty, and that cross-strait talks should resume first with discussions on economic ties, civilian exchanges and technical issues, and eventually proceed to government-to-government negotiations.[51] The DPP is becoming much more pragmatic than it was with regards to the independence issue. Some members even suggest that Taiwan should not waste taxpayers' money by maintaining diplomatic relations with a few small countries. The Formosa Faction also urged a bold step to fully open trade relations with the Chinese Mainland on the western side of the Taiwan Strait.

While the DPP took 70 seats in the December 1998 Legislature election, which was seen as a defeat for the party,[52] the KMT secured 123 of the 225 seats in the new Legislature, representing a solid majority.[53] Moreover, the former Justice Minister, Ma Ying-jeou, of the KMT unseated the Democratic Progressive Party's Chen Shui-bian to become the new mayor of Taipei, in the December 1998 election. Many party members of the DPP have speculated that advocacy of independence could be frightening away any voters who prefer either the status quo in Taiwan's relations with China or Chinese unification.[54] It should be noted that Chen Shui-bian, in his election campaign, has insisted that 'the biggest threat to Taiwan's security lies in its national identity', and that 'if Taiwan cannot free itself from the myth that it is part of China, it will have no future'.[55] In early 1999, many party members of the DPP argued that phrases such as 'establishment of a Republic of Taiwan' and 'determined by referendum' should be revised but this proposal was rejected. [56]

6.   Federalism and the Taiwan Issue

Overseas Chinese intellectuals, such as Yan Jiaqi, assume that Taiwanese are Chinese in their discussion of federalism. Wang Pengling, a Chinese philosopher in exile in Holland, proposes constructive nationalism which advocates the reunification of the two separate sides of the Taiwan Strait through a constitutional democratic state.[57] Federalism, as a super-national arrangement, is always called for to manage the national identity conflict. As Friedman said clearly:

> Beijing cannot insist on coercively imposing unification and Taipei cannot insist on absolute independence. That is, democratic confederation is the projected content of a greater Chinese (*Zhonghua*) nationalism that can contain all of China's challenging diversity.[58]

Since the end of the Second World War, and particularly since the late 1970s, federalism has increasingly become a paradigmatic practice. There are now twenty-one federations with about two billion people (40 percent of the world's total population).[59] Moreover, federalism has contributed to the restoration of democracy in Argentina and Brazil, to the extension of democracy in Venezuela, and to the slow transition from a one-party to a multiparty polity in Mexico.[60] Spain and South Africa, when embarking on democratization, have undertaken a transformation from a unitary to a federal state.

Federalism can also play a role in establishing democracy in China, in the sense that it can meet secessionist demands in Tibet and Xinjiang, secure unity through diversity, and thus facilitate Chinese democratization. Federalism offers not only a much better alternative to the current Chinese authoritarian control over secessionist regions, but also a means to achieve China's unification with Taiwan. In fact, both sides of the Taiwan Strait have discussed some aspects of a federal or confederate solution to the Taiwan issue. So have both sides of the Korean peninsula.[61] Moreover, Hong Kong's special status has already weakened the traditional unitary model. China is now a semi-federal state, in the sense that Hong Kong has its own currency and independent financial and legal systems. The special status of Hong Kong, with its financial and economic resources, will develop slowly into a constraint on Beijing.

Deng Xiaoping's proposal of 'one nation two systems' entails federal elements.[62] Under Deng's proposal, Taiwan would enjoy a high degree of autonomy, consisting of administrative and legislative power, judiciary power including final judgment, the power to keep its own army, and certain powers in foreign affairs, such as signing commercial and cultural agreements with foreign countries.[63] Taiwan will also have the power to issue its own currency. But only the PRC would represent China in the international arena; Taiwan would recognize the sovereignty of China; and its military arm would not constitute a threat against China. Deng Xiaoping's notion of 'one nation two systems' is interpreted by Yan Jiaqi as a federal solution with confederate characteristics, for the larger federal power of China would have a constitutional connection with the smaller federal state of Taiwan, which would maintain more autonomy than in normal federal-state relationships.[64] This notion is innovative in the Chinese context, in the sense that China would move away from a unitary notion of state and go towards a federal idea of nation-state. In fact, China has to accept and develop such notions and arrangements in order to meet complex contemporary political conditions. The concession made in the notion of 'one nation two systems' reflects the fact that China's national identity can be negotiated through bargaining. As Deng reportedly said, federalism could be considered if it was acceptable to Taiwan. Jiang Zemin went further by saying that so long as the principle of one country is upheld anything else can be negotiated.

In the eyes of Taipei, Deng Xiaoping's idea of 'one nation two systems' is inadequate in addressing the Taiwan issue.[65] Taiwan proposes 'one country, one culture, two governments', under which Taiwan would not only maintain its present system but also enjoy equal status with the PRC in international affairs (for example, dual UN representation).

Both Taiwan's 'one country, two governments' formula and China's 'one country, two systems' proposal have retreated from the idea that reunification be accomplished under a single government and with one socio-economic system. More importantly, Taiwanese Premier Lien Chan (Lian Zhan) considers federal or confederate arrangements as a way to achieve unification. Zhou Yanshan, a legislative member of the New Party, also suggests the model of a Chinese Commonwealth as a solution.[66] Beijing is now considering a federal proposal to unify China with Taiwan.[67]

The idea of federalism, no matter how attractive, faces resistance from both sides. In Mainland China, Beijing tends to emphasize the self-defeating nature of federalism and its unanticipated consequences, namely the proliferation of autonomy across China and the escalation of conflicts. According to Beijing, the central governing body would find such changes difficult to resist, and would eventually be forced to accommodate local demands. Modern Chinese history shows that federalism once gave rise to regional militarists (*geju*). If federalism was built upon the aspirations of regional militarists, it could never achieve national unity and strength (see section 2 of chapter 7).[68]

In Taiwan, it is often said that Taiwan is bigger than Singapore, and if Singapore has its own nation-state, then why doesn't Taiwan? The desire for an independent nation-state is strong in Taiwan, and, moreover, Taiwan does not meet certain conditions for federalism. Among other things, one necessary condition for federalism is that one state should not be so powerful as to be able to rely on its individual strength for protection against foreign encroachment.[69] A combination of the economic, military and political powers of Taiwan; the history of Taiwan's semi-independence; the democratization effect on the Taiwan question; and the worldwide secession/independence tendency, make it extremely difficult for federalism to be accepted by Taiwanese nationalism.

Federalism, and other proposals, 'one China, two governments', or 'one nation, two systems', adopt and continue to confirm the framework of the nation-state system. Under such a system, since nationalism in China and Taiwan share features such as the exclusion of other forms of state, or other orders of state, or the intensification of national identities, there is no peaceful solution to the Taiwan question. There are two alternative approaches. One is 'Confucian China' or 'cultural China', the key idea being that a 'cultural China' can allow the existence of plural political entities. Another alternative is a kind of regional arrangement, something like the institution of the European

Union, which would fulfill the PRC's desire for unification as well as Taiwan's request for its own nation-statehood, and in which the national sovereignty question does not prevail. This requires the plural idea that separate state identities are compatible with a notion of one China. We will not examine these issues further, as they are beyond the scope of this chapter.

7.   Chinese Democratization and the Taiwan Issue

In the above section, we saw that both sides recognize the necessity of a confederate or federal arrangement. Why, then, is there no action? Here, democracy seems to come into play in the politics of national identity. Politicians and commentators have often made such a claim: if China is still an authoritarian state, there is sufficient reason for Taiwan to separate from China; if Taiwan is unified with an authoritarian China, there will be no democracy in Taiwan; and if China is being democratized, there is no legitimate reason for Taiwan to become independent. To take one example, when Jiang reiterated that 'one country, two systems' would 'set an example for the final solution to the Taiwan question', Premier Lien Chan argued, 'Taiwan is governed by a democracy, and no one in Taiwan wants to live under Communism. Hence the government has to respect the wishes of the people'.[70] Koo Chen-fu, Chairperson of Strait Exchange Foundation, reiterated in his meeting with Jiang Zemin, Qian Qichen and other Chinese leaders during his trip to China in October 1998, that the democratization of China is a precondition for unification.

Putting aside the complex issue of what and how federal or confederate institutions should be adopted,[71] federal or confederate arrangements must contain democratic elements. Among other things, Chinese democratization is a precondition to establish a confederate or federal structure, in the sense that it would build trust and good will,[72] and reduce political and ideological differences. Within the current Chinese authoritarian system it is impossible to establish a federal system.

Furthermore, the way in which a federal or confederate arrangement is established must involve a democratic process. A unifying federalism must listen to public opinion, appeal to ratification by both parliaments, and finally rest upon referenda. Such a process will provide legitimacy for an emerging federal or confederate system.

Moreover, the federal or confederate arrangement may contain several democratic elements. First, the two political entities would equally share the pool of sovereignty.   Second, federalism would place constitutional constraints both on central government and on the governments of sub-units. And third, the autonomy of sub-units would be fully guaranteed. These democratic elements are necessary incentives and safeguards for Taiwan in coming to terms with a federal or confederate arrangement.

Current Chinese leaders, however, reject the above line of thinking. Qian Qichen, for example, recently said that it is a serious problem for a group of people who attempt to change the status of Taiwan through a referendum in Taiwan.[73] Tang Shubei, Vice-President of the Association of Taiwan Strait, also asserted that democracy is not an essential question and that democratic form should not constitute an obstacle to the negotiation on the reunification question. He stressed that Taiwan should not impose democracy on China, nor should China impose socialism on Taiwan.[74]

For the Chinese leadership, the idea of pan-Chinese nationalism is a guiding principle to deal with the Taiwan Strait relation. It is unlikely for current Chinese leaders to accept the idea of democratic federalism. What if China embarks upon democratization? Will unification be achieved? Or, will Taiwan gain its independence in the process of Chinese democratization? Now let us turn to various hypotheses on the likely impact of Chinese democratization on the Taiwan issue.

The democratization of China would create political systems and institutions compatible with those in Taiwan, and thereby facilitate unification. It is likely that the democratization of China will help China win an international reputation and improve its relations with the USA.[75] It is likely that the democratization of China would both intensify pro-unification pressure on Taiwan, as it would reduce the differences between political institutions,[76] and increase confidence in a peaceful solution among Taiwanese people. A democratic China, with decentralized powers and perhaps a confederation, will foster a trust between China and Taiwan. Moreover, elected leaders in Mainland China would push unification further, if they had an electoral mandate.

The democratization of China, however, does not guarantee successful unification with Taiwan. It might also facilitate the independence of Taiwan. Democratization cuts two ways when dealing with the national boundary question: it can facilitate independence or strengthen the unity of states. Spain, the Philippines, South Africa, St. Kitts and Nevis, Papua New Guinea, Nigeria and Turkey, all have been democratized in the third wave of democratization, and have maintained the unity of their states. Democratization helps them to contain the secession problem and maintain the unity of states.[77] This is because national elections legitimize the political unit and support the regime's claim to legitimacy. Democratic packages, such as decentralization and regional autonomy, have also accommodated secessionist demands.

On the other hand, democratization processes make independence or secession much more likely to succeed. Twenty-six new seceding states out of 46 new UN member states recognized by the UN between 1974-1997 are related to the democratization of parent states.[78] This means that in recent years 57 percent of new states have been formed during the democratization of their parent states. Democratization has facilitated successful secession in contexts such as the former Soviet Union, Pakistan,[79] Ethiopia and Yugoslavia. It becomes apparent that all successful secessions, without exception, have happened in the period just before to just after the initiation of democratization, usually within the first three years. When democratization is consolidated, it becomes harder for secessionists to succeed.

Here we would like to propose a hypothesis concerning the relationship between the pattern of Chinese democratization and the resolution of the Taiwan question. If the democratization of China is prompted by popular mobilization, Taiwan is more likely to gain its independence, as shown by the case of the successful secession of Mongolia from Qing, when the Manchu ruler's resistance against democratic reform led to a revolution from below. This is because popularly mandated democratization weakens the power of the center and creates an opportunity for independence. If, on the other hand, the democratization is imposed from above, through elite negotiation, Taiwan would not have a favorable opportunity to declare independence. Democratization from above can boost the legitimacy of the government and may even strengthen state power.

China would have a chance to unify with Taiwan if it were to follow Stepan and Linz's model of *sequential* democratic reform: state-wide election precedes provincial election, followed by the negotiation of an autonomy statute with Tibet and a confederal arrangement with Taiwan. China would risk disintegration if the first competitive election were at the provincial, not nation-wide level. In the USSR, democratization started with the Baltic states, not with the center. Thus the center and Gorbachev had no legitimate authority to manage the boundary problem; and democratization in the republics assisted secession. The result was disintegration.[80] In fact, Chinese leaders seem to have already learnt a lesson about this sequence. In 1993, 'multiple-candidate' elections were held for provincial leaders, by ballots in regional 'parliaments', in a few provinces, including Zhejiang and Guizhou, where officially designated candidates for governors were voted down. For fear that they would lose control of provincial leaders, as a consequence of elections, the central leaders decided that multiple candidate elections for provincial leaders should be stopped.

Moreover, one immediate effect of Chinese democratization would be that Chinese dissidents, particularly those who do not care about the Taiwan issue or who would even willingly let Taiwan gain independence, could freely express their views. Thus the myth that there is an indisputable consensus on unification might be shattered.[81] There would be competitive political parties, and the emergence of pro-Taiwan and anti-Taiwan parties or social groups. The dominant party would be likely to be a pro-unification party. Under plural and competitive politics, it might be speculated that either some democrat members, or some members of the government, might strike a political deal with Taipei that would support its independence claim in exchange for various supports from Taiwan. If this were done quickly and wisely, peace would be assured. Historically, Sun Yat-sen made such a secret deal with Japan over Northern China in the 1910s,[82] and Boris Yeltsin supported and encouraged the Baltic States to secede in order to gain power over his rival, Gorbachev, in 1991.

In short, a Chinese democrat is likely to argue for Chinese democratization, on the grounds that if China seeks to democratize itself at a national level, it has a chance to build a democratic federal or confederate system, facilitating reunification with Taiwan. By contrast, a Chinese nationalist is likely to argue against Chinese democratization, on the grounds that it is likely to facilitate the independence of Taiwan.

Conclusion

For Chinese nationalists, the unification and the unity of China is the fundamental aim, while democracy is merely a means. The Chinese nationalists take an instrumental view of democracy: they will introduce it if it can promote unification, otherwise they will reject it. The fact that Beijing talks about unification without mentioning democracy indicates that democracy is incompatible with unification in the eyes of Beijing. If Beijing perceives that the logic of the democratic effect favors Taiwan's independence, it will choose to push for unification at the cost of democracy. In the eyes of Chinese nationalists, Taiwan's democratization has gone hand in hand with Taiwanization, and the rise of Taiwanese nationalist movements. Moreover, Chinese nationalists do not feel confident that Chinese democratization will necessarily promote unification, and they worry that the democratization of China will provide a chance for Taiwan to gain its independence.

The fact that the DPP talks about both independence and democracy indicates that, in the eyes of Taiwanese nationalists, democracy is compatible with, and can assist with, independence. The DPP therefore intends to declare or maintain *de facto* independence through democratization. In short, the mutually supportive association between democratization and Taiwanization, in Taiwan, contrasts with the clash between democratization and nationalism in China, which we will revisit in chapters 7-8. The significance of democratized Taiwanization or Taiwanized democratization lies not only in its challenge to the basic assumptions of pan-Chinese nationalism, but also in its insistence on self-rule through democratization, which sets an example for the peoples of China, in particular those who demand secession. This gives rise to the question of whether China will follow the path of the Soviet Union, which will be discussed in the next chapter.

Notes

1   Baogang He's conversation with him on 23 July 1991 in Taipei.

2   Wu Naide, 'The Sense of Provincialism, Political Support and National Identity', in *Zuqun guanxi yu guojiang rentong*, Institute for National Policy Research, Chang Yung-fa Foundation, 1993, p. 48.

3   Cheng-Feng Shih, 'Emerging Taiwanese Identity', Prepared for Taiwan Update 1997, Taiwan-Hong Kong-PRC Relations, Brisbane, Queensland, Australia, Aug. 14-15, 1997, p. 25.

4   When Baogang He encountered a Uygur man in Xinjiang and asked whether he considered himself Chinese, the man replied, 'Look at my skin, the color of my hair and eyes! Am I a Chinese? No!'.

5   Writings on Taiwanese nationalism are burgeoning. In recent years, for example, Qianfeng Publisher, has published thirteen series and around 178 books on Taiwan. The topics of the series include *a Collection of Taiwan's Writers, a Study of Taiwan's Literature, a Collection of New Taiwan, a Collection of New Taiwanese, Taiwan's Literature and History, Taiwan's Winds and Clouds, Taiwan Studies, and the People of Taiwan's Nation*. For recent books on nationalism, see Cheng-Feng Shih, *Sub-ethnic Groups and Nationalism*, Taipei: Qianfeng Publisher, 1998; and Cheng-Feng Shih, (ed.), *Taiwan Nationalism*, Taipei: Qianfeng Publisher, 1994.

6   On January 27, 1999, Taiwan forged formal diplomatic ties with the Republic of
       Macedonia, bringing its number of diplomatic allies to 28. *The Free China Journal*,
       Vol. 16, No. 5, 29 Jan. 1999, p. 1.

7   Cheng-Feng Shih, 'Emerging Taiwanese Identity', p. 22.

8   Jei Guk Jeon, 'The Origin of Northeast Asian NICs in Retrospect: The Colonial
       Political Economy, Japan in Korea and Taiwan', *Asian Perspective*, vol. 16, no. 1,
       1992, pp. 71-101.

9   Similarly, through an emphasis on Japanese influences in Taiwan, the Japanese
       scholar Mitsuta contends that 'the assumption that Taiwan is nationally a part of
       China is nothing more than a conceptual one.' Wan-Lee Yin, however, comments
       that Mitsuta's account 'left out centuries of cultural heritage preserved by Chinese
       settlers in Taiwan. In the result, he almost managed to posit a state of nature for the
       islanders prior to Japanese occupation'. Yin also argues that Mitsuta's account does
       injustice to history, truth and reason. See Wan-Lee Yin, , 'On "Taiwan in the China
       Circle"', *The Journal of Contemporary China*, no. 8, Winter-Spring, 1995, pp. 102-
       105: 102.

10   Cheng-Feng Shih, 'Emerging Taiwanese Identity', p. 24.

11   Ibid., p. 17.

12   Ibid., p. 23.

13   Virginia Sheng, 'Junior high books spark controversy over content', *The Free
       China Journal*, June 27, 1997, p. 4.

14   Cheng-Feng Shih, 'Emerging Taiwanese Identity', p. 6.

15   Ibid., p. 5.

16   Ibid., p. 23.

17   Ibid.

18   Zhong Weiguang, 'Minzu, minzu zhuyi he zhongguo wenti' (Nation, Nationalism
       and the China Problem), *Modern China Studies*, No. 2, 1997, pp. 141-2.

19   See Yin Wan-Lee, 'On "Taiwan in the China Circle"', *The Journal of
       Contemporary China*, no. 8, Winter-Spring, 1995, pp. 102-105.

20   Wen-chun Chen, 'National Identity and Democratic Consolidation in Taiwan: A
       Study of the Problem of Democratization in a Divided Country', *Issues and Studies*,
       vol. 33, no. 4, Apr. 1997, pp. 1-44: 14.

21   See 'Public Opinion on Cross-Strait Relations in the Republic of China',
       www.mac.gov.tw

22   Allen Chun, 'From Nationalism to Nationalizing: Cultural Imagination and State Formation in Postwar Taiwan', *The Australian Journal of Chinese Affairs*, no. 31, Jan. 1994, p. 69.

23   Tien Hung-mao, 'Toward Peaceful Resolution of Mainland-Taiwan Conflicts: The Promise of Democratization', in Edward Friedman (ed.), *The Politics of Democratization: Generalizing East Asian Experiences*. Boulder: Westview Press, 1994, p. 189.

24   Peter Kien-hong Yu, 'Concept of New Taiwanese foresees new, unified China', *The Free China Journal*, vol. XV, no. 51, Dec. 25, 1998, p. 6.

25   Yu-tzung Chang, 'Ethnic Conflict and Democratic Consolidation in Taiwan: Dissolving the Logic of Nation-State and Democratic Policies', *Issues and Studies*, vol. 33, no. 4, Apr. 1997, pp. 77-93: 86.

26   Peter Kien-hong Yu, 'Concept of New Taiwanese foresees new, unified China', *The Free China Journal*, vol. XV, no. 51, Dec. 25, 1998, p. 6.

27   Frank Chang, 'ROC monitors Mideast tensions', *The Free China Journal*, vol. XV, no. 51, Dec. 25, 1998, p. 1.

28   Ibid., p. 1.

29   Oscar Chung also discusses the concept of New Taiwanese in detail, see 'Neither Yam Nor Taro', *Free China Review*, Vol. 49, No. 2, Feb. 1999, p. 13.

30   It should be clarified that the DDP is not identified with this radical Taiwanese nationalism, although there is an element of radical nationalism within the DPP.

31   Peter Kien-hong Yu, op. cit., p. 6.

32   *Free China Review*, Vol. 49, No. 2, Feb. 1999, editorial page.

33   See Linda Chao and Ramon H. Myers, *The First Chinese Democracy: Political Life in the Republic of China on Taiwan*, Baltimore, the John Hopkins University Press, 1998.

34   *Central Daily News*, 27 Jun. 1994.

35   This view was expressed by Liu Suli, the manager of the Wanshan bookshop in our conversation in 1993.

36   Edward Friedman, 'Chinese Nationalism, Taiwan Autonomy and the Prospects of a Larger War', *Journal of Contemporary China*, vol. 6, no. 14, 1997, pp. 5-32.

37   This comes from *Polity III* data. We acknowledge that there are huge differences in political institutions and ideology even though both have similar scores.

38   For a detailed discussion of this, see Baogang He, *The Democratic Implications of Civil Society in China*, London, Macmillan, 1997.

39   For a review of Chinese writings on nationalism, see Preface. For the view of the compatibility between democracy and nationalism in Taiwan, see Cheng-Feng Shih, (ed.), *Taiwan Nationalism*, p. 8.

40   Also see Bruce Jacobs, 'Political Opposition and Taiwan's Political Future', *Australian Journal of Chinese Affairs* 6 Jan. 1981, pp. 22-44.

41   My conversation with Professor Hu in Jul. 1991 in Taipei.

42   Yun-Han Chu, Hu Fu and Chung-in Moon, 'South Korea and Taiwan: The International Context', in Larry Diamond, Marc Plattner, Yun-han Chu, and Hung-mao Tien, (eds.), *Consolidating the Third Wave Democracies: Regional Challenges*, Baltimore: the Johns Hopkins University Press, 1997, p. 289.

43   We cannot make the general claim that democratization inevitably gives rise to independence movements, because the democratization of South Korea simply has not had such an effect.

44   Sheng Lijun, 'China Eyes Taiwan: Why is a Breakthrough so Difficult?', *The Journal of Strategic Studies*, vol. 21, no. 1, Mar. 1998, p. 69.

45   Tien Hung-mao. 'Taiwan's Transformation', in Diamond et al., *op. cit.*, p. 145.

46   See Alastair Johnston, 'Independence through Unification: On the Correct Handling of Contradictions across the Taiwan Straits', Harvard University, 1993, *Contemporary Issue*, No. 2, p. 15.

47   See Bruce Jacobs, 'China's Policies Towards Taiwan', paper given at Taiwan Update 1997: Taiwan, Hong Kong and PRC Relations, 14-15 Aug. 1997, Brisbane, p. 25.

48   Editorial commentary: 'New Trend Set in Party Politics', *The Free China Journal*, Dec. 5, 1997, p. 6.

49   Eric P. Moon and James A. Robinson, 'Past Trends Show Election Results not so Surprising', *The Free China Journal*, Dec. 5, 1997, p. 8.

50   According to Julian Kuo, a member of the Formosa Faction, the interdependence between Taiwan and Mainland China will be the best protection for Taiwan. By contrast, the New Tide Faction promoted a strategy similar to President Lee Teng-hui's 'no haste, be patient' policy, and said there is no need for cross-negotiations because the US will protect Taiwan. And Hsu Yang-ming, of the Justice Alliance Faction, urged Taiwan to abandon its so-called 'one China' policy and use its name

when it bids for membership in the United Nations. See Virginia Sheng, 'DPP's Mainland Policy Sparks Intraparty Clash', *The Free China Journal*, Jan. 16, 1998, p. 2.

51   Virginia Sheng, 'DPP's Mainland Policy Exemplifies Party's Maturity', *The Free China Journal*, Mar. 27, 1998, p. 7; 'DPP Factions United in Mainland Policy Meeting', *The Free China Journal*, Feb. 20, 1998, p. 1.

52   Myra Lu, 'KMT wins Taipei, bolsters its majority in Legislature', *The Free China Journal*, vol. XV, no. 49, Dec. 11, 1998, p. 1.

53   The KMT won, by contrast, a thin majority of 85 seats in the 164 seat law-making body in the 1995 elections.

54   Myra Lu, 'DPP Opts not to Revise Wording of Platform', *The Free China Journal*, Vol. XVI, No. 2, Jan. 8, 1999, p. 2.

55   Virginia Sheng, 'DPP election win may unite opposition forces', *The Free China Journal*, vol. XV, no. 26, Jul. 3, 1998, p. 2.

56   Myra Lu, 'DPP Opts not to Revise Wording of Platform', p. 2.

57   Wang Pengling, 'Zhongguo minzu zhuyi de yuanliu – jianlun cong geming de minzu zhuyi zhuanxiang jianshe de minzu zhuyi' (Source of Chinese nationalism – On the transformation from revolutionary nationalism to constructive nationalism), *Modern China Studies*, No. 2, 1997, pp. 101-127.

58   Edward Friedman, 'A Democratic Chinese Nationalism', in J. Unger (ed.), *Chinese Nationalism*, 1996, New York: M.E. Sharpe, Inc., p. 180.

59   Daniel J. Elazar, 'From Statism to Federalism: A Paradigm Shift', *Publius: The Journal of Federalism*, vol. 25, no. 2, Spring 1995, pp. 5-18. Also see the special issue, 'New Trends in Federalism' in *International Political Science Review*, vol. 17, No. 4, Oct. 1996.

60   Daniel J. Elazar, *op. cit.*, p. 16.

61   See Kwan Hwang, 'Korean Reunification in a Comparative Perspective', in Young Whan Kihl (ed.), *Korea and the World: Beyond the Cold War*, Boulder: Westview Press, 1994, p. 293.

62   It can be argued that Beijing may consider dropping the term 'one nation two systems' and adopt common international terms such as federalism and confederation, so as to avoid confusion and come close to international standards.

63 Chen Qimao, 'The Taiwan Strait Crisis: Its Crux and Solutions', *Asian Survey*, Vol. XXXVI, No. 11, Nov. 1996, p. 1056.

64 *China's Constitutionism Newsletter*, No. 2, Jun. 1994, 24. For Yan's ideas on federalism, see Yan Jiaqi. *Disan gonghe - weilaizhongguo de xuanze (The Third Republic - A Choice for Future China)*, New York: Global Publishing Co. Inc, 1992; *Lianbang zhongguo gouxiang (A Design for a Federated China)*, Hong Kong: Ming Bao Press, 1992. Yan attempts to combine federalism and confederation to provide an adequate solution. It is debatable whether confederation is a much better solution to the Taiwan issue than federalism.

65 For an excellent analysis of inadequacy, see C.L. Chiou, 'Dilemmas in China's Reunification Policy toward Taiwan', *Asian Survey*, Vol. 26, 1986, pp. 467-82.

66 Zhou Yanshan, 'New Thinking on the "Chinese Commonwealth"', *Modern China Studies*, No. 6, 1995, pp. 19-24.

67 *China's Constitutionism Newsletter*, No. 2, Jun. 1994, p. 24.

68 Prasenjit Duara, 'Nationalism as the Politics of Culture: Centralism and Federalism in Early Republican China', The Woodrow Wilson Center, Asia Program Occasional Paper, No, 37, Jun. 11, 1990, p. 12.

69 John Stuart Mill, *Utilitarianism, Liberty, and Representative Government*, London: J. M. Dent and Sons Ltd, 1947, p. 367.

70 Chou Yujen, 'The Impacts of Taiwan's National Identity and Democratisation on its International Stance and East Asia's Security', the paper presented at the XVIIth World Congress of the International Political Science Association, Paper No. SS-61, Aug. 21, 1997, pp. 1-39, especially, p. 35.

71 Yujen Chou argues for confederation in which the PRC does not swallow the ROC, nor does the ROC swallow the PRC. See Yujen Chou, 'The Impacts of Taiwan's National Identity and Democratization on its International Stance and East Asia's Security', paper given at the IPSA Congress, Seoul, 17-21 Aug. 1997.

72 One condition necessary to render a federation advisable, in the opinion of J. S. Mill, is that there should be a sufficient amount of mutual sympathy among the populations. See John Stuart Mill, *op.cit.*, p. 366. Chinese democratization can create an opportunity to meet this condition.

73 *The Peoples Daily* (overseas edition), 29 Jan. 1999, p. 1.

74   *The Peoples Daily* (overseas edition), 28 Jan. 1999, p. 5.

75   However, Chinese nationalists distrust the USA and wonder whether it will support the unification project when China moves towards democratization. They think that divide-and-rule is the best strategy for the USA to maintain its strategic position in East Asia.

76   Tien asks the question whether the PRC must democratize in order to appeal to newly democratic Taiwan, or whether real negotiation requires prior democratization or federalism on the mainland. See his article, 'Toward Peaceful Resolution', op. cit., p. 192, p. 195.

77   Other factors, such as the stability of a democratic regime, international relations, and diplomatic efforts, also come into play.

78   The figure comes from chapter 4 of my forthcoming book *Democracy and Boundaries in East Asia* (London: Routledge, 1999).

79   In the case of Bangladesh secession, it was a long process. Bengali became an official language together with Urdu in the 1950s. Bangladesh demanded a level of autonomy in the 1954 'Twenty-one Points', then a loose federal system in the 'Six Points' in 1966, and finally secession in 1971 in the wake of the Awami League's victory, with a 75 percent vote in the 1970 December election.

80   Juan J. Linz and Alfred Stepan, *Problems of Democratic Transition and Consolidation: Southern Europe, South America, and Post-Communist Europe.* Baltimore and London: The John Hopkins University Press, 1996, p. 34, pp. 381-384. Also see Alfred Stepan, 'Toward a New Comparative Analysis of Democracy and Federalism: Demos Constraining and Demos Enabling Federations', paper given at IPSA XVII World Congress, Seoul, Aug. 17-22, 1997, Footnote 27, p. 17.

81   Chen Qimao assumes one Chinese voice about the Taiwan issue, see Chen Qimao, 'The Taiwan Strait Crisis', pp. 1055-1066.

82   Marius Jansen, *The Japanese and Sun Yat-sen*, Cambridge: Harvard University, 1967.

6 Nationalism, National Identity, Elites and Democratization in Russia and China

There is little doubt that the collapse of the Soviet Union, democratization of Russia and economic liberalization in China have been the most important historical developments in the second half of the twentieth century. With some qualifications, these developments may be seen as a part of the 'third wave' of democratization: Russia representing a transition to 'unconsolidated democracy', and China undergoing 'creeping democratization', whereby economic reforms undermine the authoritarian political structures. Both the creeping democratization in China and the consolidation of democratization in Russia have confronted the national identity question and the rise of nationalism.[1]

The qualifications concern, first and foremost, the applicability of the words 'democracy' and 'democratization', in particular in relation to the developments in China. While few would argue that Russia has developed unambiguously democratic political institutions and practices - albeit often described as 'unconsolidated', 'weak', or 'delegative',[2] - the case of China is problematic. The economic liberalization there, although quite extensive and in many ways similar to post-Communist reforms in Eastern Europe and Russia, has been conducted under an authoritarian regime which does not fulfill even the most basic criteria of democratic polity. Lack of free elections, open political contestation, and basic civil and political freedoms exclude China from the ranks of democratic 'polyarchies', that is regimes in which plural elites share power and compete for office by subjecting themselves to free and open elections.[3] Nevertheless, the liberal economic reforms in China, especially those embraced at the 15th Party Congress, have accelerated the process of elite differentiation thus moving one step closer to a 'polyarchic' configuration. Moreover, the introduction in China of the direct election for village chiefs since 1987 indicates a movement towards a local democracy, albeit in an embryonic form. The elections for people's deputies and the increasing powers of the National People's Congress (NPC), the more open leadership selection processes within the Communist Party, and the improvement of the rule of law all can be seen as a part of the process of creeping democratization in China.[4]

The differences, however, are considerable. While Russia faces problems of democratic *consolidation*, that is strengthening the democratic institutions and practices which have already been introduced, albeit in an embryonic form, China faces, at best, the prospect of democratic *transition*. We see both processes as strongly inter-related and dependent on the same set of factors and conditions: securing state power and national integrity, and promoting differentiation and consensus among the national elites. A weakened state, and ethno-national fission, especially when with deep divisions within national elites, hinder both democratic transition and consolidation.[5]

This is the core argument of this chapter. While developing this argument, we critically address an alternative view according to which a weakened state, national fission and elite divisions *facilitate* democratic transition (though they may hinder democratic consolidation as well). Although plausible to some degree as a generalization of the Soviet/Russian experience, it is in our view based on an incorrect interpretation of the transition sequence in the Soviet Union and Russia, and on a misreading of political conditions in both countries. Prospects for securing democracy in Russia, and initiating democratic transition in China, depend, first, on the solution of the national boundary and identity problem - and this solution has to be different in Russia and China - second, on the control of ethno-national fission; and third, on elite structure, conflict management and sequencing of reforms.

1.   The National Identity Problem

Perhaps the most salient and pressing problem in Russia and China is the maintenance of national boundaries and an integral state. This reflects both the underlying fears of foreign incursions, secessionist wars and crippling border disputes, and a rather tenuous current relationship between the centers and the peripheries in both countries. The very size, ethnic composition, and the relatively recent history of political divisions and ethno-national challenges infuse this problem with special urgency, among the elites and mass populations in both countries. For the elites, national integrity is the key element of their ruling formulas; for the mass populations this is the foundation of national pride and the sense of security. Moreover, in both Russia and China the national boundary problem is fused with the question of national identity. Although, as argued below, the relations between the political (state), cultural (traditions) and territorial (lands) referents of national identities differ, both countries, nevertheless, share a strong attachment to the notion of integral country. Because of these implications, the issues of national unity and state integrity are typically placed higher on the national agendas than the issue of democratic reforms.

A more jaundiced view is that the threats to national unity and integrity are merely excuses and smokescreens used by the Communist Party leaders in opposing democratization. While partly true, such a view would miss an important point, namely, that the arguments of national unity and state integrity prove quite effective and popular. They reverberate strongly in the elites and mass populations of both countries. In the case of China, there was a strong link between the declaration of martial laws in Tibet and the crackdown on the pro-democracy movement in Beijing in June 1989. It was Tibet's separatist movement, among other things, that heightened the CCP's concerns about the centrifugal effects of democratization at the national level. In Russia, the fears of national 'dismembering' and the fate of Russians in the 'near abroad' have served as the foundations for the anti-reformist, anti-democratic opposition, both in the Communist Party and among the Zhirinovskiyite ultra-nationalists.

The collapse of the Soviet Union was first prompted by the independence bid by the Baltic republics. The most significant of all the Soviet nationality disputes began in mid-1989 on the anniversary of the very Nazi-Soviet pact which had led to the incorporation of these republics into the USSR. In December 1989, the Lithuanian Communist Party broke with the CPSU. In March 1990, elections to republican and local soviets were held, followed by victories for Popular Fronts and accompanied by a constitutional change that saw Gorbachev elected to the Executive Presidency. At the same time, the Lithuanians declared independence, followed by the Georgians. Yeltsin's victory in the Russian presidential elections (June 1991) and the failed coup attempt (August 1991) accelerated the disintegration. Armenia (23 August), Ukraine (24 August), Belarus (26 August), Moldova (27 August), Azerbaijan (30 August), Kyrgyzstan and Uzbekistan (31 August), Tajikistan (9 September), Turkmenistan (27 October), and Kazakhstan (16 December) all followed suit. The hastily stitched up Commonwealth of the Independent States (CIS), formally established in December 1993, proved unsuccessful as a unifying structure. Although it now embraces all the former Soviet republics, except the Baltic states and Moldova, it is nothing more than a loose forum for economic co-operation.

These momentous events could be accurately described as a collapse of the empire. It was unprecedented in its speed and, at least initially, remarkably non-violent in nature. Clashes erupted only briefly in Baku in 1990, in the Baltic Republics in the summer of 1991 and in Moldova in 1992 when the Russian 14th Army supported the Communist insurgency in the secessionist 'Dniestr Republic'. Serious military conflicts in Chechnia and Tajikistan started later, mainly in 1993-1995. Although bloody and prolonged, they have been relatively well insulated and contained in the regions.

In spite of this largely peaceful fragmentation, tensions related to national identities and state boundaries remain very high in Russia. There are a number of reasons for this fragility. First, the Soviet Union and the post-Communist Russian Federation have evolved historically as successors to the Tsarist empire, in which Russians were a minority (or a slim majority, if one counts partly Russified Belarussians and Ukrainians). Russian cultural identity was affected by constant accommodation and assimilation of the Slavic neighbors. Consequently, Russian national identification had evolved in a strongly étatist way, focused on the state rather than the people and their culture (*ethnos*). The collapse of the Soviet state was a serious threat to this étatist national identity, although it generated a more ethnically homogeneous entity, the Russian Federation.

The second and closely-related reason for the intensity of concerns over national identity in Russia is that the Federation is not, strictly speaking, the nation-state successor of the Russian/Soviet empire. Although the new Federation contains more than half the population of the ex-Soviet Union, three-quarters of its territory and over 60 percent of its industrial capacity, the boundaries of the Federation have been pushed to the early modern period (i.e. before the union with Ukraine in 1654). This is important, because for many Russians national identity presumes a coincidence of identities with the Slavic neighbors (especially Ukrainians). Kiev - currently in Ukraine - is regarded as the cradle of 'Russian' culture. The autonomization of the 'western republics' is thus seen by many Russians as a loss of identity and is depicted by nationalist leaders as a threat to national unity.

Third, the new Russian state has been created in a somewhat topsy-turvy manner. While the typical evolution of the nation-states in the West, and in East Asia, has extended state powers and assimilated minorities, post-Soviet Russia has 25 million ethnic Russians outside its borders. The fate of these post-imperial minorities, especially in the so called 'near abroad' (in the neighboring post-Soviet states), is the source of constant aggravation and the favorite topic of nationalistic demagogues.

Fourth, in spite of its name, the Russian Federation lacks an authentic federal structure. The autonomy enjoyed by its components is narrow and shrinking. While increased regional autonomy constituted the key slogan of Yeltsin's early electoral campaigns - aimed at weakening Soviet structures - his more recent presidential policies have been vigorously integrationist. This disparity between the federal facade and integrationist-nationalist 'content' of Russian policies is a source of aggravation not only for ethnic minorities.

The ideological complexion of the Russian population and the political orientation of their leaders are likely to remain nationalist and étatist. Yeltsin's democratic nationalism, it must be remembered, gained ground mainly in opposition to Gorbachev's more liberal (though not necessarily democratic) reforms and in reaction to what has been perceived as the fatal weakening of the state. Yeltsin's democratic breakthrough, which was aimed at strengthening his hand in dealing with the Communist leaders, was possible due to the opening up of a window of opportunity: a consensus in the circle of his (mainly nationalistic) colleagues-leaders. This explains why much of the support, that has initially helped Yeltsin to democratize Russia comes, paradoxically, from people with autocratic and authoritarian preferences: those who mourn the lost superpower status, and those who are longing for a 'strong hand' capable of strengthening law and order in Russia and 'protecting' Russian minorities in the neighboring states. This means that there is little consensus among Russian elites, and even less among the public at large, as to what would constitute 'just' national boundaries, 'proper' national identity, and the 'natural' shape of the Russian polity.

Compared with the former Soviet Union, China has been relatively successful in managing and manipulating national identity as an instrument for social and political unity. To counteract separatist tendencies, the Chinese government has been pushing for the development of a pan-Chinese nationalism (*da Zhonghua minzuzhuyi*), a set of shared values and cultural identities that could hold the Chinese peoples together. The sense of common national identity and cultural heritage are strong in China, in spite of the secession movements in Tobet and Xinjiang (They fuse with religious identities: Buddhism in Tibet and Islam in Xinjiang). Unlike the inhabitants of the Baltic republics, Ukraine and the Caucasus, Chinese minorities do not have long histories of independent statehood, and they have not spawned nationalistic elites. Tibet enjoyed only semi-independent status before annexation, and the Uygurs only had a very short period of autonomy under the Republic of East Turkestan. Furthermore, China's historical legacy was quite different from the Russian one. China was the victim of colonization by Western imperialist powers after the Opium War. This image of the 'victim' played a positive role in building a unified Chinese state. However, under the Qing dynasty China herself became an empire colonizing and assimilating ethnic minorities. This expansion and assimilation was in many ways similar to the Western process of nation-state formation - a fact seldom mentioned in official pronouncements. However, this expansion was more successful than Russian imperial expansion in assimilating minorities, partly due to the centuries-old and powerful radiation of Chinese culture in the region. When the Chinese Communist Party came to power, it not only inherited Qing traditions but also 'colonized' minorities by a strongly unificationist Chinese Communist ideology.

To sum up, there are significant differences between Russia and China in respect of state integrity and national identity, and in the way the ethno-national fissures have affected the reform paths in the two countries. For a start, the Soviet Union was a much looser entity than China, and most of the seceding Soviet 'peripheries' had strong national identities, independence movements and traditions of sovereign statehood. The etatization of Russian nationalism facilitated the split: national sentiments could be played up by Yeltsin in his attacks on the collapsing 'union' and as the foundation of the sovereign Russian state. At the same time, however, the threats to national integrity - now within the Russian Federation - and the fears of a collapsing state have been hindering democratic reforms in Russia. Both the unreformed Communists and ultra-nationalists use these fears to undermine democratic institutions.

While the fears of a collapsing state and dissipation of the nation in Russia have been fueled by the Chechen conflict and tensions in Tajikistan, such fears are reduced in China by the return of Hong Kong, the prospect of regaining control over Macau (1999), and by the increasing probability of re-unification with Taiwan. These 'gains' are widely seen - and depicted by the leaders - as strategically important for the national strength and future development of China. Similarly, the economic reforms are portrayed as potentially strengthening national integrity by bridging the economic gap between mainland China, on the one hand, and Hong Kong, Macau and Taiwan, on the other. In this context, generally speaking, the Chinese nation-state does not have a serious identity crisis, although the Communist revolutionary identity has gradually vanished and the Chinese national identity has been challenged by secessionist and independence movements in the peripheries of China.

2.   Irredentist Nationalisms

Post-Soviet Russians have discarded their heritage. The blanket rejection of values associated with the Soviet order has not released modern normative structures thought to have been present but repressed under Communism. Instead, there has been a massive resurgence of fundamentalist impulses and superstition.[6] The Russian withdrawal from Chechnya was not voluntary but the result of a stunning defeat, which was a product of low morale and bad planning and constituted a further ringing endorsement of Russia's identity crisis. Russia is gripped by a serious crisis of identity and seems incapable of crafting a new ideology or common idea that will unite the country and give it a sense of national identity and purpose. The collapse of the Soviet identity has left a vacuum. This identity vacuum has led Russia into a struggle between three principal forces – democrats, patriots and Communists – ostensibly to provide a defining set of concepts for the Russian nation.[7] Over the past couple of years a special committee, comprising leading Russian citizens, has been working to reinvent the 'Russian idea'.[8] The view that Russians should preserve their Union identity is expressed not just by those on the extreme right and Communists, but also by those who regard themselves as liberals. Several political alliances, such as the National Salvation Front and the People's Alliance, emerged during 1992-94 which united Communists, nationalists and some moderate intellectuals and politicians in their desire to recreate the great USSR.[9] In a twisted way, they had embraced Russian nationalism in the Soviet modification.[10] The withering away of a supra-ethnic Soviet identity served to increase enmity towards the Republic's minorities and has increasingly become an 'us' (ethnic Russians) against 'them' (non-Russians) situation.[11]

There are more than 80 active ultra-nationalist groups, many of which sprang from Dmitri Vasiliev, the founder of the Pamyat (Memory) group, which stands for a return to tsarism and submission to the authority of the Russian Orthodox Church.[12] Other reactionaries include the neo-Communists and the non-religious, non-Communist nationalists, the best known member of which is Vladimir Zhirinovsky, whose message was the crudely simple one that ethnic Russians should take back the empire and put minorities in their place.[13] This group of nationalists has been successful in recruiting young people into politics. Zhirinovsky's star seems, however, to have waned. Although he attracted over 23 percent of the vote in 1993 this was reduced to a mere 5.7 percent in 1996. Indeed, the hard core of the far right views him with contempt and a far more worrying development has been the development of a coolly organized neo-fascist movement, under Alexander Barkashov, the leader of Russian National Unity.[14]

In 1997 Dmitriy Rogozin, the leader of the Congress of Russian Communities (the CRC, Lebed's political base) delivered a speech on national populism, giving a list of so called enemies of the people – bureaucrats, journalists, businessmen – who should be held responsible and punished for Russia's current situation. Emphasizing spiritual nationalism the CRC concentrates attention largely on reaching regional leaders who lean towards nationalist viewpoints.[15]

The essential nature of Russian nationalism is irredentist. It holds a strong belief in the greatness of Russia, accompanied by the view that the nations of the former Soviet Union, especially Ukraine, Belarus and Kazakhstan, naturally belonged under the Russian umbrella. By the end of 1998, we have already witnessed that Russia and Belarus have agreed to form a new union and the Russian parliament has approved a friendship treaty with Ukraine. A further unification process is still on the way.

Russian nationalism is a stronger version of irredentism than Chinese pan-nationalism, for the former wants to reclaim the territories of the former Soviet Union, while the latter only insists on the unification with Taiwan. Moreover, except for the Taiwan question, Chinese nationalism is in a defensive position: it attempts to hold up the existing territories against any separatist forces. Russian nationalism wages its campaign not only against further secessionist tendencies in Russia, but also for an irredentist cause.

In the above context of the politics of irredentist nationalism, the definitions of Russian and Chinese have different content and focus. In Russia, Yeltsin's view of the 25.3 million ethnic Russians living in the newly independent republics in 1991 was that they should choose what was most convenient for them, pledging to create appropriate conditions if they wanted to return. By officially recognizing the sovereignty and present boundaries of the other republics he effectively contributed to rendering Russians living there as foreigners.[16] However, Russian nationalism has played the card of the ethnic Russians: they might be threatened by war, exclusionary politics or Islamic extremism and want to flee to their homeland. It was feared that such mass migration would exacerbate already difficult economic conditions and further radicalize domestic politics.[17] Most importantly, the ethnic Russians are regarded as the basis of the political force for the irredentist cause.

With Zhirinovsky garnering so much public support in the 1993 elections, the political center in Moscow was seen as shifting in his direction with many 'reformers' peppering their speeches with chauvinist rhetoric, taking up the cause of the 25 million Russians living in other republics and urging the West to recognize a new Russian sphere of influence. Even Yelsin had adopted the rhetoric of nationalism.[18] By 1993-94, the attitude of the Russian government towards Russians and Russian speakers in the 'near abroad' had changed and they began to be defined as an integral part of the Russian nation. Instead of recognizing the concept of a civic nation, Russianness was defined, in accordance with a long tradition, by language and culture. One can therefore regard the government's claim to represent Russian speakers abroad as a purely pragmatic tool in the quest to regain control over former colonies.[19]

By contrast, pan-Chinese nationalism emphasizes civic aspects of the nation, whose members are all citizens regardless of their ethnic and cultural background, united by loyalty to the Chinese state and to the constitution. This definition of Chinese and the Chinese nation is an attempt made by pan-Chinese nationalism to strengthen the existing nation-state. It focuses on the status quo. Certainly, the Chinese state regards 'overseas Chinese' as part of cultural China, but not citizens of the PRC. Unlike the notion of ethnic Russians living in the newly independent republics, the notion of overseas Chinese does not have any territorial implications.

3. Ethnic Composition and National Fission

In the former Soviet Union, Russians accounted for just over half (51 percent) of the total population in 1989. The ethnic composition of the peripheral regions was quite diverse. Estonians constituted 65 percent of the population in Estonia; 2.6 million ethnic Latvia constituted about 54 per cent of the population in Latvia; in Lithuania about 80 per cent of the population belonged to the indigenous nationality.[20] The Russians accounted for 30 percent of the population in Estonia, 34 percent in Latvia and 9 percent in Lithuania.[21] There was clearly a correlation between the stronger independence tendency and the higher percentage of ethnic population. It was the Lithuanian Party who was the first among the Baltic states to break with the CPSU in December 1989 and to declare independence in 1990.

After the collapse of the Soviet Union, Russia has emerged suddenly as an ethnically homogenized entity with 82 percent ethnic Russians and a much higher percentage of Russophones. However, it also has strong concentrations of Russians the in 'near abroad' and big pockets of Muslims in the Chechen-Ingushetia and central Asian regions. In both these areas ethnic dissent and separatist movements grew hand in hand with democratic reforms fanned not only by cultural and religious differences, but also memories of domination and persecution encouraged by irredentist Islamic neighbors, mainly Iran and Afghanistan.

In China, Han Chinese constitute 92 percent of the total population and form the culturally dominant group in all regions, except for Tibet and parts of Xinjiang. The Manchus' rule relied on Han Chinese cooperation and support, with many Manchus adopting Han identity and customs since the fall of the Manchu Qing dynasty. Non-Han peoples are concentrated in peripheral 'autonomous regions'. In Tibet, the indigenous people constitute 96 percent of the population. In Xinjiang, the total non-Han population is 62 percent; over seven million Uygurs constitute less than half of the local population, while Hans form a 37 percent-strong minority. Non-Hans represent 39 percent of the population in Guangxi; 33 percent in Ningxia; and 19 percent in Inner Mongolia. Needless to say, Tibet and Xinjiang, with large and concentrated minorities are centers of ethnic dissent.[22]

Ethnic problems in both countries, but particularly in Russia, are further complicated by different population growth rates. While the Russian population has been growing by about 5 percent per decade, the Caucasian and Central Asian nationalities have been growing by between

33 and 46 percent. The higher growth rate of the Muslim population has been widely seen as threatening Russian domination and contributing to the revival of Muslim nationalism. By comparison, the population growth differentials in China are lower and less likely to change ethnic balances, except for the Tibet and Xinjiang regions. In both cases internal migrations have changed ethnic balance in favor of Han nationality, especially in Xinjiang where the Uygur population has declined from 76 percent in 1949 to 55 percent in 1964, 46 percent in 1986 and 47 percent in 1990. At the same time, the Han population has increased from 7 percent in 1949 to 38 percent in 1990. Similarly, there has been a massive influx of Han Chinese into Tibet since the late 1980s, particularly since 1992. There are no figures available on this human movement.[23]

To sum up: ethnic cleavages, especially when reinforced by religious divisions, form the grounds for separatist movements, feed ethno-nationalisms and weaken the state.[24] The existence of large and territorially concentrated ethnic minorities increases the likelihood of national fissures and hinders the process of democratization. It must be stressed, however, that the sheer size and concentration of minorities are not necessarily the key determinants of ethnic strife and therefore the key obstacles to democratization. As argued in the previous section, a strong, 'over-arching' national identity inoculates societies against secessionist pressures. Another key factor includes elite type and elite 'management' of ethnic cleavages. To these factors we must now turn.

4. Elite Unity and Differentiation

Elites are the key actors controlling political outcomes. Elites can 'craft' democracy, even in the entrenched authoritarian regimes, and they may destroy democratic institutions, even if the latter enjoy popular support; Spain and Cambodia illustrate such contrasting cases. Elites can mobilize ethnic cleavages in divisive and violent ways or play down ethnic divisions and defuse ethnic tensions. Civil wars in the former Yugoslavia, and violent clashes in Russia, contrast with the 'velvet divorce' of Czechs and Slovaks and good 'management' (though not free of tensions) in the Baltic republics. The difference, as mentioned earlier, is partly due to the ethnic concentration and the strength of national integration. But the elite's conduct and strategy, the way in which ethnic tensions are managed and the way in which the democratic institutions and practices are cultivated, depends crucially, as we argue below, on elite unity and differentiation.[25]

If elites are fundamentally divided, government executive power is subject to irregular seizures, coups, elite-led uprisings, or other usurpations. Elite power struggles may then modify or topple the regime, opening the way to a more democratic alternative. But unless warring elite groups achieve consensual unity, their divisions - added to and/or fueling popular discontents - will undercut the effectiveness of the new democracy and contribute to its erosion or breakdown.

The political outcomes also differ significantly in relation to elite differentiation - the tendency of elite groups to become organizationally diverse and partly autonomous from external interference, whether from other elites or mass pressures. Differentiation increases horizontal autonomy between different elite sectors and functional domains. Budding business elites in post-Communist societies illustrate the process of differentiation and functional autonomization. They are integrated into national elites as powerful actors, often critical of government policies. Differentiation enhances the 'polyarchic' nature of elites, precluding the domination of any one elite group and ensuring political competition for mass support.[26] The Communist elites represent a narrowly differentiated and strongly (ideologically) unified type; they manage authoritarian regimes that enforce consensus and prevent diffusion of powers. Wide differentiation combined with strong unity, engender consensual elites which manage stable democracies. When accompanied by weak unity, differentiation results in elite fragmentation and unstable democracy - a configuration found in Russia. Finally, divided elites are polarized and transform the political contest into an untamed struggle. Being a winner or loser in such a struggle is a matter of not only political but also physical life and death.

Situating the Communist and post-Communist elites and regimes in China and Russia in this typology helps explain the patterns of political transformations in the Euro-Asian region. Chinese elites have maintained a degree of ideological unity, and can manage 'ethnic issues' more effectively. However, their narrow differentiation also undermines their capacity to conduct democratic reforms, which require further autonomization of sectoral elites (including business, administrative, and cultural). Elites in post-Communist Russia are deeply fragmented. Such a configuration increases the temptation for the hostile elite camps to mobilize ethnic issues in a populist and inflammatory fashion, thus sharpening elite divisions and paving the way for a possible authoritarian outcome. Let us look at the two cases in more detail.

In both Russia/Soviet Union and China the ideologically united elites originated in revolutionary takeovers. Though the authoritarian regimes created by these elites proved relatively stable and long-lasting, they were designed to prevent genuine electoral contests among elites and therefore any meaningfully democratic politics. In both cases elite unity was undermined by the processes of industrial development, political failures and succession crises. In both cases the Communist elites stifled differentiation by imposing a highly centralist system of authoritarian control. However, they could not prevent elite differentiation that accompanied industrial developments. Although this differentiation of Communist elites predated the political reforms of the 1980s, the authoritarian regime started to crumble in the late 1980s resulting in the rapid autonomization and fragmentation of elite groups.[27]

The Soviet Union/Russian trajectory represents a transformation from an ideological elite to a divided one, with some attempts at elite deals paving the way to a more stabilized regime. Prior to the mid-1980s, strong ideological unity prevailed. Marxism-Leninism constituted the political formula to which all elite persons were expected to adhere in public utterances. It defined official goals, justified institutional arrangements - especially the hegemonic-party system and the centrally-controlled economy - and it provided guiding principles and rhetorical devices for elites in their actions and discourses. The Marxist-Leninist formula was nevertheless sufficiently broad and flexible to accommodate policy changes, including some reforms. Although the differentiation of organizational sectors and of the elites heading them increased with industrialization and greater social complexity, the relative autonomy of most elite groups was still quite narrow. The principles of 'democratic centralism' and the Party's 'leading role' reinforced and justified this elite hierarchy.

The ideocratic unity of Communist elites in the Soviet Union and China, it must be stressed again, was never truly monolithic. In the Soviet Union, divisions appeared periodically, especially at times of leadership change. The most serious split occurred in the late 1980s, following Gorbachev's ascent to power and his vigorous reformist drive. In China, the deep divisions, visible at the time of the Cultural Revolution, reappeared after Mao's death, and in 1989. However, unlike in Russia after 1988, elites in China suppressed political dissent, and re-imposed the central political and ideological control. The divisions were successfully patched up under the revised ideological formula associated with Deng's reformist drive and the banner of neo-nationalism. The suppression of the Democracy Movement in June 1989, the purges that followed the crackdown, and the natural attrition of the Maoist 'old guards', ostensibly helped in restoring ideological unity. Surely, official ideology has been eroded and is no longer taken seriously by the populace and some officials. But revitalized and supplemented by neo-nationalism, it still serves well as a control mechanism (see chapter 2).

Thus in the mid-1990s the Russian elites are more plural, but also more fragmented and exposed than their Chinese counterparts. The fragmentation is both programmatic - concerning the desirability and direction of reforms - and territorial, reflecting Russia's vast size, regional fragmentation, and the legacy of Yeltsin's own attempts to bolster regionalism. By 1990, Yeltsin openly championed Russian independence, while, at the same time, encouraging autonomous republics within the Russian Federation to 'seize as much sovereignty as you can handle'. In championing Russian sovereignty, Yeltsin won favor among Russian People's Deputies, democrats and Communists alike. But he also strengthened ethnic-regional fissures culminating in the Chechen war and bloody clashes in Tajikistan.[28] These, in turn, further hindered elite accommodation and deepened elite divisions.

These fissions were aggravated by low levels of elite autonomy. Russian elites lack the insulation from immediate public pressures which a developed party system provides. Governing elites are vulnerable to demagogic and plebiscitary challenges. Ethnic separatism, loss of empire and a sense of national 'greatness', as well as the predicaments of Russians in the 'near abroad', are mobilized in political struggles by mavericks, like Vladimir Zhirinovsky. His political ascendancy in the parliamentary elections in 1995 was due mainly to skillful use of the ethno-nationalist idiom. An apparent decline in his popularity in the presidential poll in June 1996 was partly affected by the ascent of General Lebed, and partly reflected the switch of electoral allegiance to increasingly nationalistic Communists.

By contrast, the ethnicity issue cannot be mobilized by elites in local or Party elections in China. This is precluded by the Party's political formulas and policies. Although China saw differentiated elites and the growing power of provincial leaders, they hardly make any territorial or dissident claims. If they do, they are promptly punished. When the vice-governor in Guangdong advocated the introduction of a federal system in China, he was immediately removed from his position.

In China, economic reforms have resulted in *some* elite differentiation and the emergence of political bargaining between the center and the localities. 'Interest factions' have emerged. Government departments, in favor of a planned economy and those who advocate a market economy, have become the sources of pro-reformist pressures. In the armed forces, those engaged in the transformation of military industries to civilian production have also formed a special interest faction.[29] The National Peoples' Congress (NPC) has now become a formal forum where the interplay of political elites takes place. Deputies engage in debates over policies and express their local and provincial interests in regular sessions of the NPC and of local parliaments. Provincial delegation teams openly demand more power, more national appointments, and more special considerations. Much more importantly, local Party leaders support such demands.[30]

Provincial elections also encourage the development of regionalism. Some deputies of provincial People Congresses have already challenged the central government. In early 1993, for example, a group of independent-minded deputies to the Guangdong People's Congress jointly nominated their own man to compete with seven candidates hand-picked by the central authority.[31] In 1993, 'multiple-candidate' elections were held for provincial leaders during ballots in provincial 'parliaments' in some provinces, including Zhejiang and Guizhou. Victories in these provincial elections bolstered the legitimacy of provincial leaders and gave them a mandate to challenge the center. After learning that officially designated candidates for governors were voted down in Zhejiang and Guizhou, Beijing decided that multiple candidate elections for provincial leaders should be stopped. Central government leaders replaced the governor of Heilongjiang province in 1994, and in 1995 five governors and Communist Party secretaries from Hubei, Anhui and other provinces were forced to retire. Dissatisfied with Guangdong's lack of cooperation with central economic policy, Beijing leaders tried to oust the Governor Zhu Senlin from power in early 1995. But their efforts to bring the southern province in line were resisted by the local leaders who called for the re-election of Governor Zhu in February 1995.[32]

In conclusion, democratization and democratic consolidation rely on state-protected order, stability and the capacity of elites to reach minimum consensus as to the norms of restrained political engagement. As Linz and Stepan put it, paraphrasing Barrington Moore's formula: 'No state, no democracy'.[33] We supplement this formula by adding to the equation the elite variable: 'No elite consensus, no democracy'.

Elites can resolve conflicts that threaten social stability, and they can aggravate conflicts and inflame divisions. They can craft, as well as destroy, democracy.

Two points need to be stressed. First, many democratic regimes had *originated* from splits of multi-national states, typically accompanied by elite divisions: the Ottoman and Habsburg empires and, more recently, Russia and Yugoslavia. However, in all cases of such a route to 'national liberation', successful democratization was preceded - or accompanied by - effective etatization, that is the formation and consolidation of an integral state, and by the patching up of elite divisions in the process of elite settlements and transformations. Where the integrity of the state was challenged, as in Serbia or Bosnia-Hercegovina, democratic reforms were aborted. Only in the integral states one can talk about national elites, and only in such states are elites capable of unified action in crafting democratic institutions. Second, ethnic fissures often reinforce the crisis and collapse of autocratic regimes. This seemed to be the case in the Soviet Union, Bulgaria and Romania. Moreover, ethnic conflicts have subsequently hindered democratic transition and consolidation. War in Chechnya has hindered - one may say nearly derailed - Russian political reforms. Inflamed ethnic divisions and democratic reforms do not go hand in hand. What is important is that ethnic conflicts can be skillfully managed by elite strategies.

5. Elite Conflict Management Strategies

The reforms in China, unlike those in Russia, are not seen as cataclysmic events: as out of control, endangering the national integrity and reducing the living standards of the majority of the population. The liberal economic reforms are depicted - rightly or wrongly - as 'planned' and controlled by national leadership, and as bringing China the status of a superpower.

Following Mao's death, Chinese leaders reached consensus on the priority of economic development and modernization, on the need to reform, and on maintaining the unity of the state.[34] This consensus was constructed on nationalistic grounds, and it extends well beyond the territorial boundaries of China. Even opposition groups, including those overseas, subscribe to the nationalistic consensus formula of 'building a Great China'. They accuse the CCP of taking a weak position in dealing with Japanese aggression over Diaoyu (Senkaku) Island.[35] They are also committed to the unification of China with Taiwan and to maintaining Chinese rule in Tibet.[36] The areas of disagreement concern the scope and pace of political reforms, and the role of the Communist Party. Because these areas of disagreement constitute official taboos, it is hard to assess the scope of divisions within national elites. However, the personal changes and official pronouncements made during the 15th Congress seem to indicate that the divisions are relatively narrow and decreasing.

The Soviet/Russian elites show a different dynamic and strategy of reforms. The unity of Soviet elites on issues of the general soundness of the system and desirability of reforms collapsed between 1988 and 1990. Gorbachev tried hard to maintain elite unity and the integrity of the USSR, but failed. Elite divisions deepened in 1987-1988, thus opening the way for Yeltsin's bid for autonomy. Democratization of Russia was a fortuitous side effect, rather than the primary objective, of this bid. By adopting democratic practices (elections), Yeltsin strengthened his legitimacy vis-à-vis the non-elective Soviet leaders, distanced himself clearly from the Gorbachovite Soviet camp - which he could attack as 'antidemocratic' - and gained powerful allies and supporters among the separatist nationalists in the Soviet republics. Economic reforms, especially marketization and privatization, were largely bracketed or seen as secondary. The separation of the republics was the main issue and the principal concern of the leaders; it occurred in a largely revolutionary but peaceful manner, led by local nationalists and Communist reformists, but with the approval of the Russian leaders around Yeltsin.

The post-Soviet elite has emerged divided on the issues of democratization, economic strategies and national boundaries. Both the initial political strategy adopted by Yeltsin, that of fanning republican separatism, and the very process of democratic reforms, which involved awakening of national consciousness and demands for wider autonomy, deepened these divisions, undermining the prospects for further democratization. The most spectacular manifestation of elite split was the violent confrontation between Yeltsin's faction and the anti-reformist Parliament in October 1993. The splits remained deep in the mid-1990s. Opposition leaders, such as Zyuganov and Zhirinovsky, have been ambivalent about democratic procedures and openly called for the restoration of the Soviet Union. Rising leaders, such as General Lebed, are often described as 'dubious democrats' and make no secret of their nationalistic-authoritarian sympathies.[37] Thus the fragmentation of the Soviet elite proves a poor ally of democratization. It slows down the process of reforms and often threatens the very operation of budding democratic institutions. The major steps towards instituting and consolidating democratic practices have been taken by Yeltsin during the periods in which he has secured some degree of elite consensus. Following the parliamentary elections in December 1993, and again after the presidential elections in June-July 1996, the Russian elite has shown some signs of successfully managing divisions and avoiding open conflict.

Chinese elites have proved more skillful in managing the internal conflicts and divisions that followed Mao's death. A split between moderate and radical reformers led to the removal of Hu Yaobang and Zhao Ziyang in 1986 and 1989 respectively. Nevertheless, Deng Xiaoping and his supporters managed to keep the conflicts from fracturing the elite further by moderating the reform policies, isolating the dissenters (both democrats and the hard-line Communists), and finding convenient scapegoats. When Deng made errors, such as one on price reform, Hu and Zhao were declared guilty. Deng also exercised tight control over provincial leaders and military generals. These patently non-democratic practices proved successful in maintaining both elite unity and the reformist path - two factors conducive to 'creeping democratization'.

In contrast, Gorbachev failed to contain political conflicts, and he was gradually deserted by both the opponents of reforms and by the supporters of more radical changes.[38] The former coalesced around the leaders of the failed coup; the latter switched their allegiances to Yeltsin, who embraced the democratic idiom. When Yeltsin won in the first free parliamentary elections, he had a powerful democratic mandate to challenge the authority of Gorbachev. In fact, as Rutland points out, 'Gorbachev's vision of perestroika was of a carefully managed, step-by-step process, with himself playing a pivotal role, balancing the conflicting demands of the democratic left and the conservative right. As time wore on, Gorbachev found it increasingly difficult to maintain this balance, and his policy started to lurch violently from one side to the other'.[39] This lurch was reinforced by pro-autonomy pressures and by the Soviet quasi-federalist system, under which leaders of republics had much more power than Chinese provincial leaders had under a unitary system. The Constitution of the Soviet Union specified the right to secede, thus legitimating secessionist leaders of republics. By contrast, Deng and his supporters introduced only moderate political reforms, and never let these reforms weaken central Party control. Moreover, China's Constitution has got no provisions for secession.

6. Sequence of Reforms and its Impact on National Identity

These differences in elite dynamics were clearly reflected in the strategies and sequences of reforms. In China, political stability and economic modernization were paramount goals and considerations after the stormy and destructive Maoist years. These considerations dictated the sequence of reforms. Political liberalization and democratization were considered risky. Economic reforms preceded (the very modest) political reforms; economic liberalization occurred without significant political liberalization and democratization. Paradoxically, the failed Democracy Movements gave additional stimulus for such a strategy. Initially, in the early and mid-1980s, Deng advocated and called for simultaneous economic and political reforms. But when the early attempts at political reforms led to the Democracy Movement and students' demonstrations - events widely perceived as destabilizing China - he suspended democratization and called for economic reforms under the firm control of the Communist Party. The notion that only the Party can provide firm control and political stability seems to be the key plank of the reformist ideology.

The Soviet-Russian sequence was quite different. The initial political reforms in the Soviet Union, as noted above, occurred largely in spite of the intentions of the leaders. Political liberalization preceded economic liberalization and democracy preceded market economy. Gorbachev chose to begin with political rather than economic reform, but he quickly lost the initiative. While political liberalization went beyond his control - and was continued by his opponent, Yeltsin - his economic reforms never really materialized.[40]

Gorbachev also destroyed the central Party institution - the glue that held the system together - because it would not support his reforms. Under Gorbachev's reforms, power was transferred to governmental bureaucracies which represented the national principle. Moreover, he attempted to prevent the secessionist movements in a very clumsy way by setting up procedural limits on the right to secede (such as two-third majority vote) and by denying independence to the early bidders (Lithuania and Latvia). This did not work. The independence movements gained power from both glasnost and radical liberalization which Gorbachev himself had promoted, and from the powerful stream of nationalistic activism.[41]

Thus, while the Soviet-Russian sequence has been centrifugal in its political consequences, the Chinese sequential reform has strengthened national integration. The nature of commercial economies and common markets is such that they override or transcend small nationalities, accelerating the process of national acculturation and assimilation. Commercial economies and common markets have also eroded local customs and cultural symbols to the extent where people from small nationalities, rather than establishing any notion of national identity, have instead been forced to identify with the Chinese community.

Current commercial economies go well beyond particular national economies. Today's Chinese will accept the idea of buying goods from anywhere in the global market so long as they are of the highest quality. In other words, commercial economies discourage the idea that the state should dictate choice, advising people to buy, exclusively, goods produced by national industries. In commercial market based economies, people tend to buy either the best quality goods, as produced in Japan, or the cheapest goods regardless of where they were produced. While it may appear that nationalism plays a big part in the sale and export of goods – in terms of harnessing traditional cultural codes and customs – these are little more than marketing devices designed to attract customers to so-called traditional products. Indeed, in contemporary commercial societies it is increasingly difficult to locate pure authentic nationalisms. These are little more than inventions relegated to the status of mythology and found only in academic writings.

The commercial law disregards the identities of local minorities and values the quality of products alone. When carriers of cultural identity, such as the traditional clothes and costume of Yi and Bai minorities, are commodified and used for commerce, they are also reproduced and universalized by other nationalities, and thus lose their original cultural meaning.

The rapid advances in transportation and communication are further aspects of commercialization which significantly affect national identity. With the construction of infrastructure throughout China, new routes have developed giving access to remote areas and consequently bringing the attention of the world to Han cultures. One example of this is the Yi nationality. In the 1970s they were frightened of the Chinese face, when they occasionally encountered it. Now, with the development of new roads that have afforded access to a range of commercial goods, they have become open to many influences which have impacted on their cultural identity. In an effort to combat this they have established a research institute dedicated towards the support and retention of the Yi culture. Despite this it is becoming increasingly difficult to hold back the forces of commercialization. The cultural identity of the Yi has been undermined and they have been forced, through economic pressures, to identify more and more with the Chinese.

In order to be economically successful nationalities have had to learn Mandarin, which has become the common commercial language of China. Thus the widening of the commercial economy and common markets in China have promoted the universalization of standard Chinese language. In the elementary schools for the Yi, for example, children learn both Chinese and the Yi language, while at high school, they learn mathematics, physics and chemistry and the Chinese language becomes dominant, although some streams do continue to learn Yi. Economic modernization also promotes internal migration and changes the balance of the population in favor of Han nationality. Under such conditions, ethnic dissent and regional separatism are neither likely to blossom nor to be fanned by sections of elite' struggling for power.[42]

Chinese reform, with its strong emphasis on economic liberalization and integration, does not 'resolve' the national identity problem, it merely defers it. By contrast, the sequential pattern in the former Soviet Union, where resolution of the national identity problem and democratization occurred simultaneously, has some advantages in that democratization created an opportunity for the national identity question to be settled. The new government of Russia has gained regime legitimacy from general elections. Unlike the Chinese government, which still faces serious challenges from secession movements that may yet tear the country apart, the Russian government has only those minor secessionist claims to deal with in Chechnya and Tatarstan, which are unlikely to threaten the unity of the new Russian Federation.

Moreover, the Chinese sequence also carries important risks. The reforms may generate a backlash. Economic liberalization under authoritarian conditions, assists a kind of 'systemic corruption' that may be mobilized against a reformist regime. The fact that Han Chinese internal migrants in Tibet dominate small business and win major construction contracts fans resentment, and may trigger protests similar to those in the early 1990s. There is also a danger of uneven development. For example, tensions seem to be growing between Han nationality and minorities who complain that the State has been favoring the Han.[43] Finally, some observers suggest that economic development weakens the power of the central government and creates a 'kingdom economy', thus generating conditions encouraging local and ethnic separatism.[44]

7. Prospects for Democratization

There was heightened conflict in Russia between proponents of economic reform, democratization and decentralization and opponents who pushed for centralization and the recreation of the USSR.[45] If the democratization process were to be reversed in Russia, this would be mainly due to Russian irredentist nationalism over the issue of the residual national identity problem. Nationalist Zhirinovsky's victory (winning 22.9 percent of the party-list vote) in the 1993 parliamentary elections and the Communist Party's victory (winning 158 Duma seats and 22.7 percent of the party-list vote) in the 1995 parliamentary election created a possible threat to democratic consolidation.

If Yeltsin's leniency towards, and encouragement of, separatism had promoted Russia's transition to democracy in the initial stage, the sovereignty issue haunted him during the consolidation period. The dismantling of the Soviet Union sparked border conflicts, civil wars and secessionist movements and the chaos caused by the disintegration has continued to hinder the process of democratization. Moreover, the fate of 25 million ethnic Russians currently residing outside its borders, especially those in the so-called 'near abroad' regions in the neighboring post-Soviet states, is a constant source of concern and aggravation and provides a platform for nationalistic demagogues.

The tide of nationalism sweeping Russia in 1994 was said to threaten the fragile independence of former Soviet republics such as Latvia, Estonia and Lithuania. Two principal areas of trouble were Russian troop withdrawals from Latvia and the treatment of large Russian communities in Latvia and Estonia. Russians in the Baltics complained about discrimination and new citizenship laws, that required knowledge of local language, which they believed were aimed at driving them out. The foreign minister Kozyrev, claimed it may not be in Russia's interest to withdraw all its troops from the 'near abroad'.[46]

The December 1994 invasion of Chechnya was the result of a major nationalist spasm which shook the Russian leadership during 1994 and 1995, and followed sharply on the heels of Yeltsin's move to the right. The major justification for the war was the notion that Chechnya was an integral part of Russia and national borders are sacred. There was also a stated desire to protect ethnic Russians in the republic. Yet the government had been, in the main, passive with regard to ethnic Russian interests in other non-Russian republics, although there were fears at the time that other republics, especially those in the Caucasus and along the Volga, would follow Chechnya provoking further disintegration.[47] Russia's war against Chechnya was intended to demonstrate its strength and power not only to Russia's restive minorities but also to the newly independent CIS states and the West.[48]

The rise of Russian nationalism, Yeltsin's brutal war with Chechnya and his increasing estrangement from democratic forces, were instrumental in provoking a drive to expand NATO membership to include the Baltic States thereby encircling Russia with democracies. Indeed, the Baltics were themselves looking to NATO for insurance against Russia. There were fears, however, that this would further undermine the remnants of Russia's democratic faction and allow ultranationalists to portray the Russian government as little more than American stooges.[49]

Russian consolidation of democracy is further exacerbated by the lack of a common political language. While elements of the political discourse of democracy – rule of law, elections, human rights and political liberties – have become generally accepted principles (if not practices), the political rhetoric of democracy has failed to ignite popular opinion and seems already to have been exhausted. Indeed, given that liberal democratic ideology has been associated broadly with Yeltsin's reforms, which seem in the main to have been spectacularly unsuccessful in solving Russia's social, economic and political problems, it is not surprising that it has been discredited.[50]

It seems that commitments to democracy have declined markedly in Russia, as suggested by the drop in the number of Russia's respondents who believe in democratic values from 42 percent in a 1993 poll to 28 percent in that of 1996. Disenchantment with Russia's current 'democracy' has also fuelled nostalgia for the Soviet past. A 1994 poll indicated that only 29 percent thought that the breakup of the Soviet Union was a good thing for Russia, while 71 percent disagreed.[51]

During the Chechen war, increasingly the Russian people were expressing a desire for stability and order above all else and seemed to care little whether this was achieved through democracy or dictatorship. Ultra-nationalists such as Dmitri Vasiliev and Vladimir Zhirinovsky and the proto fascist, Alexander Lebed, have used these fears and concerns to their advantage, offering simplistic solutions and a sense of direction to a people in crisis. Perhaps the most potent danger posed by ultra nationalists has been the subtle way in which they have set the tone of political debate in recent years. Zhirinovsky's Liberal Democrats were, for example, the only large Duma party to support Yeltsin through the Chechen War. They have also supported him on other issues such as budgetary reform, the war against crime and a hardline approach to the defence of Russian national interests with regard to the CIS and the West.[52] Nationalist elite-inflamed mobilizations and conflicts are particularly dangerous when ethnic minorities are large and concentrated, and when ethnic divisions are deep.

The collapse of the Soviet Union and the emergence of Russian Federation illustrate the 'paradox of democratization', whereby initial democratic reforms encourage ethnic separatism, aggravates elite and ethnic divisions by awakening national consciousness through enfranchising minorities; they stimulate political competition but also trigger an anti-democratic backlash. The elites in the Russian Federation are deeply fragmented, and struggle to maintain national and state integrity. The ultra-nationalist and Communist elite groups gain considerable power and popular support.

Chinese nationalists seem to have learnt the lesson from this paradox of democratization. They are now thinking that Western advocacy of democracy and open markets has brought chaos in the former Soviet Union and Russia. If the democratization of the former Soviet Union has led to the disintegration of it, and today's Russian nationalism attempts at reunification, why do they need democracy in the first instance? In such a context, democracy is not a desirable value for Chinese nationalists. In particular, when Chinese nationalists come to confront the national identity question, in respect of Tibet and Taiwan for example, they find that nationalism, rather than democracy, offers the best solution. The rise of Russian nationalism seems to reinforce Chinese nationalist standing over the national identity question. We will discuss in detail the question of how Chinese nationalism clashes with democracy in the next chapter.

Chinese democrats, however, will doubt the intellectual validity of the so-called 'the paradox of democratization'. For them, democracy is still hoped for and the idea of a democratic and federal China offers the solution to the national identity question. We will address this issue in the concluding Chapter.

Notes

1   On the 'third wave' of democratization see S.Huntington, *The Third Wave: Democratization in the Late Twentieth Century*, Norman: University of Oklahoma Press, 1991; and, 'Democracy for the Long Haul', *Journal of Democracy*, vol. 7, no. 2, 1996, pp. 3-14. On 'consolidated democracy', see J. Linz and A. Stepan, 'Towards Consolidated Democracies', in *Journal of Democracy*, vol. 7, no. 2, 1996, pp.14-34; G. O'Donnell, 'Illusions about Consolidation', in *Journal of Democracy*, vol. 7, no. 2, 1996, pp. 34-52; G. O'Donnell and P. Schmitter, *Transitions From Authoritarian Rule: Tentative Conclusions About Uncertain Democracies*, Baltimore: Johns Hopkins University Press, 1986; J. Linz and A. Stepan (eds.), *The Breakdown of Democratic Regimes*, Baltimore: John Hopkins University Press, 1978; S. Mainwaring, G. O'Donnell and S. J. Valenzuela (eds.), *Issue In Democratic Consolidation: The New South American Democracies in Comparative Perspective*, Southbend: University of Notre Dame Press, 1992; A. Przeworski, *Democracy and the Market*, Cambridge: CUP, 1991. On the 'paradox of democracy', see S. Huntington, 'Democracy for the Long Haul', p. 6; S. Holmes, 'Precommitment and the Paradox of Democracy', in J. Elster and R. Slagstad (eds.), *Constitutionalism and Democracy*, Cambridge: Cambridge University Press, 1995, pp. 195-240. On 'creeping democratization' see Minxin Pei, 'Creeping Democratization in China', *Journal of Democracy* , vol. 6, no. 4, 1995, pp. 65-79.

2   G. O'Donnell, 'Delegative Democracy', *Journal of Democracy*, vol. 5, 1994, pp. 56-69; P. Rutland, 'Has Democracy Failed Russia?', *The National Interest*, vol. 38, 1994, pp. 3-12.

3   E. Etzioni-Halevy stresses elite differentiation and autonomy as the key condition of democratic 'check and balance', *The Elite Connection: Problems and Potential in Western Democracy*, Boston: Basil Blackwell, 1993. Democratic polyarchy involves, according to R. Dahl, free contestation and participation, *Polyarchy: Participation and Opposition*, New Haven: Yale University Press, 1971.

4   See Minxin Pei, op. cit.

5   However, we do not consider polyarchal destinations inevitable in China and Russia. Instead, we see the change in both countries as focused but not foreclosed, leading towards several possible alternative outcomes.

6   Michael Urban, 'Remythologising the Russian State', *Europe-Asia Studies*, vol. 50, no. 6, 1998, p. 982.

7   Ibid., p. 969.

8   Dmitry Shlapentokh, 'The Russian Identity Crisis', *Contemporary Review*, vol. 273, Sept. 1998, p. 125.

9   Vera Tolz, 'Forging the Nation: National Identity and Nation Building in Post-Communist Russia', *Europe-Asia Studies*, vol. 50, no. 6,1998, p. 998.

10   Dmitry Shlapentokh, 'The Russian Identity Crisis', op. cit., p. 125.

11   John Dunlop, 'Russia in search of an identity?', in Bremner, Ian and Taras, Ray (eds.), *New States, New Politics: Building the Post-Soviet Nations*, Cambridge: Cambridge University Press, 1997, p. 60.

12   'The rise of the new right: Russia after Chechnya', *The Economist*, 28 Jan. 1995, pp. 21-24; also see Walter Laqueur, 'Russian Nationalism', *Foreign Affairs*, vol. 71, no. 5, 1992, p. 103.

13   John Dunlop, 'Russia in search of an identity?', op. cit., p. 50.

14   'The rise of the new right: Russia after Chechnya', op. cit., pp. 21-24.

15   'CRC Leader Rogozin Turns National Populist', Centre for Russian Studies Database, 5 Mar. 1992; Web site address at http://www.nupi.no/russland/russland.htm.

16   John Dunlop, op. cit., p. 37.

17   Mortimer B. Zuckerman, 'Dangers on the Russian Front: nationalism in Russia', *U. S. News and World Report*, vol. 116, no. 12, 1994, p. 80. Also see Rogers Brubaker, *Nationalism Reframed: Nationhood and the National Question in the New Europe*, Cambridge: Cambridge University Press, 1996, pp. 51-54.

18   Zuckerman, op. cit., p. 80.

19   Vera Tolz, 'Forging the Nation', op. cit., p. 1009.

20   S. White, A. Pravda and Z. Gitelman (eds.), *Developments in Soviet and Post-Soviet Politics*, Hampshire: Macmillan, 1992, p. 127.

21   Victor Gray, 'Identity and Democracy in the Baltics', *Democratization*, vol. 3, no. 2, 1996, p. 76.

22   C. Mackerras, *China's Minority: Integration and Modernization in the Twentieth Century*, Hong Kong: Oxford University Press, 1994, p. 253; *China's Minority Cultures*, Melbourne: Longman, 1995, p. 173; *China's Ethnic Statistical Yearbook,* 1995, p. 208.

23   C. Mackerras,*China's Minority*, op. cit., pp. 250-9; Z. Gietlman, 'Nations, Republics and Commonwealth', in S. White, et al., *Developments in Soviet and Post-Soviet Politics*, op. cit. p. 124; S. Cook, 'Tibet in Transformation: The Consequences of Economic Interactions with Han China', paper presented at the Conference of China's Provinces in Reform: Social and Political Change, Suzhou University, 23-27 Oct., 1995.

24   As suggested by Huntington in *The Third Wave*, op. cit. Also see J. Linz and A. Stepan, 'Towards Consolidated Democracies', op. cit.

25   G. L. Field and J. Higley, *Elitism*, London: Routledge, 1980; M.G. Burton and J. Higley, 'Elite Settlements', *American Sociological Review*, vol. 52, 1987, pp. 295-307; R. D. Putnam, *The Comparative Study of Political Elites*. Englewood Cliffs: Prentice-Hall, 1976; G. Sartori, *The Theory of Democracy Revisited: The Contemporary Debate*, Chatham: Chatham House Publishers, 1987; J.Higley and M. G. Burton, 'The Elite Variable in Democratic Transitions and Breakdowns', *American Sociological Review* , vol. 54, 1989, pp. 17-32; J. Higley and R. Gunther, *Elites and Democratic Consolidation in Latin America and Southern Europe*, New York: Cambridge University Press, 1992; E. Etzioni-Halevi, *The Elite Connection*, op. cit; J. Higley and J. Pakulski, 'Elite Transformations in Central and Eastern Europe', *Australian Journal of Political Science*, vol. 30, no. 3, 1995, pp. 415-35; and J. Higley, J. Pakulski and W. Wesolowski (eds.), *Postcommunist Elites and Democracy in Eastern Europe*, New York, St. Matin's Press, 1998.

26   S. Keller, *Beyond The Ruling Class: Strategic Elites in Modern Society*, New York: Random House, 1963; E. Etzioni-Halevi, *The Elite Connection*, op. cit.

27   The process of early differentiation has been analysed by, amongst others, A. H. Brown *Soviet Politics and Political Science*, London: Macmillan, 1974. For the analysis of the Soviet elite differentiation and political division in the late 1980s also see D. Lane and C. Ross, 'Limitations of Party control: the government bureaucracy in the USSR', in *Communist and Post-communist*

Studies, vol. 27, no. 1, 1994, pp. 19-38; and D. Lane, 'The Gorbachev Revolution: the Role of the Political Elite in Regime Disintegration', in *Political Studies*, vol. XLIV, 1966, pp. 4-23.

28   These moves are analysed by M. McFaul in 'Prospects for Democratic Consolidation in Russia', paper presented at the International Conference on Consolidating the Third Wave Democracies, Taipei, 27-30 Aug. 1995, pp. 19-20; and 'Russia Between Elections: The Vanishing Center', *Journal of Democracy*, vol. 7, no. 2, 1996, pp. 90-105. Rogers Brubaker also analyzes the key role of elite in the breakup of the Soviet Union. See, *Nationalism Reframed*, op. cit., p. 41.

29   Wu An-chia, 'Mainland China's Political Situation in the Post-Teng Era: A Forecast', in *Issues and Studies*, vol. 29, no. 6, 1993, p. 14.

30   Yang Shengchun, 'An Analysis of the Operational Relation between the Party and Government in the Current National People's Congress', in *Gongdang wenti yanjiu*, vol. 21, no. 10, 1995, pp. 23-4.

31   See the *South China Morning Post*, 8 February 1993.

32   *Nikkei Weekly*, 30 January 1995.

33   J. Linz and A. Stepan, 'Towards Consolidated Democracies', op. cit. pp. 14, 23.

34   H. Harding, *China's Second Revolution: Reform after Mao*, Sydney: Allen and Unwin, 1987, pp. 77-83.

35   See *FDC Newsletter*, no. 19, Nov. 1990, pp. 15-21; *Democratic China*, no. 6, Feb. 1991, p. 82.

36   Some members of the FDC, such as Wu'er Kaixi, support Tibet's self-determination. But the FDC as a whole does not. As the Manifesto of the FDC states, 'the FDC is seriously examining the long-standing neglect by the forces of Chinese democracy of the Tibetan people's struggle for democracy, and believes that the Tibetan issue, as well as other races' issues, require a free, democratic foundation, with a sound human rights and law, before it can be resolved.' Note that the Tibetan people's struggle for self-determination is not mentioned. Also, in 1989 most of the intellectuals and students were silent on the imposition of martial law in Tibet, except for Wang Ruowang's denouncement of it. See M. Goldman, *Sowing the Seeds of Democracy in China*, Cambridge: Harvard University Press, 1994, p. 296.

37   As the commander of the Russian 14th Army in Moldova region, Alexaner Lebed actively supported the formation of the secessionist 'Dniestr Republic'. In the presidential election campaign, he stressed a need for strong authoritarian rule.

38   D. Lane and R. Cameron, 'The Social Backgrounds and Political Allegiance of the Soviet Political Elite of the Supreme Soviet of the USSR: The Terminal Stage, 1984 to 1991', *Europe-Asia Studies*, vol. 46, no. 3, 1994, pp. 437-63; D. Lane, 'The Gorbachev Revolution', op. cit.

39   Peter Rutland, 'Economic Crisis and Reform', in S. White, et. al., *Developments in Soviet and Post-Soviet Politcs*, op. cit., p. 215.

40   Ibid., p. 208.

41   M. McFaul, 'Prospects for Democratic Consolidation in Russia', op. cit.

42   It is estimated that 10 million Han Chinese have gone to minority areas for commercial activities, while around 2-300, 000 people from minorities are living in Shanghai, ten thousand people in Shengzhen. Weng Jiemin et. al. (eds.) (1997), *Status and Trend of Development in China 1995-1996*, Beijing: China Social Science Press, 1997, pp. 208-9. On the effects of modernisation and population movements see C. Mackerras, *China's Minority Cultures*, op. cit., pp. 218-20.

43   For example, the annual income of peasants or herdsman is 24222 Chinese *yuan* in Beijing, 2225 in Zhejiang, and 555 in Tibet. The annual income of workers is 5100 in Zhejiang, and only 3493 in inner Mongolia. Weng Jiemin et. al.(eds.), *Status and Trend of Development in China 1995-1996*, op. cit., p. 210.

44   Some rich minorities have put their money into developing their cultural identities. For example, a research institute of Yi nationality has been established. However, economic development makes it difficult to resist Sinicization. Take an example of the bi-lingual policy which stresses the use and study of the language of minorities. Because of the domination of Han language, minorities tend to study and use the Chinese standard language much more rather than their own languages.

45   John Dunlop, 'Russia in search of an identity?', op. cit., p. 52.

46   Victoria Pope and Douglas Stanglin, 'Too close for Comfort', *US News and World Report*, vol. 116, no. 5, 1994, p. 40. Russian troops eventually withdrew

from Latvia on 30 August 1994, despite continuing Russian anger over the citizenship laws, warning the Baltic States to expect Russia to react (and expect assistance from those countries who had insisted on the Russian withdrawal) if ethnic Russians rights were violated. See 'Russian Troops Withdraw from Latvia', RFE/RL Newsline, Sept. 1994, Centre for Russian Studies Database, Web site address at http://www.nupi.no/russland/russland.htm.

47   'How many other Chechnyas?', *Economist*, 14 Jan. 1995, p. 43.

48   John Dunlop, 'Russia in search of an identity?', op. cit., p. 65.

49   Paul Cook, 'Extending borders for a new NATO', *Insight on the News*, 13 Mar. 1995, pp. 6-11.

50   Michael Urban, 'Remythologising the Russian State', op. cit., p. 974.

51   Michael McFaul, 'Russia's Rough Ride', in Diamond et. al., op. cit., pp. 64-94. Frederic J. Fleron has also discussed the decreasing support for democracy by comparing the public opinion surveys conducted between 1989 and 1994. However, he cautiously notes that it is quite possible that surveys conducted recently are more reflective of deeply held values and attitudes than those done earlier since Russians are accustomed to free speech without negative repercussions. See his article, 'Post-Soviet Political Culture in Russia: An Assessment of Recent Empirical Investigations', *Europe-Asia Studies*, vol. 48, no. 2, 1996, pp. 225-260, particularly p. 252.

52   John Dunlop, 'Russia in search of an identity?', op. cit., p. 69.

7 The Clash between State Nationalism and Democratization over the National Identity Question

The previous chapters have offered a comparative examination of how democratization contributed to the development of an independence movement in Taiwan and to the breakdown of the former Soviet Union. It appears that the Chinese leadership has been strongly influenced by the experiences of the former Soviet Union and Taiwan and, as a result, is reluctant to attempt a large scale democratization in China. Indeed, Chinese state nationalists oppose democratization which they see as threatening national unity and the control of the territories. This chapter aims to examine the areas where, and conditions under which, Chinese nationalism can be said to constitute an obstacle to democratization. It also seeks to demonstrate the logic of the conflict between democracy and nationalism in the Chinese context.

The chapter comprises seven sections. Section one offers some general remarks on the relationship between nationalism and democracy, while section two gives a brief historical account of the various episodes where the national identity question has clashed with democratization. Sections three, four and five examine further the clash between democratization and nationalism in today's China, with particular focus on Hong Kong, Tibet and Taiwan. Section six considers the tension that exists between the national identity question and democratization in a broad comparative context, and, finally, in Section seven, the asymmetric effect of democratization is identified and employed in an effort to explain why the question of national identity provokes a clash between democratization and state nationalism in China.

It should be acknowledged, at the outset, that the question concerning the clash between democratization and nationalism is only important when there is a commitment to democratic values such that there is a desire to reduce the tension. For nationalists who are not interested in democratic values it is not an issue. The only issue with which they are concerned is the maintenance of national unity and power. It is only when it comes to undermine national unity that the question of democratization is considered. Their purpose in so doing, however, is not to reduce the tension and find a way to introduce democracy. Instead, as discussed in chapter 2, they are more concerned with promoting a scare campaign that highlights the dangers of democracy as part of an attempt to manipulate and delay its introduction.

1.　General Remarks: Is nationalism an ally or enemy of democracy?

Generally speaking, nationalism can be both an ally and an enemy of democracy. That is, it may be a necessary condition for democratic transition as well as being an obstacle to it.

Nationalism as Ally

As distinguished in chapter 1, different versions of nationalism have different relationships to different models of democracy.[1] Indeed, it would be inaccurate to argue that Chinese state nationalism is completely opposed to any form of democracy. For example, Chinese state nationalists see their cause as compatible with, and even promote, a version of paternalistic 'democracy'. They have, for instance, supported village committee elections, which are a form of 'guided democracy' conducted under the control of the central authority. It would seem, therefore, that Chinese state nationalists will not hesitate in incorporating certain elements and procedures of democracy, such as the manipulation of local democracy, if this is seen as the best way to promote the unity of the Chinese nation-state.

　　It is possible for the cultural nationalist construction of pan-Chinese national identity to co-exist with liberal democracy because of its emphasis on equal and civic citizenship. This civic national identity is compatible with democracy in the sense that its definition of 'we the people', in terms of citizenship, will provide the foundation for a Chinese democratic order. It will, on the other hand, be in a tension with liberalism in the sense that its communitarian principles override and undermine individual liberty.

Clearly, Chinese nationalists will not venture to openly reject the principle of democracy. This is because the age of modern nationalism is one linked to the modern idea of 'the people'. The people, that is the mass of ordinary human beings, are believed to have a sense both of their own worth and of their rights. Indeed, Chinese nationalist leaders from Mao Zedong, and Deng Xiaoping to Jiang Zeming have, for the purposes of political mobilization, been forced to use some form of democracy and speak in the name of the people. This is also true of fascism. As Emerson points out:

> Even in the Fascist variants the role which the people play is sharply distinguished from their role in the earlier type of dictatorship or monarchy, as witness the efforts of Fuehrer and Duce to carry the masses with them, to give the appearance of popular consultation through plebiscitary techniques, and to spread the tentacles of the Party down into every cranny of the society. This, certainly, is not democracy, and yet it is equally certainly a perverse offshoot from democratic roots, a post-democratic phenomenon.[2]

In the history of Chinese democratization, there have been countless attempts by Chinese nationalists to bring about liberty and democracy. In the latter part of the last century and earlier this century, Liang Qichao urged the development of a sense of Chinese nationalism. He criticized the 'slavish character' of the Chinese people and advocated the development of an assertive and intellectually free body of 'citizens', as he believed that such a citizenry was fundamental to China's progress and national survival. Underlying his fervent espousal of liberty was an assumption that there was an identity of interests between his liberal ideals and his nationalistic concerns. Energetic individuals would, he thought, contribute to a dynamic society, and 'liberty' would foster the growth of such individuals, who would, in turn, assure the modernization and power of the Chinese nation. As Emerson claims: 'National forces are inherently and inevitably "democratic" in the sense that they mobilize formerly submerged elements and classes of society into new social roles, eat away at traditional relationships, and work toward the building of a new great society into which, in principle, all men are actively drawn.'[3]

In contemporary China, students have used both nationalism and democracy as tools for political mobilization. For instance, the 1988-1989 Nanjing Anti-African student protests combined justifications for anti-government action, based on Chinese nationalism, with support for democracy and political reforms. Like the student demonstrators in the pro-democracy movement, in the Spring of 1989, the Nanjing students sought to promote China's national strength and dignity through the implementation of democratic political reforms that guaranteed human rights and equality before the law. In both cases the students regarded themselves as the embodiment of Chinese patriotism and the vanguard of the legal and political reforms needed to end China's stagnation.[4] Nevertheless, the Nanjing incident also revealed that democratic groups in China have been constrained by a racially-defined nationalism which is common to both present-day conservative leaders and reform minded intellectuals.[5]

It is quite conceivable, however, that nationalist democrats can make nationalism a constructive force for democracy. As argued in chapters 3 and 4, this is because popular or cultural nationalism has undermined the foundation of the CCP. Thus it is possible for democrats to mobilize popular nationalism in order to push for democratization, build a just nation-state and struggle against corruption.

Nationalism as Enemy

On the other hand, although nationalists sometimes appeal to the idea of democracy, Chinese nationalism is not necessary for the establishment of a democratic political system or a society striving towards democratic values. In another context, it is possible to see how nascent democracy was destroyed by military nationalism in Japan during the 1930s because democracy was seen as a barrier to the military cause. Moreover, nationalism may become anti-democratic when it is associated with independence movements. For example, post-colonial independence movements, which gave rise to the establishment of democracy, were frequently followed by the failure of the new democratic regimes, the logic being that the deepening process of democratization undermined the elite's domination, which in turn undermined the unity of the nation-state; causing dictatorships to be restored in order to hold together the post-colonial nation-state.

The idea of democracy is contradicted and undermined by ethnic nationalism if it holds an exclusively ethnic notion of nation (which denies membership to other minority groups), and if the state uses one particular ethnic group as its vehicle. Moreover, in multi-national states, ethnic nationalism tends to refuse the democratic path.[6] Mill questions whether homogenous nation-states are more likely than multi-national states or federations to protect democratic procedures and the freedoms of thought, speech and association, and concludes that, 'free institutions are next to impossible in a country made up of different nationalities'.[7]

Mill's view can be applied to the Chinese scenario. It is much more difficult to build a democracy in China than in the more homogenous Japan. Currently state nationalism in China is anti-democratic and refuses to take a democratic path. This is due partly to the fact that nationalists believe democratization is likely to empower ethno-nationalism, and thus undermine state nationalism. Chinese leaders seem to believe democracy is something that threatens the unity of China and undermines the pan-Chinese national identity project, and state nationalists tend to regard the USA's promotion of democracy as a conspiracy aimed at China's disintegration.

Any fighting over national territorial integrity is likely to alter the direction of democracy for, as a general rule, whenever the unity of China has been threatened, the course of democracy has changed. In the case of such a conflict the drive for national unity is sure to subordinate the claims of the individual, and liberal democracy would give way to an authoritarianism in which the actual and diverse wills of the people are replaced by a leader who, in some mystical fashion, is able to express the national ethos. This, the central argument of the chapter, can be demonstrated by analyzing the impact of the national identity problem on the process of democratization in modern China.

2. The Clash Between Democracy and Nationalism in Modern China

Early liberals saw democracy as an instrument with which to build a strong nation-state and gain legitimacy for the Chinese state. They contended that democracy would make the nation the people's concern and strengthen the Emperor's authority, bringing thousands of ears and eyes into his service, thus enabling him to withstand the foreigner.[8]

The Hundred Days of Reforms, the earliest partial democratic reform in China, faced a serious challenge: which nationality would dominate a constitutional China? Would the Manchu maintain their rule? Would Han Chinese take over? The ethnic tension between the Han and Manchu made it difficult, both to achieve an overriding sense of national unity and identity, and develop a political opposition (or a royal opposition) – one of the touchstones of political democracy. In Japan, by comparison, the emperor was *native*. Not only was there little ethnic tension when Japan introduced the first parliament and elections in East Asia, but the native throne was used as the central symbol of national reconstruction. As Emerson remarks, 'The Japanese Emperor served as the rallying point for the forces which sought to modernize Japan, whereas the Manchu regime effectively blocked China's passage into the modern world'.[9]

The failure of the Hundred Days of Reforms led to Sun Yat-sen's 'ethnic revolution', in which the Han Chinese overthrew the Manchu regime. In building a new nation-state, Sun Yat-sen developed the three fundamental principles of the people, combining democracy with nationalism and the people's livelihood. In 1924 he addressed the national identity problem, writing in the manifesto of the 1st Chinese Nationalist Congress:

> The Kuomintang solemnly declares that the right of self-determination is recognized for all the nationalities inhabiting China; following the victory of the revolution over the imperialists and militarists there will be established a free and united (formed on the basis of a voluntary union of all nationalities) Chinese republic.[10]

Later this policy of self-determination was completely abandoned, both in theory and practice, by the Kuomintang. Sun Yat-sen also advocated a federal system that would curb the power of the central government and grant autonomy to the provinces and minority regions. This was abandoned by Sun himself when he witnessed the rise of regional militarists (*geju*). Chen Duxiu, a radical Marxist, also discredited the idea of federalism. Chen, who had originally favored self-government and federalism, realized that the circumstances of feudalistic politics meant the self-governing movement was doomed to become a pawn in the game of the militarists. If federalism was built upon the aspirations of regional militarists, it could, he concluded, never achieve national unity and strength.[11]

From 1934 to 1935, the national identity and unity issue again rose to prominence. This time there was heated debate among Chinese intellectuals over the 'democracy versus dictatorship' question. In rejecting 'military unification', Hu Shi favored 'political unification' – which involved the establishment of a national congress where people from different provinces would be invited to take part in national politics. This, he believed, would cultivate the centripetal force of locality that would help to build a strong national identity.[12] By contrast, Jiang Tingfu and Chen Zhimai expressed a preference for an authoritarian leadership that could unify China by force. They asserted that the political reality of China was such that the parliament could be closed down by a few soldiers. For them, even though a few representatives were sent to central governmental organizations, those who did not favor unification were considered untrustworthy as it was felt they might use parliament for political purposes.[13] Here, the problem of fostering national identity was intertwined with the problem of choosing a political system. For liberal intellectuals, democracy was seen as the best means to overcome local division and develop a national identity, while anti-liberal intellectuals saw dictatorship as the best option. In the end, rather than adopting the idea of a democratic national identity and unification, Chiang Kai-shek opted for an authoritarian one-party government to combat the warlords and Communists. The Chiang regime had an outward parliamentary form that made no attempt at revolutionary translation of power to the masses. Moreover, when the Japanese army invaded and occupied northern China, most Chinese liberal intellectuals and democrats gave up the democratic enterprise and became nationalists in defence of China's national unity.

Initially, the Chinese Communist Party entertained the idea of self-determination. The Constitution of the Chinese Soviet Republic declared in November 1931:

> The Soviet government in China recognizes the right of self-determination of the national minorities in China, their right to complete separation from China, and to the formation of an independent state for each national minority. Thus the Mongols, Moslems, Tibetans, Koreans and others inhabiting the territory of China enjoy the complete right to self-determination, that is, they may either join the Union of Chinese Soviets or secede from it and form their own state as they may prefer.[14]

In 1945, Mao Zedong wrote, in 'On a Coalition Government', that the future People's China would 'grant nations the right to be their own masters and to voluntarily enter into an alliance with the Han people'. 'All national minorities in China must create, along voluntary and democratic lines, a federation of democratic republics of China.' In the later edition of Mao's *Selected Works* that passage had vanished, and the original words of 'granting of the right to national self-determination to all national minorities' were replaced by the phrase 'the granting of the right to national autonomy to all national minorities'.[15] Soviet-style federalism was also rejected by the CCP, in the early 1950s, on the grounds that it would enable various nationalities of China to form separate states and thus allow the national autonomous regions to secede.[16]

By the 1950s and 1960s, the CCP were committed to a Marxist class approach, which held that class division is much more important than ethnic division, and that the working classes across different nationalities should be unified against their common enemy, the exploiting class. This class-based approach empowered the CCP to implement a radical program to promote a new socialist national identity. In practice this program failed as, instead of reducing ethnic conflicts, it intensified them. In the case of Tibet, for example, it forced a change to the structure of religious politics that endangered Tibetan culture to the extent that it prompted a Tibetan separation movement in China. The failure of the Marxist approach reflects a deeper weakness in its doctrine stemming from an insistence that working men 'have no country'. The failure also signals for some contemporary Chinese liberals that the time is ripe to give liberal democracy a try.

The above observations lead to the following conclusions. China has confronted the national identity or unity problem and, among the various options for dealing with it, nationalist and democratic approaches have been advocated and attempted. Ideas of self-determination and federalism, that is elements of the democratic approach to managing the national identity problem, were adopted by both the nationalist and communist parties but abandoned immediately after they became powerful. It would seem, therefore, that the fundamental statist traditions override all the differences between the nationalists and Communists.

The building of a democratic nation-state was advocated by democrats in the later Qing period, and by liberal-minded intellectuals in the 1930s, but it was not taken seriously and implemented. The winners were always the nationalists, authoritarians or centralists. This was because it was perceived that democracy would undermine the unity of China.

During the 1980s and 1990s rising nationalism, and the debate over democracy versus neo-authoritarianism, has again raised the issue of the national identity problem, and some of the themes of the debates in modern history have been revisited. The national identity problem that China faces today is a deep-rooted, and fundamental issue. However its form and content are different. If it was the case that the Qing court faced a challenge from the Han Chinese, the scenario today is that the Han-dominated leadership is confronting a challenge from minorities located at the peripheral borders of China. Furthermore, China faces not only the secessionist claims in Tibet and Xinjiang, but also an independence claim in Taiwan, where an independent political entity has existed for around fifty years. This raises a difficult issue for Chinese democrats: how can they unify China and Taiwan through democracy? This question is different from combating secessionism through democracy. The next three sections will, therefore, give consideration to the impact of the national identity question on contemporary Chinese democratization, and analyse the tension between Chinese nationalism and democracy in the contexts of Hong Kong, Tibet and Taiwan.

3.   Democratization of Hong Kong Denied[17]

The democratization of Hong Kong began in 1982 with elections for some district direct board seats, followed by direct elections for 12 out of 56 members of the Legislative Council (Legco), in 1985. During the events of 1989, one million people in Hong Kong demonstrated their support for Chinese students in Beijing. Since then, the British government has attempted to introduce a bill of rights, and a report by the House of Commons Foreign Affairs Committee proposed that 50 percent of Legco members be elected by citizens in the 1991 election, with all Legco members to be directly elected by 1995. The 1991 election was won by the newly formed Hong Kong Democratic Alliance (HKDA), led by Li Zhuming. In 1992 a battle between China and Britain ensued when China refused to accept Governor Christopher Patten's Democratic Plan. Indeed, when China took over Hong Kong in 1997 the Legco was dismantled.

The democratization of Hong Kong has largely been conditioned and constrained by China. Beijing's concern with and obstruction of the further democratization of Hong Kong can be understood in the context of the rise of a distinctive Hong Kong identity. In a 1985 survey, 59.5 percent of respondents identified themselves as 'Hongkongnese'; 23.7 percent professed a 'very strong' sense and 55.8 percent a 'strong' sense of belonging to Hong Kong. In a 1988 survey, identification with 'Hongkong-ness' was registered by 67.4 percent of the respondents, and in the same survey, 44.3 percent of respondents agreed with the statement that Hong Kong should not be returned to China but should become independent.[18]

Chinese nationalism has sought to appeal to the people of Hong Kong using the notion of pan-Chinese nationalism and there has been resistance to Hong Kong's democratization by Beijing, as it is seen to be opposed to China's rule and have the potential for independence. The fate of Hong Kong's democracy appears to be linked, not only to the rise of Chinese nationalism, but also to the rivalry between China and the United Kingdom. Democracy in Hong Kong is unlikely to take root and develop into an entrenched institution when it is opposed to Chinese nationalism. Thus we can understand why, after the take-over in July 1997, Beijing replaced the Legco with its own sponsored legislature.

Moreover, for Chinese state nationalists, it was not democracy that contributed to the return of Hong Kong to China, but the tough stance adopted during diplomatic negotiations, and the strength of Chinese political, military and economic forces. In other words, it was through political, military and economic powers that the lost territory was reclaimed and the national boundaries expanded. In the eyes of Beijing, had the people of Hong Kong been allowed a referendum to decide their political fate, separatist tendencies were likely to have been provoked.

It should be noted that, as the national identity question of Hong Kong has been settled through its return to China, it is unlikely that further democratization would encourage separatist tendencies. For this reason, the 1998 Hong Kong election has been tolerated, even as it was manipulated, by Beijing.

Although the return of Hong Kong has satisfied Chinese irredentist nationalism and strengthened national identity, it has also provoked new issues and challenges. In the first place, the democratization of Hong Kong has now become an issue relevant to political life within China, and as, such will continue to pose a challenge to China's political system. Second, for practical reasons it is not a necessary requirement that one has to accept socialism in order to be a good Hong Kong patriot. This anomaly means that the ideology of official state nationalism, which requires Chinese patriotism to embrace socialism, is effectively undermined.

4. Nationalist Management of the Tibet Question

In dealing with the Tibet issue, the nationalist Chinese approach seems to have adopted three main measures. First, the Chinese state has used force to crush any rebellion in Tibet, and employed divide-and-rule tactics to control the Tibetan elite. This approach has, however, failed to neutralize the secessionist movement, but driven it under-ground, so that it is likely to re-emerge as political and military control is weakened.

The second measure has been to financially 'buy off' secessionists with promises of wealth and the provision of funding. For example, in recent years the Chinese government has funded fifty development projects in Tibet. But it seems that economic 'sweeteners' cannot staunch secessionist aspirations. Nor can economic integration deflect the demand for political and cultural identity by Tibetans.[19] In short, Tibetan secessionism is not a matter of economics but one of politics.

The third measure is to accommodate secessionist claims by offering a kind of semi-autonomy and an affirmative policy towards minorities. In the eyes of Chinese state nationalists the art of ruling consists of employing all three methods. An affirmative policy towards minorities must prevent minorities from forming a privileged social group that may undermine the unity of the state.

In short, Chinese state nationalists reject a democratic solution to the Tibet problem. In their opinion, it is democracy and human rights discourses that have brought down the USSR. They argue further that if there is no solution to the Tibet problem, there should be no democracy in Tibet even if democratization takes place in other parts of China.[20]

The Chinese state's fear of the disintegrating effects of democratization has resulted in resistance to democratic procedure in handling the Tibet issue. Moreover, the CCP has little faith in democracy. Its monopoly on political power makes it difficult for a solution based on the devolution of power to take place. Because China has always been a unitary state, it will continue to resist any type of federalism that would result in a transfer of power from the center to localities. Since Han Chinese have the predominant position and bargaining power, they, unlike the Indonesian government, which is willing to grant concessions to East Timor and Aceh, are reluctant to make concessions to Tibet. The rise of China as a world power may make it even more unwilling to accept a democratic solution based on compromise and power-sharing. Moreover, China's self-righteousness about its control of Tibet, and its sense of having suffered under Western imperialism, exclude any democratic thinking on the Tibet issue.

Furthermore, the CCP does not recognize the right to self-determination nor does it allow for the right to secede. In China, only the state has the right to define territorial boundaries, and it does so through diplomatic efforts rather than through democratic mechanisms, as shown by

China's settlement of the Hong Kong issue. Chinese leaders strongly believe that the state has the right to suppress any secessionist movements by whatever measures (carrot and stick). The argument against secession is grounded on communitarian (or collectivist) claims that are supported by state-sponsored nationalism. Individual consent has little value in this regard and is, at best, a supplement to the power of the state. Furthermore, in the Confucian tradition, secessionists will lose their appeal if their claim is grounded on selfish considerations. What has happened in the Baltic republics would be quite inconceivable in China. It would be regarded as selfish, and secessionists are not able to mobilize people on such grounds. For this reason, the disparity between rich and poor regions may not lead to support for secession, but may undermine the unity of the state by changing the power balance between the center and local regions.

In comparison, Tibetan nationalists demand democracy because they believe it will support their cause. The separation of Tibet from China, they argue, will not damage China's integrity, because it has no legitimate claim over Tibet in the first place. Some Tibetan nationalists cherish the idea of a 'Greater Tibet', one autonomous region which extends into three provinces in China. This radical faction of Tibetan nationalism has been committed to a pan-Tibetan identity since 1959 and are on a collision course with Chinese nationalists over the sensitive internal boundary question. If neither is willing to compromise conflicts are inevitable.

By contrast, some more moderate Tibetans argue that Chinese nationalism actually has much to gain from democratization, because it will serve to legitimize the Chinese state and make secession difficult. They maintain that as human rights violations decrease, so the moral force for secession will diminish accordingly. If Tibet enjoys freedom why should it continue to demand secession? If, despite democratization, it still wanted to secede, this would be seen as little more than a political power struggle among the Tibetans, which would be unlikely to attract international support. If so, radical Tibetans argue, the most favorable timing for Tibetan secession would be before Chinese democratization, not after it.[21]

The Dalai Lama advocates regional autonomy, rather than independence and seeks to resolve the Tibet question along the lines of the Hong Kong model. His train of thought seems to be: according to international and Chinese laws we cannot ask for the whole of Tibet, so if we ask for secession our demands will be restricted to the 1959 internal boundary. That is, secession will make Tibet smaller, so autonomy will be the more beneficial option.[22] Moreover, autonomy will ensure Tibet continues to gain economic and security benefits through its links to China.

5. The Taiwan Question: Unification or Independence?

In approaching the Taiwan question Chinese nationalists appeal to common traditions, history and Chinese culture, because it is the shared history and culture that legitimates Chinese claims over the territories of Taiwan. Thus Chinese nationalists insist that the fact that Taiwan was historically a province under Qing's rule cannot be denied.

Beijing considers a democratic solution to the Taiwan issue unfeasible and undesirable. Qian Qichen, Vice-Prime Minister, for example, said it is illegitimate, fruitless and pointless to declare Taiwan's independence through a referendum.[23] For Chinese nationalists, the 'One China' policy will never be compromised by democracy or anything else. They see the unification of Mainland China and Taiwan as a primary task in building a strong nation-state. The rationale is that 'Taiwan was an inalienable part of China, thus any self-determination process that might result in a permanent separation was totally unacceptable'.[24] In the eyes of Beijing, the One-China policy is rooted in Chinese history and culture; it presupposes the membership of the political community of China and the precedence of Chinese national identity over the democratic enterprise. For Chinese nationalists, when there is a dispute over what constitutes 'the people', Chinese nationalism provides the answer. It is a guiding principle for unification, that overrides the ideological competition between socialism and the three principles of the people.[25]

Chinese nationalists see the return of Hong Kong to China as significant, bringing China and Taiwan closer together by providing an intermediate place of trade and culture across the Taiwan Strait. Thus Hong Kong has struck a blow at secessionist forces within China and, most importantly, it has provided a model for the resolution of the Taiwan issue.

By contrast, the democratic logic in Taiwan is that Taiwan's democratization makes it difficult for one party or government to make a promise not to become independent because such a promise cannot be made against the will of the people. Since the democratization of Taiwan, any significant change with regard to the national identity question cannot take place without consulting the people. As Tien remarked, 'Democratization helps open up the debate over legitimacy of the ROC identity, defined by the KMT ruling elite but increasingly challenged by the advocates of an independent Republic of Taiwan'.[26] Neither can the diplomatic negotiation model of Hong Kong be applied to Taiwan for diplomacy alone cannot decide its status.

By comparison, authoritarian logic states that because it lacks democratic legitimacy the Chinese leadership is to a large degree, dependent on the Taiwan issue for its survival. As Wang points out:

> The theme of reunification is at the heart of restoration nationalism. Restoration is not only an essential part of the structure of legitimacy, the supremacy of continental interests. It is also the best defense against other threats to the sanctity of China's borders. The tense developments of 1995-1996 in cross-straits relations testify to the emotional force that this view of its destiny can still generate.[27]

A further aspect of this authoritarian logic is that the authoritarian state not only refuses to resolve the national identity question through democratic procedure, but it also refuses to rule out the use of force. Thus Beijing does not want to promise it will not use force if Taiwan continues to pursue independence. Indeed, it insists on military options as a preventive measure against Taiwanese independence, that is, it will not use force to conquer Taiwan, but rather to prevent it from gaining independence. China will use force only under two types of circumstances: (1) a declaration of independence or (2) foreign intervention. Liu Huaqing, Vice-Chairperson of the Central Military Commission, has said clearly that if Taiwan moves towards independence, China will use force to defend its sovereignty.[28] Beijing believes only military force can deter an independence movement in Taiwan. In terms of Machiavellian politics, Beijing does not need to please the 'enemy' by renouncing the use of force. For Beijing, force is a necessary resort.

Moreover, Chinese politics of national identity operate within the framework of nationalism, where, 'Any leader who is perceived as soft on this issue [Taiwan] and fails to protect Chinese sovereignty and territorial integrity would be regarded as another Li Hongzhang and discarded by the people'.[29] In fact, Jiang Zemin was accused of adopting a soft policy on Taiwan and, in 1994, a tough stance was demanded. Containing Taiwan's independence was, and is, a major task for Chinese nationalism for no one dares to let Taiwan go. Chinese leaders would not survive if they could not prevent Taiwan from achieving independence. In the light of this nationalist framework, therefore, political actors are likely to become more radical and adopt more extreme policies in order to combat Taiwan's independence movement.

Two other factors contribute to a clearer understanding of the conflict between the two logics outlined above. First, both are concerned with identifying the agents which deal with the Taiwan question. The authoritarian state of China recognizes only the right of the state to deal with the national identity problem; while democratizing Taiwan increasingly recognizes the important role of the people, civil society, public opinion and referenda. The statist solution to the Taiwan question clashes with the belief, held by some members of the DPP, that referenda should decide the question of Taiwan's international position. It should be pointed out that the key issue here is not so much the CCP's slow recognition of, or passive reaction to, democratic development in Taiwan, as Bruce Jacobs suggested,[30] but more with the nature of political regimes and the ways in which they gain legitimacy.

Second, the conflict of logic is also revealed by the difference in attitude towards democracy in respect to the Taiwan question. A Chinese nationalist must be a unionist in the sense that she or he must be committed to the cause of unification with Taiwan. For Chinese politicians, the unification of China with Taiwan is a fundamental aim, while democracy is merely a means.[31] The Chinese nationalists take an instrumentalist view of democracy: if it can promote unification, they might introduce it; if not, they will reject it. The fact that Beijing talks about unification without mentioning democracy indicates that, in its eyes, democracy is incompatible with unification. When Beijing realises that, in effect, the logic of democratization favors Taiwan's independence, it will choose to push for unification at the cost of democracy. The fact that the DPP talks about both independence and democracy indicates that, in the eyes of Taiwanese nationalists, democracy is compatible with, and can assist, independence. The DPP therefore intends to declare or maintain *de facto* independence through democratization and referenda.

6. Democracy and the National Identity Question in a Comparative Context

There are many examples which demonstrate the extreme complexity of the relationship between democratization and the national identity problem. On the one hand, we have witnessed how, in 1989, democratization in the former Soviet Union and East Germany enabled unification of the two Germanys. In the case of the Soviet Union, elections facilitated the secessionist movements, and finally led to the breakdown of the Russian empire.[32] By contrast, the democratization of Spain, the Philippines and South Africa demonstrates that it helps to manage the national identity problem through a democratic accommodation of secessionist demands. In China, democratization may provide an opportunity for Tibet to separate from China, and for Taiwan either to establish an independent state, recognized by the international community, or to unify with Mainland China. In other words, Chinese democratization could facilitate a diverse range of outcomes.

There is sufficient empirical data to suggest that a correlation exists between the question of national identity and the success or failure of democratization. In Asia, for example, multi-ethnic states were established under colonial rule in Burma and Indonesia, but after independence, both returned to authoritarian rule following a short period of democracy. One argument for authoritarianism was that it would effectively prevent secessionist movements. In Malaysia, ethnic cleavages and conflict have provided an excuse for the imposition of increasingly authoritarian measures. In Sri Lanka, ethnic tension has been identified as a primary factor in the deterioration of democracy; and in Pakistan, ethnic conflict has also played a significant role in domestic instability and failed attempts at democracy.[33] The near universal failure of democracy in post-colonial Africa is first and foremost attributed to 'deep ethnic divisions' and 'a very shallow sense of nationhood', although it must be added that the 'historical and structural handicaps' also included weak political institutions, lack of indigenous managerial personnel, economic dependence, and popular expectations generated by the independence struggle.[34]

Furthermore, when a state disintegrates, democratization is usually difficult to consolidate. This was the case with China in the early republican period and, when Singapore seceded from Malaya in the 1960s, Malaysia suspended parliamentary democracy. Indeed, we can see how today's Russian nationalists regard democracy as the primary obstacle to their irredentist cause.

Post-Communist developments illustrate the striking positive relationship that exists between ethnic homogeneity and the success of democratic reforms. With the small, but notable, exception of the Baltic states (which, one may argue, constitute a somewhat special case), democratic stabilization has progressed faster in the more ethnically homogeneous nation-states of Poland, the Czech Republic and Hungary. It is slower and less successful in countries with large and assertive minorities (See Table 7.1). While some ethnic fissures seem to have reinforced anti-Communist mobilizations, speeding the collapse of Communist regimes in the Soviet Union, Bulgaria and Romania, they have subsequently hindered democratic transition and consolidation. That is, articulated ethnic divisions and democratic reforms do not go hand in hand.

It is easy to pinpoint the reasons for this regularity: ethnic cleavages, especially when reinforced by religious divisions, form the grounds for separatist movements, which feed authoritarian nationalisms and weaken the state.[35] One can even suggest that ethnic homogeneity is an important condition of democratization. Where large and territorially concentrated ethnic minorities exist the likelihood of national fissures is increased and the process of democratization hindered. Indeed, Table 7.2 demonstrates that when the percentage comprised by a dominant ethnic group drops below 50 per cent, democracy is always threatened, either from ethnic conflicts, civil war or a military coup, all of which destroy or suspend democracy.

Certainly, there are exceptions. For example, democracy survived in both Gambia, where the Malinke (tribe) constitutes 43 percent of the population, and in Botswana, where the Bamankwato (tribe) constituted 34 percent. It might be noted, however, that nearly all tribes belong to the same ethnic group, Tawana. Other exceptions are those cases where the breakdown of democracy corresponds to the high percentage of one dominant ethnic group. For example in Argentina where 97 percent of the population was European, the 1966 Coup destroyed democracy. Similarly, Chile experienced a coup in 1973, despite the fact that 90 percent of its population was of European origin. These exceptions suggest that the composition of ethnicity is only one factor influencing the outcome of democratization; and that the domination of one ethnic group does not guarantee the consolidation of democracy.

These exceptions also indicate that ethnic divisions will not necessarily render democratization impossible. India and Pakistan are good examples. Their democracies have survived intact, despite both being ethnically fragmented countries.

Table 7.1 **Ethnic Composition of Post-communist Societies**

Countries and Population (mil.)		Ethnic Majority (%)		Main Ethnic Minorities (%)	
Poland	38	Polish	96	Ukrainian	1
				Belorussian	1
Czech Republic	10	Czech	94	Slovak	4
				Romanes	2
Hungary	10	Hungarian	92	Romane/Gypsy	5
				German	2
Slovakia	5	Slovaks	82	Hungarian*	11
				Romane	5
Bulgaria	8	Bulgarian	86	Turkish*	10
				Romane/Gypsy	3
Romania	23	Romanian	89	Hungarian*	7
				Rom/Gypsy	2-8
Croatia	5	Croat	78	Serb*	12
Bosnia-Herceg	4	Musli	44	Serb*	31
				Croat*	17
Macedonia	2	Macedonian	65	Albanian*	21
				Turkish	5
Serbia	10	Serb	66	Albanian*	17
				Hungarian	4
Slovenia	2	Slovene	88	Croat*	3
				Serb	2
Albania	3	Albanians	98	Greek*	2
Russia	149	Russian	82	Tatar	4
				Ukrainian	3
Lithuania	4	Lithuanian	81	Russian*	9
				Polish*	7
Ukraine	52	Ukrainian	73	Russian*	22
				Tartar*	3
Belarus	10	Belarussian	78	Russian*	12
				Polish	4
Estonia	2	Estonain	62	Russian*	30
				Ukrainian	3
Latvia	3	Latvian	52	Russian*	34
				Belorussian	5

* denotes minorities demanding autonomy or extended rights
Source: RFE/RL Research Report, *1993: The Year in Review*

Table 7.2   Democracy Destroyed or Suspended

Country	Dominant group	Percentage	Related Outcome
Malaysia	Malay Muslims	44	democracy suspended 1969
Nigeria	Hausa-Fulani	29	1966 coup
Uganda	Baganda (tribe)	18	One-party hegemony 1960
Fiji	Fijian	46	1987 coup

Source: Compiled by the authors

Also some African democracies, such as Nigeria, Uganda, Ghana and Zimbabwe, have been able to weather wide-spread ethnic conflict which has posed a strong challenge to political stability.[36] Perhaps we can say then that it is the nature and degree of ethnic division that matters more than the fact that such divisions exist.

In China, Han Chinese constitute 92 percent of the total population, with non-Han peoples being concentrated in peripheral 'autonomous regions' and in Tibet; the indigenous people make up 96 percent of the population; while in Xinjiang, the total non-Han population is 62 percent. While the domination by Han, in most areas of China, subdues ethnic conflicts, the concentration of non-Han population in the peripheral areas creates volatile conditions for secessionism.

It must be stressed, however, that it is not the sheer size and concentration of minorities that is necessarily the key determinant of ethnic strife, and therefore the principal obstacle to democratization. Other factors include the strength of the supra-ethnic national identity - a strong 'over-arching' national identity inoculates societies against irredentist pressures; and elite 'management' of ethnic cleavages - consensual elites can manage ethnic divisions and play down ethnic fissures, while divided elites can inflame them (chapter 6).

7.   An Explanation of Asymmetric Effects

Here we attempt to understand through an identification and explanation of the asymmetric effect, why China does not favor democratization as a solution to its national identity question. If democratization is regarded as an independent variable, and the national identity question as a dependent variable, the impact of democratization on secession and unification is asymmetric. In the context of the global trend towards independence or secession, and the marginalization of reunification, democratization -other things being equal - plays a bigger role in facilitating independence than it does in encouraging reunification.[37] In other words, democratization is associated with far more political divorces than marriages. Statistically, among the 47 new member states in the UN since 1974, 26 have won independence whilst their 'parent states' were democratizing. By comparison, among those states which have successfully achieved reunification since 1974, such as Vietnam, Germany, Yemen and China-Hong Kong, only the unification of the two Germanys and the two Yemens was related to democratization. China's reunification with Hong Kong was through diplomatic negotiation, while the reunification of Vietnam was achieved through war, following the surrender of the southern government on April 30, 1975.

In the case of East Germany, democratization broke down the Communist state thereby facilitating its reunification.[38] Indeed, experiences of democratization in Eastern Europe served as examples that influenced the unification of the Yemens, by pushing the Marxist government of the former People's Democratic Republic towards reunification and democratization. However, the reunification took place in 1990 prior to the national election in 1993, and this sequence of events should not lead us to overestimate the role of democratization in promoting unification in Yemen.[39] In the case of Taiwan, its democratization has resulted in a virtual abandonment of the project of reunification with China, and thus a de facto independence. Also of note is the fact that while the democratization of Moldova supported its independence from the former Soviet Union it did not enable its reunification with Romania.

How can the asymmetric effect be explained? Three tentative answers can be offered. First, it is the political autonomy of 'the people' rather than the reunification of 'peoples' that is presupposed by the notion of democracy. In other words, inherent in the idea of democracy is a greater likelihood that it will facilitate independence or secession rather than unification. Second, people tend to use democracy to support their independence rather than unification because democratization creates favorable conditions for the construction of new national identities. Democratization programs have empowered ethno-nationalism and contributed greatly to the cause of independence and/or secession. On the other hand, it is much more difficult to bring different people into a nation through democratization than it is to establish an independent state. The third possible explanation concerns the distribution of state power among nationalities. In a divided nation, it is more difficult for those who already have control of the state to yield or share power with others, through democracy, than it is for those who have not yet tasted state power, as in the case of secession movements, who are fighting for power through democracy. Political elites have an incentive to establish their own state rather than be incorporated into a large political unit. Above all, democratization provides them with such an opportunity.

Conclusion

An analysis of the centrality of the national identity problem, and its impact on Chinese democratization, demonstrates the reasons why nationalism has prevailed and democratization has been delayed in China. The prediction that rapid democratization would follow in the wake of Deng Xiaoping's death has not been realized. On the contrary, post-Deng Xiaoping China has witnessed the very slow progress of democratization. This is because, fearful of repeating the Soviet experience, Chinese leaders have delayed full-scale democratization in order to enhance the strength of the nation's identity and thus avoid the potential threat of disintegration.

The fact is, however, that initiation of democratization in China not only requires the monopoly of power to be broken up, but it also needs the national identity issue to be addressed. If Chinese democratization is seen to threaten the unity of China, history may repeat itself so that democracy is sacrificed in the higher interest of saving the nation-state. We can say, therefore, that state nationalism and democracy are in an intrinsic state of constant tension and contradiction. This inherent tension creates an ominous prospect for democratization in China. We will revisit this theme in the concluding chapter.

Notes

1   For a discussion of three models of democracy in China, see Baogang He's *The Democratization of China*, London, Routledge, 1996.

2   R. Emerson, *From Empire Nation: the Rise to Self-determination of Asian and African Peoples*, Cambridge, Harvard University Press, 1960, pp. 214-5.

3   Ibid.

4   Michael J. Sullivan, 'The 1988-1989 Nanjing Anti-African Protests: the Tension between Chinese nationalism and Democracy', Department of Political Science, University of Wisconsin-Madison, Sept. 1991.

5   Ibid.

6   Emerson, op. cit., p. 214.

7   John Stuart Mill, *Utilitarianism, Liberty, and Representative Government*, London: J. M. Dent and Sons Ltd., 1947, p. 361.

8   Emerson, op. cit., p. 261.

9   Ibid., p. 260.

10   Cited in Victor Louis, *The Coming Decline of The Chinese Empire*, New York: Times Books, 1979, p. 114.

11   Prasenjit Duara, 'Nationalism as the Politics of Culture: Centralism and Federalism in Early Republican China', The Woodrow Wilson Center, Asia Program Occasional Paper, No, 37, Jun. 11, 1990, p. 12.

12   Cheng Yishen, *Dulipinglun de minzhu sixiang (The Democratic Ideas of the Journal of Independent Forum)*, Taiwan: Lianjing chuban Gongsi, 1989, pp. 88-91.

13   Ibid., chapter 3.

14   Cited in Louis, *The Coming Decline of The Chinese Empire*, pp. 114-5.

15   Ibid., p. 115.

16   Ibid., p. 116.

17   See Lo Shui-Ling, 'Democratization in Hong Kong: Reasons, Phases and Limits', *Issues and Studies*, Vol 26, No 5, May 1990; Kuan Hsin-chi, 'Power Dependence and Democratic Transition: The Case of Hong Kong', *China Quarterly* 128, Dec. 1991, pp. 774-93; 'Hong Kong: Pattern Won', *The Economist*, Jul. 2nd-8th 1994, p. 24; Kathleen Cheek-Milby and Miron Mushkats (eds.), *Hong Kong: The Challenge of Transformation*, Hong Kong,: Centre of Asian Studies, University of Hong Kong, 1989; Joseph Y S Cheng, 'The democracy movement in Hong Kong', *International Affairs* 65, 1989, pp. 443-62; Michael C Davis, *Constitutional Confrontation in Hong Kong*, London: Macmillan, 1989; Yash Ghai, 'The Past and Future of Hong

Kong's Constitution', *China Quarterly* 128, Dec. 1991, pp. 794-813; Lau Siu-kai and Louie Kin-sheun (eds.), *Hong Kong Tried Democracy: The 1991 Election in Hong Kong*, Hong Kong: Hong Kong Institute of Asian Pacific Studies, No. 15, 1993; Ian Scott, *Political Change and the Crisis of Legitimacy in Hong Kong*, London: Hurst, 1989; Steve Y. S. Tsang, *Democracy Shelved: Great Britain, China, and Attempts at Constitutional Reform in Hong Kong, 1945-1952*, Hong Kong: Oxford University Press, 1988; Alvin Y So and L Kwitko, 'The New Middle Class and the Democratic Movement in Hong Kong, *Journal of Contemporary Asia* 20, 1990, pp. 384-98; Jermain T.M. Iam, 'Chris Patten's Constitutional Reform Package: Implications for Hong Kong's Political Transition', *Issues and Studies*, No 7, Jul. 1993.

18　Kuan Hsin-chi, 'Power Dependence and Democratic Transition: The Case of Hong Kong', *China Quarterly* 128, Dec. 1991, p. 774.

19　A political and cultural solution is required. See Alan P. Liu, *Mass Politics in the People's Republic: State and Society in Contemporary China*, Colorado, Westview, 1966.

20　Baogang He was fortunate to attend a debate on this issue which took place at the European Association of Chinese Studies Conference in 1996. While some Chinese scholars advocate the delay of democratization so that the national boundary problem can be dealt with first, Western scholars, such as Brian Hook, contend that such an approach is likely to delay democracy indefinitely. In contrast, one Russian scholar suggests Communism is the best medicine for national integration.

21　The discussion below benefits from Baogang He's conversations, on 20-21, 24 and 28 April, 1998, with Professor Samdhong Rinpoche, Speaker of the Tibetan Parliament in Exile and Director of the Central Institute of Higher Tibetan Studies, which were held in Hobart.

22　Professor Samdhong Rinpoche's interpretation.

23　*The People's Daily* (overseas edition), 29 Jan. 1999, p. 1. See also C. L. Chiou, 'Dilemmas in China's Reunification Policy toward Taiwan', *Asian Survey*, Vol. 26, 1986, p. 481.

24　Chiou, 'Dilemmas in China's Reunification Policy toward Taiwan', p. 480.

25   See Zhao Quansheng, 'A Proposed Model of Unification and Plural Politics', *China Forum*, vol. 26, no. 5, 1988, pp. 54-5.

26   Tien, 'Toward Peaceful Resolution', op. cit., p. 190.

27   See Wang Gungwu, 'The Revival of Chinese Nationalism', Lecture Series 6, International Institute for Asian Studies, Leiden 1996, p. 22.

28   *Cheng Ming*, Sept. issue 1994, p. 24. For a discussion of the conditions under which China will use force, see Lin Gang, 'The Conditions, Consequences and Prevention of Conflicts between Mainland China and Taiwan', *Modern China Studies*, No. 2, 1996, pp. 93-7.

29   Chen Qimao, 'The Taiwan Strait Crisis', op. cit., p. 1059.

30   Jacobs, 'China's Policies Towards Taiwan', op. cit.

31   Achievement of national goals also took priority over the implementation of liberal ideals in South-eastern Europe. See, Emerson, *From Empire to Nation*, p. 220. Indeed, nationalism played a more important role than democracy in the unification of the two Germanys. The renewed legitimacy of nationalist discourse allowed West German political parties to dominate the political landscape of East Germany between the January and March elections. Because the new Forum refused to participate in this discourse it was marginalized politically. As a result the conservative parties of the National Alliance won the election because they categorically rejected socialism, and unequivocally embraced national unification. The general results of the election were: CDU 41 percent, SPD 22 percent, PDS 16 percent, DSU 6 percent, liberals 5 percent, New Forum 3 percent, and Green Party 2 percent. Helmut Walser Smith, 'Socialism and Nationalism in the East German Revolution, 1989-1990', *East European Politics and Societies*, Vol. 5, No. 2, Spring 1991, p. 243.

32   McAuley, 1992, op. cit., p. 105.

33   L. Diamond, J. Lintz, and S. Lipst, (eds.), *Democracy in Developing Countries: Asia*, Boulder, Colorado: Lynne Rienner Publishers, 1989, p. 18.

34   Ibid., p. 4.

35   As suggested by Huntington in *The Third Wave: Democratization in the Late Twentieth Century* and 'Democracy for the Long Haul'. Also see Linz and Stepan

'Towards Consolidated Democracies', *Journal of Democracy*, vol. 7, no. 2, 1996, pp.14-34.

36   L. Diamond, J. Lintz and S. Lipst, eds., *Democracy in Developing Countries: Africa*, Boulder, Colorado, Lynne Rienner Publishers, 1988, pp. 19-12.

37   We make a conceptual distinction between the maintenance of existing national unity and the reunification of different sections, states, countries and societies into one political community, and focus on the latter. It should be acknowledged that democratization programs have contributed to the unity of nation-states in the Philippines, Spain and other countries. One can also note regional differences: East Asia has witnessed two cases of unification (China-Hong Kong and the two Vietnams), but no secession since 1974. In addition, we have omitted the controversial question concerning the European Union, which can be interpreted as either reunification or federation.

38   In the case of Germany, the 1972 agreement affirmed the 'inviolability' of the existing border and provided for the exchange of 'permanent representative missions' by the two governments, basically ruling out the possibility of German reunification. In 1989, however, anti-regime demonstrations erupted in East Berlin and the East German authorities abolished restrictions on foreign travel for GDR citizens on Nov 9, 1989. On August 23, 1990, the East German parliament passed a resolution ceding the five newly restored eastern Länder to the FRG. Reunification was not supported either by referendum or parliamentary approval.

39   The merger of the former Yemen Arab Republic and the Marxist People's Democratic Republic took place in 1990. In 1981, a Yemen Council, that embraced the two chief councils, and a Joint Ministerial Council, was established, promising to submit a draft constitution for a unified Yemeni Republic to referenda in the two states. However, there was no such referendum and the constitution was ratified by the respective parliaments in 1990.

8 Concluding Remarks

Let us first briefly summarize the contents of the book, then extend our discussion to some of the essential questions which confront China as a modern nation-state. In the first three chapters, we have addressed the multiple faces of nationalism. It is suggested that Chinese nationalism is essentially a state nationalism sponsored and manipulated by the Party-state, which is inventing a pan-Chinese national identity to protect the Chinese nation-state from secessionist tendencies. It is recognised, however, that Chinese nationalism is not monolithic and also contains popular elements that undermine the CCP's rule. Indeed, popular Chinese nationalism attempts to exclude the role of the Party-state in defining national identity, and its vision of a new Chinese national identity goes against the official, socialist self-imposed definition. Its anti-Communist, anti-Party-state thrust can create a condition, or intellectual environment, for Chinese democratisation. It should be stressed that cultural nationalism and its construction of pan-Chinese national identity, such as the notion of Cultural China, or all other competing notions of 'nation' (chapter 3), will not necessarily contradict the idea of democracy. Instead, the cultural nationalist dimension of pan-Chinese national identity should be, and can be, seen as a step toward a plural construction of new national identity from below, although it is not necessarily democratic (to be discussed in section 4). In this sense, cultural nationalism can be seen as neither pro-democratic, nor anti-democratic. Most importantly, we argue, it has the potential to demand democratic reform and push for democratization in China. Nevertheless, the alliance between nationalism and democracy will be expedient. Chinese nationalism, whether official or popular, comes into conflict with democracy when it confronts the national identity/boundary problem. They clash with each other where territoriality is involved.

This is well demonstrated in the second part of the book where it is shown, in chapter 5, that democratization has assisted Taiwan's independence movement and empowered Taiwanese nationalism. Chapter 6 reveals how democratization led to the break up of the Soviet Union (chapter 6). There are inherent tensions between democracy and Chinese nationalism, and chapter 7 considers the difficulties faced by Chinese democrats in trying to achieve a democratic state in China, when confronted with the national identity/boundary question.

1. The Nature and Poverty of Chinese Pan-Nationalism

There are signs that liberal-minded Chinese intellectuals are aware of the poverty of Chinese nationalism. Ge Hongbing, for example, points out that narrow nationalism has resulted in slow development in China, and warns that the combination of narrow nationalism and autocracy will lead to state nationalism, that is militarism, even going so far as to equate nationalism with danger, disorder and fascism.[1] Chen Xi recognizes nationalist fears of the USA, but opposes them, making use of nationalistic emotions to carry out an ideological war against the USA.[2] In a book review published in the *China Economic Times* on 8 August 1996, Zhang Jianjin argued that an up-surge of ultra-nationalist emotions is leading the country astray by re-installing isolationist policies. Zhang criticized *China Can Say No* for being 'full of artificial angers' and said that '...it is just like a commercial that has nothing but instigation'.[3] He went on to say that 'If we do not have a correct assessment on our strength, there is a danger of abusing the strength. History has repeatedly proven that an emerging country often overestimated its strength and eventually brought disasters to itself'.[4] Overseas Chinese intellectuals tend, therefore, to propose a rational, constructive and responsible nationalism, rather than one which is narrow, aggressive and military in orientation.[5] Nevertheless, as our discussion in chapter 7 shows, no matter how rational, constructive and responsible nationalism might be, it is likely to conflict with democracy when it confronts the boundary question. We will focus on this issue in this the concluding chapter.

State nationalism lacks genuine popular support

The book has provided a detailed documentary description of the rise of state nationalism, and offered comprehensive discussion on Chinese pan-national identity (chapters 2-4). It is argued that state nationalism has been unable to rally the Chinese people behind the Party-state for lack of *genuine* popular support. The lack of genuine popular support for state nationalism is well indicated by general apathy to the official propaganda. Take, for example, a movie about Kong Fansen, a model government officer who spent most of his life 'serving the people' in the remote Tibetan plateau. This movie won the 'best feature film' award at the Changchun Film Festival in 1996 and was a box-office hit. However, according to a study report, it was work units - not individual Chinese – who bought 99.5 percent of the tickets.[6] Moreover, the Party-state's national project has also encountered wide-spread resistance on many a front, e.g., ethnic, cultural, and cross-Taiwan-Strait. In particular, it has been demonstrated that it is challenged with considerable force by cultural nationalism.

It should be added, however, that cultural nationalism is, in the main, a resurgent elitism. The privileged attention given to the Confucian doctrine by pan-Chinese cultural nationalists, their praise of Zeng Guofan as an ideal hero, and indeed the whole imagining of a pan-Chinese nation, based on common history and culture, is highly elitist. The influence of cultural nationalism will be limited unless it strikes an accord with the populace and persuades them to accept its message. It is also to be stressed that the deliberate choice of Confucianism as the core of Chinese identity, rather than Taoism and Buddhism, reflects a power relationship between the Chinese intellectual elites. The imagining of the nation inevitably entails a contest over what constitutes 'Chineseness', and power is one of the main things at stake in this contest over the content of national identity, its symbolization and institutionalization. In this sense, the contest is primarily one between those who seek a share of cultural or political power and those who are eager to maintain and strengthen their established, but shaken, dominance. In the current circumstances of today's China, these elites are roughly divided into two camps, Marxists and pro-Marxists on the one hand, and anti-Marxists and non-Marxists on the other; whereas different factions in the non-dominant camp, such as Confucianists, Buddhists, and Taoists, are unified in their common endeavor to subvert the Marxists' dominance and wrench from them the power to claim 'We the people'. Arguments between the factions take place as they move beyond the subversion of the old into the construction of the new identity. They compete and compromise; and at the same time neither Confucianism, Buddhism or Taoism is static: each in its own way has been adapting to changing realities. As a result, whatever emerges naturally as the most prominent will be a new version.

The Strength and weakness of pan-nationalism in dealing with the national identity question

The book's critical assessment of pan-Chinese nationalism leads to the conclusion that its nationalist principles and objective of inventing a pan-Chinese national identity have both advantages and disadvantages.

As discussed in chapter 4, pan-Chinese nationalism has moved away, or played down, Wang Fuzhi's kind of Han-centric ethos of Chineseness. Chinese pan-nationalism can also be seen as a move towards civic nationalism, in the sense that it emphasizes equal citizenship regardless of ethnic, cultural and 'racial' backgrounds. This contains a modern liberal element of national identity and citizenship. Theoretically speaking, such pan-nationalism, with limited civic elements, can co-exist with democracy without too much tension. Practically speaking, if it can develop further and is increasingly shared by the majority of people, including minority groups in China, it may promote equality between nationalities and reduce ethnic tensions and conflicts; and in so doing, create favourable conditions for Chinese democratization.

However, we are not doubtful about pan-nationalism playing any role in avoiding territorial disputes or managing the national identity problem.[7] Pan-nationalism seems to be inadequate and insufficient in dealing with the national identity question in today's world. Such a nationalist approach may be desirable for an elite minority, but it is inappropriate and difficult to deploy in an age of globalization and democratization in which minorities and ethno-nationalities are given special attention and collective rights. The key issue is whether minorities will recognize and identify themselves with pan-Chinese national identities. While there are minorities, such as Yi and Bai, who may recognize the basic elements of Chinese identity as their own, there are others, such as some Tibetans who, actively resisting sinicization, have demanded political independence from China and sought to defend and construct their own political identities. It is likely for pan-nationalists to support the use of force against secessionist movements while rejecting democratic procedure in managing the national identity question. It is here that the pan-nationalists' half-hearted acceptance of civic elements of the nation is tested to the limit.

Pan-Chinese nationalism poses a dilemma in a multinational state like China. If Chinese pan-nationalism appeals to the *Han* tradition, this is too narrow to address the complexity of the modern state. For example, if knowing standard Han Chinese language is a necessary criterion for being Chinese, many minorities who do not speak this language would be excluded. Yet, if Chinese pan-nationalism appeals to traditions outside *Han*, including those of the Yi, Tibetans and Mongolians, it is too loose and diverse to constitute a stable foundation upon which to develop a single national identity that can be shared by all peoples living in China.

Contemporary Chinese intellectuals, like their predecessor Liang Qichao, have actively searched for traditional cultural resources upon which to found the Chinese nation. It should come as no surprise to learn that, in trying to develop contemporary Chinese nationalist thought, they looked to Confucianism, so frequently seen as the heart of traditional Chinese culture. While Confucianism has a certain function in unifying society, its role in this regard is strictly limited and it is much too restrictive for pan-Chinese nationalism to privilege Confucianism as the core of Chinese national identity at the expense of Buddhism, Islam and even Marxism. Confucianism is too limited because it fails to provide a shared public culture as a basis for national identification. To strengthen national identity, particularly in Tibet and Xinjiang, a broader public culture would be more useful than Confucianism. On the other hand, in a sense, Confucianism is too broad because it is a universal way of thought in East Asian civilizations and therefore can hardly be said to be uniquely Chinese.

Moreover, careful consideration should be given to the ways in which a traditional moral consciousness can be turned into a modern civic consciousness, and family-based Confucian ideas transformed into modern national thought. These would certainly not be easily achieved. While the traditional Chinese culture, represented by Confucianism, may have a socially unifying function, it also has the tendency to induce in the Chinese harmful psychological diathesis such as conservatism without the desire for progress.

As discussed in the chapter 4 on Zeng Guofang, it is insufficient merely to advocate a pan-Chinese national identity. Even though Liang and Sun have proposed a pan-Chinese notion, they have failed to build such a notion and, to some degree, China was and still is, what Fitzgerald calls, 'a nationless state'. Today's Chinese intellectuals continue to follow the tradition of trying to construct a pan-Chinese nationalism as a way to strengthen national identity. But cultural construction is not enough. What is required is structural transformation with a thoroughgoing institutional redesign that combines the collective rights of nationalities with individual rights, together with the crafting of democratic federalism and an electoral sequence of elections, and the promotion of multiple and complementary identities. All are key factors that make democracy possible in a multinational state,[8] and it is argued that their introduction and implementation can reduce the tension between Chinese nationalism and democracy, and so facilitate the democratization process.

The weakness of nationalist thinking

Chinese state nationalism proves just as problematic as official socialist ideology for the state. Within the broader framework of nationalism generally, it can be argued that weak and small nations who proudly wave the flag of nationalism tend to resist the values, outlook and cultural traditions of large nations; while bigger more powerful nations, who highly value nationalism, usually regard their cultural tradition, values and outlook as the only desirable one, and have the tendency to impose them on weaker smaller nationalities. As a result, nationalism tends to go against multi-cultures, exclude universal values, lead to the intolerance of different cultures, and lay the cultural and moral basis for political autocracy.

As chapter 5 demonstrates, nationalisms in both China and Taiwan cannot offer an appropriate solution to the Taiwan question if they stand firmly behind their own nationalist positions and refuse to compromise. If this remains the case, the national identity question is likely to trigger war between China and Taiwan.

Moreover, when Chinese nationalists demand equal treatment from the West, they must also satisfy the same demand from minorities within China. In other words, if Westernization is seen as a threat to Chinese national culture, then sinicization must also be regarded as a threat to minority cultures. If equal status is not accorded to other nationalities and minorities, it will be difficult to implement the policies of genuine autonomy and cultural rights. Only if these policies are taken seriously, can the national identity question be settled in a fair way so that China's stability will be ensured. Nevertheless, ethnic Han nationalism constitutes an obstacle to implementing the equality principle because the hidden assumption and practice is that Han Chinese are entitled to be the core nationality of the Chinese nation-state who should command arms and hold key positions in the machinery of state.

2. Democratic or Greater China?

Through an analytical and comparative study, the book has examined a central issue concerning the relationship between the national identity problem and democratization (chapters 5-7). The key question that inheres is whether China will become democratic but smaller, greater but undemocratic, or both democratic and greater.

It is necessary to point out the inaccuracy of the concept of a 'Greater China'. Some scholars, such as eminent historian Wang Gungwu, have strong reservations about the concept of 'Greater China' and Chinese academics generally tend to avoid it, because of its expansionist or chauvinistic connotations, preferring the term 'cultural China' or something similar. At one stage, Western scholars almost dismissed the utility of this term, but now there seems to be a consensus that it is a useful way 'to describe the activities in, and interactions between, mainland China, Hong Kong, Macao, Taiwan and offshore islands, and Chinese overseas'.[9]

Here we use the term 'Greater China' to describe the aims and objectives of Chinese pan-nationalism, and speculate about the potential implications for Chinese democratization. For Chinese nationalists, a great China is far more important than democracy. They will build a great China even if democracy is denied and sacrificed (sections 3-4 of chapter 2). For they are consequentialists: If democratization is no good for China, if it might lead to the split of the whole nation, why do we need it? If something does not produce good outcomes, then it is not desirable, no matter how noble it may sound. Chinese nationalists are highly suspicious of the constant praise accorded democracy and see the endless talk of human rights, that occurs in the West and especially in the United States, as reflective of the West's ideological opposition to Communism. They believe there is nothing wrong with pan-Chinese nationalism. Indeed, in their eyes China needs it, in a competitive international environment, to motivate people's commitment to economic development. It is only through a nationalist ethos, they believe, that China can maintain control over Tibet and reclaim the lost territories of Taiwan. This stream of pan-Chinese nationalist thought has accompanied, and will continue to accompany, the process of transition from a modern nation-state to a new 'greater' China.

Chinese nationalists feel China today is a rising super-power which is undergoing a period of rapid industrialization, and it is thus in a favourable position to deal with secessionist or independence movements. While ethnic relations still pose a problem for China's national identity, the balance of ethnic power relations has changed in favor of the Han Chinese.

For the Chinese leadership, an important issue is for China to achieve a proper balance between liberty and authority. On the question of democratization, this balance is concerned with the appropriate pace and timing of reform. It was the case in Taiwan, for example, that local elections preceded a national election (local elections in the 1960s were followed, in 1986, by the freedom to establish an opposition party, legislative elections in 1992, governor elections in 1994, and the 1996 presidential elections). The gradual process of such a sequence was of benefit to rulers who, not having to face rapid and serious change, were able to consolidate their power by incorporating local elites and having the chance to set up the rules and learn to play the 'democratic' game.

The Taiwan experience demonstrates that there is an art to politically managing the pace of democratization. Full-scale, radical democratization is likely to empower minorities and the wealthy regions thereby intensifying ethnic tensions and encouraging separatism. A partial democratization, on the other hand, is more likely to help in managing the national identity issue. This is happening in today's China where a general direct election for the head of the state is to be delayed for 50 years, as reportedly suggested by Deng Xiaoping, although local village committee elections and a village representative meeting systems have been established by the centre and are now widespread throughout China. Such an uneven strategy of democratic development serves to maintain a balance between the meeting of democratic demands and limiting the right to self-determination so that domination by the Han is maintained and ethnic conflicts reduced and controlled. It can be seen as an attempt to separate the 'triple transformations' of boundary reshaping, economic liberalization and political democratization, that have occurred simultaneously in the former Soviet Union, and to have these different stages occur separately. In other words, it is designed to separate democratization from the secessionist problem in the short term. If the triple transformations had occurred simultaneously, Chinese democratization would have failed because it would require too many tasks to be solved at a critical time, constituting a gigantic decision-making obstacle and thus a mutual blockage of solutions (see chapter 6).

It is possible, however, that China could take a different path in the passage from 'empire' to nation. Under this scenario, China must dismantle the old 'empire' if it wants to build a modern state. If democracy was a significant part of this rebuilding process, and the national boundary question was managed democratically, then a peaceful resolution to the national boundary problem could be found.

The analysis of the Chinese situation has highlighted the tensions that exist between nationalism and democracy. If nationalism is associated with 'empires' that aim to hold on to their territories, it is likely to go against democracy in today's China, as well as in other cases, such as Turkey's Empire and the former Soviet Union. In such circumstances, democracy is the best tool to break down the empire system because it enables multi-ethnic groups, or nations, to be empowered. By contrast, if nationalism is associated with independence movements, which mobilise against foreign rule, monarchy or empire, it almost always appeals to popular sovereignty and seeks mass participation. Such a form of nationalism is not only compatible with, but also demands, democracy. One obvious example of this was the movement in the United States which sought independence from British rule. Another is Taiwan's neo-nationalism that has pushed for democracy because it has helped Taiwan to secure an international reputation, as well as empowering independence movements.

In short, there are more tensions between nationalism and democracy, in the process of nation-state building, in those countries where history and culture override democratic procedure, than in those where democratic procedure is adopted to provide legitimacy for the nation-state. Also of importance is what form the national identity question takes as there are, for instance, more tensions between nationalism and democracy in the case of unification than there are in the case of independence (chapter 7).

In such a context, it is difficult to be both a democrat and a patriot in China. This is because the liberal and democratic camp appears fundamentally against Chinese nationalism. This is why this group is 'unpopular' with the nationalist camp. Equally, it is difficult for today's Chinese democrats to overcome the tensions between democracy and nationalism. Indeed, some contemporary Chinese liberals face a dilemma in their attitude towards the USA. While they favour the political institutions of the USA, they are opposed to its Tibet and Taiwan policies. If they do not exhibit an anti-American stance on these questions they are likely to be criticized as 'traitors.' Hence the political space for Chinese liberals or democrats is becoming increasingly limited as they face the difficult questions posed by the national identity problem.

By highlighting the tensions that exist between nationalism and democracy, the book illustrates the tragic fate of Chinese democracy. This tragedy, concerning the transition from 'empire' to nation-state, has been played out throughout China's history. As ethno-nationalisms have threatened to break down the 'empire', pan-Chinese nationalists have attempted to maintain it at the cost of democracy. For Chinese state nationalists to be patriotic they must support an authoritarian state. This is a major problem for contemporary China and if it cannot be resolved it will be difficult for democracy to flourish. This is the crucial connection between democracy and the question of national identity; between democracy and the existence of the Chinese nation state. Democratization threatens the very existence of the Chinese nation-state.

It should be stressed again that the clash between pan-Chinese nationalism and democracy derives from China's unique position as a multi-national country with a historical legacy of 'empire'. Pan-Chinese nationalists are born only in China and are driven to defend their nation even at the cost of democracy if it threatens to break up China. Hypothetically, if they had been born in Taiwan or Tibet, they would have more likely demanded an independent state, and importantly, would probably have cherished the idea of referendum, as a democratic procedure, to solve the national identity question. From this hypothetical point of view, the logical tension between nationalism and democracy can be seen as a 'historical accident'. It is 'accidental' in the sense that the historical circumstance of each country, as a starting point, is highly contingent. Australia as a new nation-state was formed through referenda (this will be discussed in section 4) and parliamentary vote, because of the influence of the British democratic tradition and the nature of its immigrant society. Taiwan is now a semi-independent state and can easily win full independence without having to worry about its disintegration. China, like the former Soviet Union, has its historical burden as an 'empire', and its state was formed through wars. It is difficult for China, therefore, to reconstruct a new nation according to democratic procedure. In short, the special context and circumstances of China do not favour the adoption of democratic procedure by any type of Chinese nationalists in order to settle the national identity question. Chinese nationalists' commitment to the historical principle (China as a nation is entitled to claim its territories on historical grounds) is understandable, and such commitment has contributed to the tension between nationalism and democracy.

The above view of the 'contingent and accidental' clash may enhance the belief that the tension between democracy and nationalism can be reduced, if not totally dissolved. In particular, if Chinese liberals are committed to democratic principles, they can develop a bold democratic solution to the national identity question.

3.   A Democratic Solution to the National Identity Question

A few Chinese democrats have already advocated as an alternative, the possibility of a democratic and federal China. Through federalism, a grand-coalition government, and genuine autonomy, China might, they think, be able to maintain its size and unity while also democratizing itself. A federal and democratizing China may also offer a solution to the Tibet question, and establish a confederation or federation with Taiwan (section 6 of chapter 5). In this way it may be possible for China to be both strong and democratic. The success of democratization in China will greatly depend on the kind of democracy that is adopted, at the outset, to deal with the national identity question and, perhaps more significantly, on the choices, behaviour and decisions of political leaders and groups (for a detailed discussion of this, see section 7 of chapter 5).

Chinese liberal attitudes towards the national identity question are different from those of state nationalism. Dissidents have already outlined their new policies toward the national identity question.

The Taiwan Policy

Fang Jue writes,

> The People's Republic of China and the Republic of China should have equal status under international law. Each has its own territory and citizens. In reality, neither entity has ever had legal and administrative jurisdiction over the other. The above statement should be the starting point for an understanding between people on both sides of the Taiwan Straits and for the international community. If mainland China and Taiwan conduct political negotiations, they should be carried out only on an equal basis

between the government of the People's Republic of China and the government of the Republic of China.[10]

On the unification vs. independence issue, Wei Jingsheng, for example, emphasizes the need to respect the right of the Taiwanese people to determine the course of their future. However, he acknowledges that a move towards independence could provoke the 'pro-violence' Chinese Communist regime.[11] Wei also claims that Beijing does not care what the Taiwanese people think, and that the Mainland authorities simply want Taiwan to accept dictatorship by Beijing.[12] He suggests that Beijing should be made fully aware that the Taiwanese people loathe the Mainland's isolation policy towards the island.

The Tibet Policy

For Chinese liberals, the violation of human rights, and the denial of cultural autonomy in Tibet, create potential instability. Chinese liberals employ liberal democratic procedure to deal with the national boundary problem even if it allows secession. They suggest two main policies toward the Tibet issue.[13] First, liberals favor referenda, important mechanisms of voluntary agreement and consent. They also hold that parliamentary ratification is required as a procedure to deal with the national boundary problem. Ngapoi Ngawang Jigme proposed a two-step solution. Initially, Tibet should stay within China for 20 years under a federal system; when Tibetans should have referenda to decide their status and the nature of their relationship with China. This proposal is backed and praised by Yan Jiaqi as realistic and creative.[14] If referenda were held, liberals believe unity rather than secession is a much more likely outcome.

The second policy is concerned with the autonomy of Tibet and federal arrangements. Liberals assert that 'full autonomy' should take into account the following important issues: 1) Tibet's diplomatic and military affairs should be administered by the Chinese central government; 2) Tibet should enjoy broad true autonomy in the legislative, administrative, legal, religious, and cultural arenas; and 3) major Tibetan leaders should be elected through direct elections by universal suffrage. [15]

This autonomy policy is advocated by Wei Jingsheng and Yan Jiaqi, supported by Ngapoi Ngawang Jigme,[16] and echoed by Taiwanese Premier Lien Chan (Lian Zhan). Yan argues that federalism is the most rational, just and realistic solution to the problems of Taiwan and Tibet. The Dalai

Lama proposes that Tibet should be an autonomous political entity, while China maintains responsibility for Tibet's diplomacy and the right to garrison Tibet. He also supports a negotiated solution.

One dissident outlines the main reasons for an autonomy policy:

> Throughout history, Tibet has maintained high political autonomy vis-a-vis China. Before 1950, China had only limited suzerainty over Tibet. The former Tibetan government has already publicly announced that it will no longer pursue the complete independence of Tibet. Therefore, establishing a system of 'full autonomy' may be a realistic policy that can bring long-term stability to Tibet, take account of the interests of all parties, and be accepted by the international community. Given that the Dalai Lama was once the highest leader of Tibet and continues to enjoy broad prestige among the Tibetan people, the Chinese government should conduct political dialogue and negotiations with the former Tibetan government within the basic framework of 'full autonomy' to help resolve the Tibetan problem. Any institutional plan for Tibet should take full consideration of the Tibetan people's opinions through the democratic process. Under special situations, the possibility of employing the internationally recognized principles of ethnic self-determination should not be ruled out.[17]

Two questions arise. The first concerns the size of Tibet: For the Dalai Lama, Tibet compromises some areas now in Gansu, Qinghai, Sichuan and Ningxia; while for Beijing, Tibet is only today's Tibetan autonomous region. The second question concerns the kind of autonomy Tibet should have. Which form of federalism is suitable to China? The Soviet, Australian, Canadian or other model? It is likely for China to be more attracted to a strong centralized US-style federalism than a weak and devolutionary Indian-style model. Moreover, China is likely to adopt congruent rather than incongruent federalism. In congruent federalisms, such as in Australia, Austria, Germany and the USA, the political boundaries between the component units cut across the social boundaries between groups, and religious and ethnic boundaries. Such a system has not been challenged by serious secessionist movements. In incongruent federalisms such as Belgium, Canada and Switzerland, where the political and social boundaries tend to coincide, there are strong secessionist movements, even in Switzerland. Decentralized federalism in Canada seems to be dysfunctional.

In summary, there are two opposite approaches to the Tibet issue. One asserts that democratization will facilitate secession, and therefore should be postponed. State nationalism holds such a view, therefore it resists the full-scale democratization of China. It is in this context that state nationalism clashes with democracy. The other view, held by Chinese liberals, is that the national identity question does not constitute a convincing excuse to delay or reject democratization in China. Moreover, democratization should be encouraged as it can help to resolve the national identity issue. Chinese liberals argue that if the Hong Kong model were applied to the Tibet question, Chinese democratization would not conflict with Chinese nationalism. Here, the development of democratic national identity is, not only possible, but also desirable. If democratization were imposed from above, through elite negotiation, Tibet would not have a favorable opportunity to declare independence. Democratization from above can boost the legitimacy of the government and may even strengthen state power. In short, democratization can help to manage the issues of Tibet and Taiwan, as demonstrated by the successful cases of Spain, the Philippines and South Africa.

Nevertheless, if China wants to address the national boundary question democratically, this may lead to its disintegration and contraction to a much smaller state. Some democrats think that a smaller but democratic state would be more beneficial for the people and there are a few supporters of Taiwanese and Tibetan independence, who are prepared to confront the tough question of national identity and accept that, in an age of nationalism and democratization, an 'empire' has to be broken up. Such views are, however, very rare and unlikely to attract popular support. In any case it is unclear whether Chinese democrats genuinely support these secessionist movements or simply pay them lip service in order to garner support from the West, Taiwan and Tibet. Clearly the idea of democratic management lacks the political force necessary to its implementation, and is heavily overshadowed by a vigorous Chinese nationalism at work. When there is a conflict between democracy and nationalism in China, nationalism always wins out at the cost of democracy. The Chinese instrumentalist view of democracy, that has prevailed in the past, continues to dominate today and under such circumstances, it is difficult to create and maintain, what Edward Friedman calls, a democratic national identity.[18]

While the book is reluctant to speculate as to which possibility is most likely to occur in China, it emphasize the role of democracy in all of the three possibilities addressed above. In the first scenario, a great China assisted by Chinese pan-nationalism may deny democracy. The second possibility is of a disintegrating and smaller Chinese state experiencing a rapid and dramatic development of democratization. In the third scenario, China may maintain its unity and expand its territory through reunification via a gradual democratization (see section 7 of chapter 5). In this context, democratic management of the identity question will be contested and certain strategies, to reduce the tensions between democracy and nationalism, will need to be employed. One way of achieving this is by developing a strong democratic commitment and by adopting and developing a democratic national identity, and a form of civic nationalism that is based on citizenship and consent.

4.   Searching for Democratic National Identity

An extraordinary transformation in Chinese national identity has taken place. As discussed in the book, state nationalism faces challenges from cultural nationalism (chapter 3-4), and Taiwan's nationalism (chapter 5). Popular nationalists put forward various competing views of nations and national heroes: murderers and robbers can be patriots; military officers of the KMT are presented as national heroes in the anti-Japanese war; and the Chinese nation is deemed to be above the political ideologies of Communism or the doctrine of three peoples (sections 3-5 of chapter 3). Claiming 'we the nation', they stand up against the CCP whose conception of the nation is shaken. The redefining of nation by popular Chinese nationalists can be seen as an initial step towards 'democratic' national identity, although their imagined nation is far from what we can call a 'democratic national identity'.

The first point Friedman makes about a 'democratic identity' in China, is that the Chinese are no longer thought of as people descended from an isolated northern-plain culture but, instead, as intermingling with the southern Chu and other cultures, all of whom are involved with influences outside China.[19] He identifies two competing forms of national identity: a northern identity which is perceived as anti-imperialist, conservative, and chauvinistic; and a southern-oriented identity, which is open and tied to an Asian-Pacific economic dynamism that brings in most of China's foreign exchange earnings and investment.[20] Second, he points to the fact that Chinese popular opinion seems to reject the claim that He Zhili (who emigrated to Japan and adopted the name of Chire Koyama) was a traitor, seeing this as testimony to a striking change in Chinese identity - towards openness, pluralism and tolerance. Third, he suggests that *it is* increasingly recognised, not only by independent intellectuals, but also some government officials, that China can only hold itself together if it loosens up. According to this view, regional conflict will explode unless China constructs a decentralized federal or confederate system. There has been much speculation on this issue with conferences being held to discuss the prospect of a federal China and books written proposing a federal solution to China's national identity crisis.[21] According to Friedman, these new developments help explain why the conservative, Confucian, authoritarian identity, propagated by Beijing, has not taken hold, has failed to win popular support,[22] and hold 'far more promise for achieving democratic political forms than is believed possible by superficial realist still mesmerized by the former hegemony of Mao's anti-imperialist nationalism or by Deng's and Lee Kuan Yew's concocted, palpably political East Asian Confucian authoritarianism'.[23] Friedman cautiously acknowledges, however, that unless a new and open national identity is embraced by the Chinese, any prospect of democratic progress is likely to be tenuous.[24] He goes on to celebrate the southern form of national identity, suggesting that a Chinese democratic potential has come to be identified with a more open, southern national project and an end to northern parasitism.[25]

While we acknowledge Chinese people have embraced a more open, plural identity, as discussed above, we contend that an open, plural and tolerant Chinese identity is not a *democratic* national identity. Democratic national identity can be defined generally in two ways - in terms of content; and the manner of construction. In the first sense, a democratic national identity denotes that democratic institutions are the essence of national, or daily, life of people. In other words, democracy is a built-in mechanism of national characters. In the second sense, a democratic national identity refers to a national identity that is achieved democratically through management and negotiation.

It can be argued that democratic national identity is very 'empty' in the sense that the democratic idea and institutions (such as general elections, multi-party systems and parliaments) are universally the same or similar, therefore they do not reflect distinctive national identity. It is national culture, history and language that make a distinctive national identity. In this context, it can be argued that 'democratic' national identity is not enough and has to be supplemented, in practice, by national history, culture, customs and traditions, be they imaginative, mythical, or actual.

However, when we blend democracy and nationalism, much tension arises between them.

Chinese have experienced, and will continue to experience, extreme difficulty in developing a democratic national identity because of the inherent tension between democracy and nationalism that is peculiar to the Chinese situation. To illustrate this point, we would like to offer a comparison between China and Australia where rational, moderate, national democrats and democratic nationalists are able to co-exist. It is hoped that the next generation of Chinese democrats can draw from the Australian experience inspiration and knowledge that will help them overcome the difficulties identified in this book.

The Australian nation was established on the basis of a series of referenda, which were held to settle the question of nation-building. In 1898 referenda for a confederation were held in four colonies (NSW, South Australia, Tasmania and Victoria) and a 67 percent approval rate was secured. In 1899-1900, all six colonies (NSW, South Australia, Tasmania, Victoria, Queensland, and West Australia) voted for a Federal Constitution, with a 72.4 percent approval rate. Western Australia warrants special attention, in our context, because in 1900 there was a separation movement conducted by farmers who believed they would be economically disadvantaged by federation. Nevertheless, when put to the vote in a referendum, Western Australians decided by a ratio of 44,800 to 19,691 to join the federation.[26] In April 1933, however, voters agreed, by an overwhelming majority of 139,653 to 70,706, that Western Australia should secede from the federation of Australian states and revert to its former status as an independent self-governing member of the British Empire. Nevertheless, this result can be interpreted as an expression of opposition against the Federal Government of the day because, on the same day, the same voters also voted for a Labor government that was opposed to secession, while the National-Country Party, who initiated the secession referendum, was defeated in the election.[27] In any event, the secession proposal was rejected by the British Parliament.

All of these activities were conducted peacefully, according to certain procedures. The Australian nation-state has long been regarded as a voluntary association based on the consent of individuals. Australian nationalism takes the form of a civic nationalism which is compatible with democracy, and has a very complex relationship to democratic assumptions and practices.[28] The Australian conception of national identity occurs within a liberal society which contains democratic elements; that is, the nation's formation and development has been closely associated with a democratic process.

By contrast, the Chinese conception of the nation-state is not based on the idea of civic association or the idea of consent. The Chinese nation-state was never built on democratic process. It was a Party-state created through violent revolution and based merely on history, ethnicity, culture and Chinese language. Chinese writings on state nationalism are predominantly bound up with collectivism, loyalty to the state, and the protection of national territories at any cost. Ideas of state nationalism in Chinese discourse are distinctive from civic nationalism and there is no place for an individualist perspective. If the Chinese state attempts to legitimatize itself through democratic principles and processes, it will be confronted with the independence claims of Taiwan, where the Democratic Progress Party demands an independent state be established through referenda. In such a context, Chinese nationalists understandably look to strengthen national identity by appealing to tradition and culture, rather than democratic procedure and principle. It is here that the clash between Chinese nationalism and democracy is so evident. Indeed, the tensions are so fraught that there seems little cause for hope that China will be able to develop a democratic national identity.

Like the United States and Britain, Australia is proud of its democratic tradition upon which its nationalism was founded.[29] One would have to say that Australian democracy and nationalism combine well so that an Australian can be both a patriot and a democrat. Australians are generally patriotic - they are proud of their nation, their heritage and their environment, especially their beaches! One recent survey showed that Australians feel very 'emotionally attached' to their country, with 94 percent of the respondents saying they feel close or very close to it.[30] It also showed that Australians feel moderately proud of their armed forces (68 percent), the country's history (67 percent) and the way democracy operates (64 percent).[31] Yet this nationalism does not generally lead to an inward looking racism, as was demonstrated by the recent defeat suffered by Pauline Hanson's One Nation Party at the 1998 federal election. Australians love their country, protect their environment, and support national and local products. They also outwardly support the cause of international justice, through government and voluntary aid programs which go to help some of the poorest nations in the world. In this country, people can be nationalists, internationalists and democrats. The Australian Republican movement, which is gathering momentum, can be seen as a new nationalism movement which appeals to democratic procedures and follows democratic rules through public debate, civil forums, and a people's convention. Ultimately, the question of whether Australia should remain part of the British monarchy, or move to establish a republic, will be settled by a referendum in 1999. Thus the whole process of deciding the question of national identity in Australia is fundamentally reliant on the democratic process. This is a good example of how Australia's nationalism combines with its democratic spirit. Even the One Nation Party, an extreme, conservative nationalist movement, has to operate and rely on democratic procedures and must compete for political power through the electoral process. When the Party's leader, Pauline Hanson, and top officials, David Oldfield and David Ettridge refused to open the party up and introduce more democratic procedures, systematically purging disgruntled members, they were punished by three of One Nation's Queensland MPs' who resigned from the Party.[32] The One Nation Party appears more moderate than its European counterparts. While it does not seem to be violent, members are sometimes very vocal and have a tendency to adopt threatening language, directed particularly against minorities.

In Australia to be democratic one does not necessarily have to be patriotic. Indeed, it is argued by some that, in an age of globalisation, to be truly democratic Australians have to go beyond the nation-state, and become citizens of global civil society. Sadly, China is a long way from reaching this point and is only at the fledgling stage of developing citizenship. In China, to be a democrat, one must be patriotic; that is, democracy must strengthen, rather than weaken, the nation-state. By contrast, to be a patriot one does not necessarily have to be a democrat. In fact, current Chinese state nationalism demands that patriotic Chinese be anti-democratic. Surely, Chinese democrats have redefined and, will continue to redefine, patriotism. For them, the introduction of democracy can save China from disintegration and strengthen China's international status; thus Chinese democrats are entitled to be seen as genuine patriots.

Australia provides China with a model of a society where citizens can be both patriotic and democratic, or, if they choose, they can be democrats without being patriots. This is a society which appeals to the authors, and hopefully to the peoples of China.

Notes

1   Ge Hongbing, 'Jingti xiaai de minzu zhuyi' (On guard against narrow nationalism), *Zhonggu qingnian yanjiu* (*China Youth Studies*) No. 1, 1998, pp. 32-33. On this matter, John Dunn points out that, normatively, 'nationalism is simply one version of the self-righteous politics of ethical relativism'. 'The prevalence of nationalism is a moral scandal because the official ethical culture of almost the entire world is a universalist ethical culture.' Nationalism is nothing more than a form of collective egoism. John Dunn, *Western Political Theory in the Face of the Future*, Cambridge: CUP, 1979, pp. 61-2.

2   Chen Xi, 'Nationalism Among Chinese Intellectuals', in *China Strategic Review*, Vol. 1, No. 6, 1996, p. 14.

3   Zhou Yi, 'Before and After the Publication of *China Can Say No*', in *China Strategic Review*, vol. 1, no. 7, 1996, p. 20.

4   Ibid., pp. 20-1.

5   For example, see Gong Nanxiang, 'Making Nationalism a Constructive Force for Democratization', *China Strategic Review*, Vol. 2, No. 2, 1997, pp. 14-30; Wang Pengling, 'Zhongguo minzu zhuyi de yuanliu – jianlun cong geming de minzu zhuyi zhuanxiang jianshe de minzu zhuyi' (Source of Chinese nationalism – On the Transformation from revolutionary nationalism to constructive nationalism), *Modern China Studies*, No.2, 1979, pp. 101-127.

6   Yu Wong, 'Boy Wonder', *Far Eastern Economic Review*, Vol. 159, No. 40, 3 Oct. 1996, p. 28.

7   There are other limits and weaknesses of pan-nationalism which have been discussed in section 6 of chapter 4.

8   Linz and Stepan, *Problems of Democratic Transition and Consolidation: Southern Europe, South America, and Post-Communist Europe*, Baltimore, The John Hopkins University Press, 1996, pp. 33-4.

9   Harry Harding, 'The Concept of "Greater China": Themes, Variations and Reservations', in David Shanmbaugh (ed.), *Greater China: A New Superpower?*, Oxford: Oxford University Press, 1995, pp. 8-11.

10   Fang Jue, 'A Program for Democratic Reform', *The Journal of Democracy*, Vol. 9, No. 4, 1998, p. 18.

11   Myra Lu, 'Democracy the word during Wei visit', *The Free China Journal*, vol. XVI, no. 1, Jan. 1, 1999, p. 1.

12   Ibid.

13   For a full account of dissidents' view on Tibet, see Cao Changching and James D. Seymour (ed.), *Tibet through Dissident Chinese Eyes: Essays on Self-determination*, Armonk: M. E. Sharpe, 1998.

14   *China's Constitutionism Newsletter*, No. 2, Jun. 1994, pp. 22-23. Yan says that the period of 20 years is appropriate, and the timespan of 50 years is too long (p. 23).

15   Fang Jue, 'A Program for Democratic Reform', *The Journal of Democracy*, Vol. 9, No. 4, 1998, pp. 17-18.

16   *China's Constitutionism Newsletter*, op. cit., pp. 9-11.

17   Fang Jue, op. cit.

18   Edward Friedman, *National Identity and Democratic Prospects in Socialist China*. NY: M. E. Sharpe, 1995.

19   Edward Friedman, 'A Democratic Chinese Nationalism', in J. Unger (ed), *Chinese Nationalism*, New York: M.E. Sharpe, 1996, p. 175.

20   Ibid., p. 59. Here, it is unclear whether, what Friedman calls northern versus southern-oriented identity, is regional identity or national identity, or whether the people the southeners misleadingly present their regional identity as national identity. We should also stress that Chinese nationalists regard his view as an aggressive and fictionalized idea of Chinese national identity put forward by Americans to create internal tensions among Chinese.

21   Ibid., p. 177.

22   Ibid., p. 182.

23   Ibid.

24   Ibid., p. 19.

25   Ibid., p. 326.

26   F.K. Crowley, *Australia's Western Third: A History of Western Australia from the first Settlements to Modern Times*, London: Macmillan, 1960, p. 152.

27   Ibid., pp. 272-5.

28   See Liah Greenfeld, *Nationalism: Five Roads to Modernity.* Cambridge: Harvard University Press, 1992; Emerson, *From Empire to Nation,* p. 216; A. Smith, *National Identity.* London: Penguin Books, 1991, p. 82.

29   Shlomo Avineri points out the imperialist nature of the French and English culture with the ideas on rights and liberal democracy. See Diamond, Larry and Marc F. Flattner, *Nationalism, Ethnic Conflict, and Democracy,* Baltimore, The Johns Hopkins Press, 1994 p. 29.

30   Michael Bachelard, 'Hearts swell to sport and science', *The Australian,* 9-10, Jan. 1999, p. 3.

31   Ibid.

32   See *The Australian,* 6-7 Feb. 1999, p. 1. Also, Scott Emerson, 'Hanson Target as MPs Resign', *The Australian,* 6-7 Feb. 1999, p. 4.

Bibliography

Ah, Cheng (1985), 'Wenhua zhiyue zhe renlei' (Mankind Bound by Culture), *Wenyi bao*, 6 July, cited by Wang Lin (1994) in 'On the Mythical Quality of the Search for Roots in Literature' (Xungen wenxuede shenhua pinge), *Shehui kexue yanjiu* 4, pp. 108-114.

Avtorkhanov, A. (1966), *The Communist Party Apparatus*, Regnery, Chicago.

Barmé, G. (1995), 'To Screw Foreigners is Patriotic: China's Avant-Garde Nationalists', in Jonathan Unger (ed.), *Chinese Nationalism*, M. E. Sharpe, Armonk, New York.

Baum, Richard (1997), 'The road to Tianamen: Chinese politics in the 1980s', in Roderick MacFarquauhar (ed.), *The Politics of China*, Cambridge University Press, New York.

Breuilly, J. (1994), 'The sources of nationalist ideology', in J. Hutchinson and A.D. Smith (eds.), *Nationalism*, Oxford University Press, Oxford.

Brown, A. H. (1974), *Soviet Politics and Political Science*, Macmillan, London.

Brubaker, R. (1996), *Nationalism Reframed: Nationhood and the National Question in the New Europe*, Cambridge University Press, Cambridge.

Burton, M. G. and Higley, J. (1987), 'Elite Settlements', *American Sociological Review*, vol. 52, pp. 295-307.

Cai, Xiaoping (1996), 'Lun minzu zhuyi yu quanqiu yitihua de guanxi' (On the relationship betwen nationalism and globalisation), *Qinghai minzu xueyuan xuebao: Sheke ban*, No. 3, pp. 26-31.

Cao, Changching, and J.D. Seymour, (eds.) (1998), *Tibet through Dissident Chinese Eyes: Essays on Self-determination*, M. E. Sharpe, Armonk, New York.

Cao, Yueming (1992), 'Zhongguo xiandaishi shang de sanda sichao yu minzu zhuyi yundong' (Three big trends of thought and nationalists movements in modern Chinese history), *Tianjin Social Science*, No. 1, pp. 84-89.

Chang, Y. (April 1997), 'Ethnic Conflict and Democratic Consolidation in Taiwan: Dissolving the Logic of Nation-State and Democratic Policies', *Issues and Studies*, vol. 33, no. 4, pp. 77-93.

Chao, L. and Myers, R.H. (1998), *The First Chinese Democracy: Political Life in the Republic of China on Taiwan*, the John Hopkins University Press, Baltimore.

Cheek-Milby, K. (1989), *Hong Kong: The Challenge of Transformation*, Centre of Asian Studies, University of Hong Kong.

Chen, Mingming. (1996), 'Zhengzhi fazhan shijiao zhong de minzu yu minzu zhuyi', (Nation and nationalism from the angle of political development), *Strategy and Management*, Feb., pp. 63-71.

Chen, Qimao (1996), 'The Taiwan Strait Crisis: Its Crux and Solutions', *Asian Survey*, vol. XXXVI, no. 11, Nov., pp.1055-1066.

Chen, Shaoming (1996), 'Minzu zhuyi: fuxing zhi dao?' (Nationalism: the route to renaissance?), *Dongfang*, No. 2, Beijing, pp. 74-76.

Chen, Wen-chun. (1997), 'National Identity and Democratic Consolidation in Taiwan: A Study of the Problem of Democratization in a Divided Country', *Issues and Studies*, vol. 33, no. 4, pp. 1-44.

Chen, Xi (1996), 'Nationalism Among Chinese Intellectuals', *China Strategic Review*, vol. 1, no. 6, pp. 9-14.

Cheng, F.S. (1997), 'Emerging Taiwanese Identity', Paper prepared for Taiwan Update 1997, Taiwan-Hong Kong-PRC Relations, Aug. 15-15, Brisbane, the University of Queensland, Australia.

Cheng, J.Y.S. (1989), 'The democracy movement in Hong Kong', *International Affairs*, vol. 65, pp. 443-62.

Cheng, Xiaojun. (1991), Zeng Guofan yu xiandai Zhongguo wenhua (*Zeng Guofan and modern Chinese Culture*), Hunan renmin chubanshe, Changsha.

Cheng, Y. (1989), Dulipinglun de minzhu sixiang (*The Democratic Ideas of the Journal of Independent Forum*), Lianjing chuban gongsi, Taiwan.

China's Constitutionism Newsletter, No. 2, Jun. 1994, pp. 22-24.

Chiou, D.L. (1986), 'Dilemmas in China's Reunification Policy towards Taiwan', *Asian Survey*, vol. 26, pp. 467-82.

Chou, Yujen. (1997), 'The Impacts of Taiwan's National Identity and Democratization on its International Stance and East Asia's Security', the paper presented at the XVIIth World Congress of the International Political Science Association, Seoul, pp. 1-39.

Chun, Allen. (1994), 'From Nationalism to Nationalizing: Cultural Imagination and State Formation in Postwar Taiwan', *The Australian Journal of Chinese Affairs*, no. 31, Jan., pp. 49-69.

Constitution of the People's Republic of China (1954). For an English version see S.B. Thomas (1955), *Government and Administration in Communist China*, Institute of Pacific Relations, New York, pp. 181-96.

Constitution of the People's Republic of China (1982), Zhongguo fazhi chubanshe, 1997, Beijing. For an English version, see *Beijing Review*, No. 52, Dec. 27, pp. 10 - 18.

Cook, P. (1995), 'Extending borders for a new NATO', *Insight on the News*, 13 Mar, pp. 6-11.

Cook, S. (1995), 'Tibet in Transformation: The Consequences of Economic Interactions with Han China', paper presented at the *Conference of China's Provinces in Reform: Social and Political Change*, Suzhou University, 23-27 Oct.

Croce, B. (1960), *History: Its Theory and Practice*, Russell & Russell, New York.

Crowley, F.K. (1960), *Australia's Western Third: A History of Western Australia from the first Settlements to Modern Times*, Macmillan, London.

Dahl, R. (1971), *Polyarchy: Participation and Opposition*, Yale University Press, New Haven.

Dahl, R. (1989), *Democracy and Its Critics*, Yale University Press, New Haven.

Dai, Xueji and Xu, Ru (1984), 'Zeng Guofan de "yuyi" sixiang lunlüe' (Zeng Guofan's strategies to defend China against invasion), *Fujian luntan* , vol. 2, pp. 36-41.

Davis, M.C. (1989), *Constitutional Confrontation in Hong Kong*, Macmillan, London.

Deng, Xiaoping (1993), 'Disandai lingdao jiti de dangwu zhiji', in *Deng Xiaoping wenxuan* (*Selected Works of Den Xiaoping*), vol. 3, Renmin, Beijing.

Deng, Yunsheng. (1988), 'Zeng Guofan Hanjian maiguozei bian' (A challenge to labeling Zeng Guofan a 'traitor to the Han' and 'a traitor to his country'), *Qiusuo*, vol. 1, Changsha, pp. 122-30.

Deng, Yibing, Wang, Jiping and Cheng, Xiaojun, cited by Rao Huaimin and Wang Xiaotian (1986), 'Zeng Guofan yanjiu shuping' (An overview of Zeng Guofan studies), *Hunan shifan daxue shehui kexue xuebao* 5, p. 8.

Diamond, L. and Flattner, M.F. (1994), *Nationalism, Ethnic Conflict, and Democracy*, the Johns Hopkins University Press, Baltimore.

Diamond, L., Lintz, J., and Lipst, S. (eds.) (1988), *Democracy in Developing Countries: Africa*, Lynne Rienner Publishers, Boulder, Colorado.

Diamond, L., Lintz, J., and Lipst, S. eds. (1989), *Democracy in Developing Countries: Asia*, Lynne Rienner Publishers, Boulder, Colorado.

Dirlik, A. (1996), 'Reversals, ironies, hegemonies: Notes on the contemporary historiography of modern China', *Modern China*, vol. 22, no. 3, Jul. pp. 243-84.

Dong, Caishi (1986), 'Lüelun Zeng Guofan' (A brief evaluation of Zeng Guofan), *Suzhou daxue xuebao* 1, Suzhou, pp. 91-97.

Dong, Qing (1983), 'Zeng Guofan de yisheng' (A sketch of the life of Zeng Guofan), *Shandong daxue xuebao* 1, Ji'nan, pp. 27-36.

Duara, Prasenjit (1990), 'Nationalism as the Politics of Culture: Centralism and Federalism in Early Republican China', The Woodrow Wilson Center, *Asia Program Occasional Paper*, no. 37, Jun. 11.

Duara, Prasenjit (1996), 'De-constructing the Chinese nation', in J. Unger (ed.), *Chinese Nationalism*, M.E. Sharpe, Armonk, New York.

Dunlop, J. (1997), 'Russia in search of an identity?', in Bremner, Ian and Taras, Ray (eds.) *New States, New Politics: Building the Post-Soviet Nations*, Cambridge University Press, Cambridge.

Dunn, J. (1979), *Western Political Theory in the Face of the Future*, Cambridge University Press, Cambridge.

Economic Department of State Ethnic Affairs Commission and Department of Integrated Statistics of State Statistical Bureau (ed.), (1995) *China's Ethnic Statistical Yearbook 1995*, Ethnic Publishing House, Beijing.

Elazar, D.J. (1995), 'From Statism to Federalism: A Paradigm Shift', *Publius: The Journal of Federalism*, vol. 25, no. 2, Spring, pp. 5-18.

Emerson, R. (1960), *From Empire to Nation: the Rise to Self-determination of Asian and African Peoples*, Harvard University Press, Cambridge.

Etzioni-Halevy, E. (1993), *The Elite Connection: Problems and Potential in Western Democracy*, Basil Blackwell, Boston.

Fang, Jue (1998), 'A Program for Democratic Reform', *The Journal of Democracy*, vol. 9, no. 4, pp. 9-19.

Fewsmith, Joseph (1997), 'Relations, resurgence, and succession: Chinese politics since Tiananmen', in Roderick MacFarquauhar (ed.), *The Politics of China*, Cambridge University Press, New York.

Field, G.L. and Higley, J. (1980), *Elitism*, Routledge, London.

Fitzgerald, John (1996), 'The Nationless State: The Search for a Nation in Modern Chinese Nationalism', in Jonathan Unger (ed.), *Chinese Nationalism*, M.E. Sharpe, Armonk, New York.

Fleron, F. J. (1996), 'Post-Soviet Political Culture in Russia: An Assessment of Recent Empirical Investigations', *Europe-Asia Studies*, vol. 48, no. 2, pp. 225-260.

Friedman, E. (1995), *National Identity and Democratic Prospects in Socialist China*, M. E. Sharpe, New York.

Friedman, E. (1996), 'A Democratic Chinese Nationalism', in J. Unger (ed.), *Chinese Nationalism*, M.E. Sharpe, Inc., New York.

Friedman, E. (1997), 'Chinese Nationalism, Taiwan Autonomy and the Prospects of a Larger War', *Journal of Contemporary China*, vol. 6, no. 14, pp. 5-32.

Ge, Hongbing (1998), 'Jingti xiaai de minzu zhuyi' (On guard against narrow nationalism), *Zhongguo qingnian yanjiu (China Youth Studies)*, no. 1, pp. 32-3.

Gellner, E. (1996), *Conditions of Liberty: Civil Society and its Rivals*, Penguin Books, London.

Gellner, E.(1983), *Nations and Nationalism*, Oxford University Press, Oxford, England.

Ghai, Y. (1991), 'The Past and Future of Hong Kong's Constitution', *China Quaterly*, No. 128, pp.794-813.

Ghia, Nodia, (1994), 'Nationalism and Democracy', in L. Diamond and M.F. Plattner (eds.), *Nationalism, Ethnic Conflict, and Democracy*, the Johns Hopkins University Press, Baltimore.

Gietlman, Z. (1992), 'Nations, Republics and Commonwealth', in S.White, A. Pravda and Z. Gitelman (eds.), *Developments in Soviet and Post-Soviet Politics*, Macmillan, Hampshire.

Goldman, M. (1994), *Sowing the Seeds of Democracy in China*, Harvard University Press, Cambridge.

Gong, Nanxiang (1997). 'Making Nationalism a Constructive Force for Democratization', *China Strategic Review*, vol. 2, no. 2, pp. 14-30.

Gong, Shuduo (1995), 'Yuan Shikai zhi an fanbude', (The verdict on Yuan Shikai must not be reversed), *Zhongliu* , vol. 11, Beijing, pp. 36-37.

Gray, V. (1996), 'Identity and Democracy in the Baltics', *Democratization*, vol. 3, no. 2, 69-91.

Greenfeld, L. (1992), *Nationalism: Five Roads to Modernity*, Harvard University Press, Cambridge.

Han, Shaogong (1994), 'Yexingzhe mengyu' ('Dream Talk of a Night Walker'), in Lin Jianfa (ed.), *Zhongguo zuojia mianmian guan*, (*Modern Chinese Writers*), Shidai wenyi chubanshe.

Harding, H. (1987), *China's Second Revolution: Reform after Mao*, Allen and Unwin, Sydney.

Harding, H. (1992), *The fragile relationship: The United States and China since 1972*, Brookings Institution, Washington, D.C.

Harding, H. (1995) 'The Concept of "Greater China": Themes, Variations and Reservations', in David Shanmbaugh (ed.), *Greater China: A New Superpower?* Oxford University Press, Oxford.

He, Baogang (1996), *The Democratization of China*, Routledge, London.

He, Baogang (1997), *The Democratic Implications of Civil Society in China*, Macmillan, London.

He, Baogang (1998), 'Can W. Kymlicka's liberal theory of minority rights be applied in East Asia?', in P. van der Velde and A. McKay (eds.), *New Developments in Asian Studies*, Kegan Paul, London, pp. 20-44.

He, Baogang (2000), *Democracy and Boundaries in East Asia*, Routledge, London.

Hermann, M.G. and Kegley, C. (1996), 'Ballots, A Barrier against the Use of Bullets and Bombs', *Journal of Conflict Resolution*, vol. 40, no. 3, pp. 436-460.

Hertz, F. Otto (1945), *Nationality in History and Politics: A Study of the Psychology and Sociology of National Sentiment and Character*, Kegan Paul, London.

Higley, J. and Burton, M.G. (1989), 'The Elite Variable in Democratic Transitions and Breakdowns', *American Sociological Review*, vol. 54, pp.17-32.

Higley, J. and Gunther, R. (1992), *Elites and Democratic Consolidation in Latin America and Southern Europe*, Cambridge University Press, New York.

Higley, J. and Pakulski, J. (1995), 'Elite Transformations in Central and Eastern Europe', *Australian Journal of Political Science*, vol. 30, no. 3, pp. 415-35.

Higley, J., Pakulski, J., and Wesolowski, W. (eds.) (1998), *Postcommunist Elites and Democracy in Eastern Europe*, St. Martin's Press, New York.

Holmes, S. (1995), 'Precommitment and the Paradox of Democracy', in J. Elster and R. Slagstad (eds.), *Constitutionalism and Democracy*, Cambridge University Press, Cambridge.

Hsieh, J. F. and Niou, E.M.S. (1996), 'Issue Voting in the Republic of China on Taiwan's 1992 Legislative Yuan Election', *International Political Science Review*, vol. 17, no. 1, pp. 13-27.

Hu, B., Kong, L., Qi, Q. and Chen, Y. (1983), 'Guanyu Zhongguo jindaishi jiben xiansuo wenti' (A few questions about the basic framework of modern Chinese history), *Wenshizhe*, vol. 3, Ji'nan, pp. 49-56.

Hua, Ming (1989), *Qiushi*, no. 15, Beijing, pp. 17-20.

Huntington, S. (1991), *The Third Wave: Democratization in the Late Twentieth Century*, University of Oklahoma Press, Norman.

Huntington, S. (1993), 'The Clash of Civilizations?' *Foreign Affairs* vol. 72, no. 3, Summer, pp. 22-49.

Huntington, S. (1996), 'Democracy for the Long Haul', *Journal of Democracy*, vol. 7, no. 2, pp. 3-14.

Hutchinson, J. (1994), 'Cultural nationalism and moral regeneration', in J. Hutchinson and A.D. Smith (eds.), *Nationalism*, Oxford University Press, Oxford.

Hutchinson, J. and Smith, A.D. (1994), *Nationalism*, Oxford University Press, Oxford.

Hwang, K. (1994), 'Korean Reunification in a Comparative Perspective', in Yong Whan Kihl (ed.), *Korea and the World: Beyond the Cold War*, Westview Press, Boulder.

Jacobs, B. (1981), 'Political Opposition and Taiwan's Political Future', *The Australian Journal of Chinese Affairs*, 6 (Jan. 1981), pp. 22-44.

Jacobs, B. (1997), 'China's Policies Towards Taiwan', paper presented at Taiwan Update 1997: Taiwan, Hong Kong and PRC Relations, 14-15 Aug., Brisbane.

Jaivin, L. (1993), 'Life in a Battlefield', *Asian Wall Street Journal*, 24-25 Dec., cited by Barmé, G. (1995), 'To Screw Foreigners is Patriotic: China's Avant-Garde Nationalists', in Jonathan Unger (ed.), *Chinese Nationalism*, M. E. Sharpe, Armonk, New York.

Jansen, M. (1967), *The Japanese and Sun Yat-sen*, Harvard University, Cambridge.

Jei Guk Jeon, (1992), 'The Origin of Northeast Asian NICs in Retrospect: The Colonial Political Economy, Japan in Korea and Taiwan', *Asian Perspective*, vol. 16, no. 1, pp. 71-101.

Jermain T.M. Iam (1993), 'Chris Patten's Constitutional Reform Package: Implications for Hong Kong's Political Transition', *Issues and Studies*, no. 7.

Ji, Xianlin (1989), 'The Patriotic Tradition among Chinese Intellectuals' (Zhongguo zhishifenzi de aiguo chuantong), *Xinhua Wenzhai*, May, p. 164.

Jia, Pingao (1995), *Shangzhou: Endless Tales, Huaxia chubanshe*, vol.3, Beijing.

Jiang, Duo (1989), 'Lüelun Zeng Guofan qi ren' (A brief evaluation of Zeng Guofan), *Shehui kexue*, Shanghai, vol. 2, pp. 74-77.

Jiang, Niantao (1996), 'Dui minzu ziwo zhongxin de fanbo' (A Critique upon the Selfcentralism of Nationality), *Jianghan Tribune*, no. 3, pp. 33-35.

Jiang, Yihua (1993), 'Lun 20 shiji zhongguo de minzu zhuyi' (On Chinese nationalism in the 20th century), *Fudan xuebao (Shehui kexue ban)*, no. 3, pp. 8-13.

Jiang, Zemin (1997), 'Speech at the 40th Aniversary of the People's Republic of China', in *A Work Manual for the Construction of Socialist Civilization*, the Office for the Construction of Spiritual Civilization, the Department of Propaganda, Zhonggong dangshi chubanshe, Beijing.

Jiang, Zemin (1997), 'Speech at the closing session of the Sixth Plenum of the 14th Congress of the CCP', in *A Work Manual for the Construction of Socialist Civilization*, the Office for the Construction of Spiritual Civilization, the Department of Propaganda, Zhonggong dangshi chubanshe, Beijing.

Johnston, A. (1993), 'Independence through Unification: On the Correct Handling of Contradictions across the Taiwan Straits', Harvard University, *Contemporary Issue*, no. 2.

Kamenka, E. (ed.) (1976), *Nationalism: The Evolution of the Idea*, Edward Arnold, London.

Keller, S. (1963), *Beyond The Ruling Class: Strategic Elites in Modern Society*, Random House, New York.

Kohn, H.(1944), *The Idea of Nationalism*, Macmillan, New York.

Kuan, Hsin-chi, (1991), 'Power Dependence and Democratic Transition: The Case of Hong Kong', *China Quarterly*, no. 128, Dec., pp. 774-93.

Kwan, Hwang (1994), 'Korean Reunification in a Comparative Perspective', in Young Whan Kihl (ed.), *Korea and the World: Beyond the Cold War*, Westview Press, Boulder.

Lane, D. (1996), 'The Gorbachev Revolution: the Role of the Political Elite in Regime Disintegration', *Political Studies*, vol. XLIV, pp. 4-23.

Lane, D. and Cameron, R. (1994), 'The Social Backgrounds and Political Allegiance of the Soviet Political Elite of the Supreme Soviet of the USSR: The Terminal Stage, 1984 to 1991', *Europe-Asia Studies*, vol. 46, no. 3, pp. 437-63.

Lane, D. and Ross, C. (1994), 'Limitations of Party control: the government bureaucracy in the USSR,' in *Communist and Post-communist Studies*, vol. 27, no. 1, pp. 19-38.

Laqueur, W. (1992), 'Russian Nationalism', *Foreign Affairs*, vol. 71, no. 5, p. 103.

Lau, Siu-kai and Kin-sheun, L. (eds.) (1993), *Hong Kong Tried*

Democracy: The 1991 Election in Hong Kong, Hong Kong Institute of Asian-Pacific Studies, Shatin, No. 15.

Leng, Shao-chuan and Lin, Cheng-yi (1995), 'Political Change on Taiwan: Transition to Democracy', in D.L. Shambough (ed.), *Greater China: the Next Superpower?* Oxford University Press, New York.

Li, Jiefei (1996), (*Xungen wenxue: gengxin de kaishi*), 'The Search for Roots in Literature: A New Beginning', *Wenxue Pinglun*, Aug. 1996, pp. 101-13.

Li, Rui.(1992), 'Wei shenme 'dufu Zeng Wenzheng' (Why did Mao admire Zeng Guofan?), *Dushu*, vol. 2, Beijing, pp. 8-17.

Li, Ruihuan (1990), 'Some Questions Relevant to Enhancing the Outstanding Elements of National Culture', *Qiushi*, no. 10, Beijing, pp. 2-15.

Li, Weihan (1951), 'The Chinese Communist Party and the People's Democratic United Front', *People's China*, IV: 1, 1 Jul. p.38.

Li, Xing (1995), 'Lun guojia minzu zhuyi gainian' ('On the concept of state nationalism'), *Beijing daxue xuebao (zhexue shehui kexue ban)*, no.4, pp. 74-80.

Li, Zehou (1994), 'Guanyu wenhua xianzhuang daode congjian de duihua' (A dialogue about moral reconstruction in contemporary culture), *Dongfang* 5 (extracted in *Zhongliu*, Oct. 1995, Beijing, p. 29).

Li, Zehou and Liu, Zaifu (eds.) (1995), *Gaobie geming: Huiwang ershi shiji Zhongguo (Farewell to revolution: Looking back upon twentieth-century China)*, Tiandi tushu youxian gongsi, Hong Kong.

Lin Gang (1996), 'The Conditions, Consequences and Prevention of Conflicts between Mainland China and Taiwan', *Modern China Studies*, no. 2, pp. 93-7.

Linz, J. and Stepan, A. (1996), 'Towards Consolidated Democracies', *Journal of Democracy*, vol. 7, no. 2, pp. 14-34.

Linz, J. and Stepan, A. (1996), *Problems of Democratic Transition and Consolidation: Southern Europe, South America, and Post-Communist Europe*, the John Hopkins University Press, Baltimore and London.

Linz, J. and Stepan, A. (eds.) (1978), *The Breakdown of Democratic Regimes*, the John Hopkins University Press, Baltimore.

Liu, A.P. (1966), *Mass Politics in the People's Republic: State and Society in Contemporary China*, Westview, Colorado.

Liu, Junning (1997), 'Minzu zhuyi simianguan' (Four Dimensions of Nationalism), *Nanfang wenhua*, no. 6, pp. 25-28.

Liu, Leyang (1987), 'Lüetan Zeng Guofan de lishi gongzui yu xueshu diwei' (A brief evaluation of Zeng Guofan's merits and demerits and his intellectual influence), *Jianghai xuekan*, vol. 4, Nanjing, pp. 82-86.

Liu, Xiaobo, 'Chinese Ultra-Nationalism in the 1990s', Internet: http://bjs. org/bjs/44/31.

Lo, Shui-Ling (1990), 'Democratization in Hong Kong: Reasons, Phases and Limits', *Issues and Studies*, vol. 26, no. 5.

Louis, V. (1979), *The Coming Decline of The Chinese Empire*, Times Books, New York.

Ma, Y. (1987), 'Zeng Guofan 'Hanjian' shuo zhi yi' '(Questioning Zeng Guofan's label of "a traitor to the Han"), *Nei Menggu minzu shiyuan xuebao*, vol. 1, pp. 82-84.

Mackerras, C. (1994), *China's Minority: Integration and Modernization in the Twentieth Century*, Oxford University Press, Hong Kong.

Mackerras, C. (1995), *China's Minority Cultures*, Longman, Melbourne.

Mainwaring, S., O'Donnell, G., and Valenzuela, S.J. (eds.) (1992), *Issue In Democratic Consolidation: The New South American Democracies in Comparative Perspective*, University of Notre Dame Press, South Bend.

McFaul, M. (1996), 'Russia Between Elections: The Vanishing Center', *Journal of Democracy*, vol. 7, pp. 90-105.

McFaul, M. (1997), 'Russia's Rough Ride', in *Larry Diamond, Marc Plattner, Yun-han Chu, and Hung-mao Tien*, (eds.), *Consolidating the Third Wave Democracies: Regional Challenges*, the Johns Hopkins University Press, Baltimore.

Mill, J. S., *Representative Government* (1861), quoted in Alfred Zimmern (1939), *Modern Political Doctrines*, Oxford University Press, London.

Mill, J.S. (1947), *Utilitarianism, Liberty, and Representative Government*, J. M. Dent and Sons Ltd, London.

Miller, D. (1995), *On Nationality*, Clarendon Press, Oxford.

Mo, Yan (1986), *Hong gaoliang* , Xueshu chubanshe, Hong Kong.

Mu, Fu (1996), (Yangniur Zhongguo ze xu), 'Foreign Girls Find Husbands in China', *Literature and Life (Wenxue yu rensheng)*, no. 138, Apr. pp.16- 21.

Mu, Fu-sheng (1962), *The Wilting of the Hundred Flowers: The Chinese Intelligentsia under Mao*, Praeger, New York.

O'Donnell, G. (1994), 'Delegative Democracy', *Journal of Democracy*, vol. 5, no. 1, pp. 56-69.

O'Donnell, G. (1996), 'Illusions about Consolidation', *Journal of Democracy*, vol. 7, no. 2, pp. 34-52.

O'Donnell, G. and Schmitter, P. (1986), *Transitions From Authoritarian Rule: Tentative Conclusions About Uncertain Democracies*, the Johns Hopkins University Press, Baltimore.

Oksenberg, M. (1987), 'China's Confident Nationalism', *Foreign Affairs*, vol. 65, no. 3, pp. 501-23.

Pakulski, J. (1986), 'Bureaucracy and the Soviet System', *Studies in Comparative Communism* , vol.19, no. 1, pp. 3-21.

Pei, Minxin (1995), 'Creeping Democratization in China', *Journal of Democracy*, vol. 6, no. 4, pp. 65-79.

Peng, Qian (1986), 'Tantan Zeng Guofan yanjiu wenti' (On the study of Zeng Guofan), *Qunyan*, vol. 1, Beijing, pp. 33-35.

Pi, Mingyong (1996), 'Minzu zhuyi yu rujia wenhua'(Nationalism and Confucian culture), *Strategy and Management*, Feb., pp. 51-57.

Plaks, A.H. (1997), 'Towards a Critical Theory of Chinese Narrative', *in Chinese Narrative: Critical and Theoretical Essays*, Princeton University Press, Princeton.

Pope, V. and Stanglin, D. (1994), 'Too close for comfort', *U. S. News & World Report*, vol. 116, no. 5, 7 Feb., pp. 40-43.

Przeworski, A. (1991), *Democracy and the Market*, Cambridge University Press, Cambridge.

Putnam, R.D. (1976), *The Comparative Study of Political Elites*, Prentice-Hall, Englewood Cliffs.

Rao, Huaimin and Wang, Xiaotian (1986), 'Zeng Guofan yanjiu shuping' (An overview of Zeng Guofan studies), *Hunan shifan daxue shehui kexue xuebao*, vol. 5, Changsha, pp. 3-10.

Renan, E. (1939), 'What is a Nation?', in A. Zimmmern (ed.), *Modern Political Doctrines* , Oxford University Press, London.

Rosen, Stanley (1993), 'The Effect of Post-4 June Re-education Campaigns on Chinese Students', *The China Quarterly*, no. 132, Jun. pp. 311-34.

Rustow, D. A. (1967), *A World of Nations: Problems of Political Modernization*, Brookings Institution, Washington, D.C.

Rutland, P. (1992), 'Economic Crisis and Reform', in S. White, A. Pravda and Z. Gitelman (eds.), *Development in Soviet and Post-Soviet Politics*, Macmillan, Houndmills.

Rutland, P. (1994), 'Has Democracy Failed Russia?', *The National Interest*, vol. 38, pp. 3-12.

Sang, Ye (1996), (*Zhunbei haole ma*?) 'Are You Ready?', translated by Barmé with Jaivin, in *The Year the Dragon Came,* Queensland University Press, Brisbane.

Sartori, G. (1987), *The Theory of Democracy Revisited: The Contemporary Debate,* Chatham House Publishers, Chatham.

Scott, Ian. (1989), *Political Change and the Crisis of Legitimacy in Hong Kong,* Hurst, London.

Sha, Yexin (1997), (Zhongguoren de zunyan buke ru), 'Chinese Dignity Is Not for Sale', *Dongxi nanbei, (Four Corners),* Mar., pp. 4-5.

Shen, J. (1987), 'Zeng Guofan yu Hong Xiuquan bijiao' (A comparison of Zeng Guofan and Hong Xiuquan), *Guangming ribao* , vol. 3, 5 Aug., Beijing, p. 3.

Shen, J. (1990), 'Zeng Guofan 'maiguozei an' xintan' (A revaluation of the Zeng Guofan "case of treason"), *Shixue yuekan,* vol. 1, Kaifeng, pp. 45-50.

Sheng, L. (1998), 'China Eyes Taiwan: Why is a Breakthrough so Difficult?', *The Journal of Strategic Studies,* vol. 21, no. 1, p. 69.

Shi, X. (1987), 'Dui Zeng Guofan pingjia de zhenglun' (Contending evaluations of Zeng Guofan), *Jiefang ribao,* vol. 4, Shanghai, 25 Jan.

Shih, Cheng-Feng (1997), 'Emerging Taiwanese Identity', Paper prepared for Taiwan Update 1997, Taiwan-Hong Kong-PRC Relations, Brisbane, Queensland, Australia, Aug. 14-15, pp. 1-30.

Shlapentokh, D. (1997), 'The Chechen war and Russia's identity crisis', *Contemporary Review,* vol. 270, Feb., pp. 72-78.

Shlapentokh, D. (1998), 'The Russian Identity Crisis', *Contemporary Review* , vol. 273, Sept., pp. 125-135.

Slyke, Lyman P. Van (1967), *Enemies and Friends - The United Front in Chinese Communist History,* Stanford University Press, Stanford, California.

Smith, A. (1991), *National Identity,* Penguin Books, London.

Smith, A. (1995), *Nations and Nationalism in a Global Era,* Polity Press, Cambridge.

Smith, A.D (1994), 'The Problem of National Identity: Ancient, Medieval and Modern?', *Ethnic and Racial Studies,* vol. 17, no. 3, Jul., pp. 375-99.

Smith, A.D. (1981), *The Ethnic Revival,* Cambridge University Press, Cambridge, England.

Smith, H.W. (1991), 'Socialism and Nationalism in the East German Revolution, 1989-1990', *East European Politics and Societies,* vol. 5, no. 2, Spring, p. 243.

Snyder, J. (1994), 'Russian backwardness and the future of Europe', *Daedulus*, vol. 123, Spring.

Snyder, L.L. (1968), *The New Nationalism*, Cornell University Press, Ithaca.

So, A.Y and Kwitko, L. (1990), 'The New Middle Class and the Democratic Movement in Hong Kong, *Journal of Contemporary Asia*, vol. 20, pp. 384-98.

Song Quan (1996), 'Guanyu minzu zhuyi de jige wenti' (On several Topics about nationalism), *Heilongjiang congkan*, no. 2, Harbin, pp. 31-34.

Song, Liming (1997), 'Minzuzhuyi yu xizang wenti' (Nationalism and the Tibet problem), *Modern China Studies*, no. 2, pp. 159-167.

Song, Ping (1991), '*Zai quanguo zuzhi buzhang huiyi shang de jianghua*' (Talk to national meeting of organization department heads), in *Shisanda yilai zhongyao wenxuan xuanbian, zhong, xia (Important documents since the Thirteenth Party Congress, vol. 2)*, Renmin chubanshe, Beijing.

Song, Ping (1995), in *A New Work Manual for Party Affairs*, Zhongguo yanshi chubanshe, Beijing.

Song, Q., Zhang, Z., and Qiao, B. (1996), (*Zhongguo keyi shuo bu*), *China Can Say No, Zhonghua gongshang lianhe chubanshe*, Beijing.

Stepan, A. (1997), 'Toward a New Comparative Analysis of Democracy and Federalism: Demos Constraining and Demos Enabling Federations', paper presented at *IPSA XVII World Congress*, Seoul, Aug., pp. 17-22.

Sullivan, M. J. (1991), *The 1988-1989 Nanjing Anti-African Protests: the Tension between Chinese Nationalism and Democracy*, Sept., Department of Political Science, University of Wisconsin-Madison.

Tang, Y.S. (1996), 'Minzu zhuyi yu guoji zhixu' (Nationalism and international order), *Strategy and Management*, Mar. issue, pp.76-79.

Tao, Dongfeng (1994), 'Xiandai Zhongguo de minzu zhuyi' (Nationalism in Modern China), *Academic Monthly*, Jun. issue, pp. 6-9.

Thomas, S.B. (1955), *Government and Administration in Communist China*, New York: Institute of Pacific Relations, pp. 181-96.

Thompson, M.R. (1996), 'No Exit: 'Nation-stateness' and Democratization in the German Democratic Republic', *Political Studies*, vol. XLIV, pp. 267-8.

Tian, Tong (1997), 'Guanyu minzu zhuyi lilun de ruogan jiexi' (Various analyses on nationalism theory), *Shisue yuekan* , no. 5, Kaifeng, pp. 9-13.

Tien, Hungmao (1994), 'Toward Peaceful Resolution of Mainland-Taiwan Conflicts: The Promise of Democratization', in E. Friedman (ed.), *The Politics of Democratization: Generalizing East Asian Experiences*, Westview Press, Boulder.

Tien, Hungmao (1995), 'Prospects for Democratic Consolidation in Taiwan', Paper presented at the International Conference on Consolidating the Third Wave Democracies, 27-30 Aug., Taipei.

Tikhy, S. (1995), 'Struggle for Influence continues in Crimea', *Moscow News*, 7 April, p. 4.

Tolz, V. (1998), 'Forging the Nation: National Identity and Nation Building in Post-Communist Russia', *Europe-Asia Studies*, vol. 50, no. 6, pp. 993-1022.

Townsend, J. (1996), 'Chinese nationalism', in J. Unger (ed.), *Chinese Nationalism*, M.E. Sharpe, Armonk, New York.

Tsang, Steve.Y.S. (1988) *Democracy Shelved: Great Britain, China, and Attempts at Constitutional Reform in Hong Kong, 1945-1952*, Oxford University Press, Kong Kong.

Unger, J. (ed.) (1993), *Using the Past to Serve the Present: historiography and politics in contemporary China*, M.E. Sharpe, Armonk, New York.

Unger, J. (ed.) (1996),*Chinese Nationalism* , M.E. Sharpe, Armonk, New York.

Urban, M. (1998), 'Remythologising the Russian State', *Europe-Asia Studies* , vol. 50, no. 6, pp. 969-992.

Vanhanen, T. (1992), *Politics of Ethnic Nepotism: India as an Example*, Link Press & New Delhi, Sterling Publishers Ltd, Berkshire.

Wang, D. (1993), *From May Fourth to June Fourth - Fiction and Film in Twentieth-Century China*, Harvard University Press, Cambridge.

Wang, Gungwu. (1996), 'The Revival of Chinese Nationalism', Lecture Series 6, *International Institute for Asian Studies*, Leiden, p. 20.

Wang, Jianwei (1995), 'It is in the best interest of the people all over the country to safeguard the authority of the centre', *Qiushi*, no.8, Beijing, pp. 26-29.

Wang, L. (1996), 'Rujia lunli guannian zhidao xia de Zeng Guofan hua yang jiaoshe sixiang' (Zeng Guofan's thought on Sino-foreign negotiations guided by Confucian ethics), *Jindaishi yanjiu*, vol. 3, Beijing, pp. 165-89.

Wang, Pengling (1997), 'Zhongguo minzu zhuyi de yuanliu – jianlun cong geming de minzu zhuyi zhuanxiang jianshe de minzu zhuyi' ('Source of Chinese nationalism – On the transformation from revolutionary nationalism to constructive nationalism'), *Modern China Studies*, no. 2, pp. 101-127.

Wang, Shaopu (1983), 'Zeng Guofan yangwu sixiang de xingcheng, xingzhi he zuoyong' (The formation, nature, and role of Zeng Guofan's ideas on modernization), *Lishi yanjiu*, vol. 2, Beijing, pp. 164-77.

Wang, Zhanqui (ed.) (1997), *The National Flag, State Insignia, and National Anthem - Questions and Answers*, University of Public Administration Press, Beijing.

Wang, Zhengping (1996), 'U.S. Human Rights Diplomacy Is Doomed to Fail', *The People's Daily*, 4 Mar., trans. in FBIS-CHI-96-054, 19 Mar. 1996, p.10.

Wen, L. (1993), in Wenyi lilun yu pinglun (Literary Theory and Criticism), Mar., p. 132.

Weng Jiemin et al. (eds.) (1997), *Status and Trend of Development in China 1995-1996*, China Social Sciences Press, Beijing.

Whelan, F.G. (1983), 'Prologue: Democratic Theory and the Boundary Problem', in J. Roland Pennock and J.W. Chapman (eds.), *Liberal Democracy: Nomos XXV*, New York University Press, New York.

White, S., Pravda, A., and Gitelman, Z. (eds.) (1992), *Developments in Soviet and Post-Soviet Politics*, Macmillan, Hampshire, p. 127.

Whiting, A. (1983), 'Assertive Nationalism in Chinese Foreign Policy', *Asian Survey*, vol. 23, no. 8, pp. 913-33.

Whiting, A. (1995), 'Chinese Nationalism and Foreign Policy after Deng', *The China Quarterly*, Jun. no. 142, pp. 295-316.

Wong, Yu (1996), 'Boy Wonder', *Far Eastern Economic Review*, 3 Oct., p. 25.

Wu Guoguang (1996), 'Rational Nationalism as a Counterbalance against "Containing China"', *Twenty-First Century*, no. 34, Apr., pp. 25-33.

Wu, An-chia (1993), 'Mainland China's Political Situation in the Post-Teng Era: A Forecast', *Issues and Studies*, vol. 29, no. 6, p.14.

Wu, Chuke (1996), 'Dui Dangdai minzu zhuyi sichao fanlan de pingxi' (Comment and analysis on the spreading of the trend of thought of nationalism in the present age), *Neimenggu shehui kexue, Wenxueshi ban*, no. 3, Huhehaote, pp. 6-12.

Wu, Naide (1993), 'The Sense of Provincialism, Political Support and National Identity', in *Zuqun guanxi yu guojiang rentong*, Institute for National Policy Research, Chang Yung-fa Foundation, Taibei.

Xong, Kunxin (1996), 'Guanyu minzu zhuyi zhenglun zhong de jige redian wenti' (On several hot topics concerning nationalism), *Guizhu minzhou yanjiu*, no. 4, Guiyang, pp. 1-6.

Xu, Shanhe (1989), 'Zeng Guofan shi aiguozhe' (Zeng Guofan was a patriot), *Xiangtan daxue xuebao (sheke ban)*, vol. 1, Xiangtan, pp. 86-90.

Yan, J. (1992), Disan gonghe - weilaizhongguo de xuanze (The Third Republic - A Choice for Future China), Global Publishing Co. Inc., New York.

Yang, Guoqiang (1987), 'Zeng Guofan jianlun' (A brief evaluation of Zeng Guofan), *Lishi yanjiu*, vol. 6, Beijing, pp. 97-100.

Yang, Guoqiang (1989), 'Zeng Guofan he chuantong wenhua' (Zeng Guofan and traditional culture), *Jindaishi yanjiu* 1, Beijing, pp. 58-83.

Yang, Nianqun (1994), 'Wo kan 'Zeng Guofan xianxiang'' (My views on the 'Zeng Guofan phenomenon'), *Ershiyi shiji (Twenty-First Century Bimonthly)*, Oct., Hong Kong, pp. 132-35.

Yang, S. (1995), 'An Analysis of the Operational Relation between the Party and Government in the Current National People's Congress', *Gongdang wenti yanjiu*, vol. 21, no. 10, pp. 23-4.

Yash, Ghai, (1991), 'The Past and Future of Hong Kong's Constitution', *China Quarterly*, no. 128, Dec., pp. 794-813.

Ye, Zhi (1982), 'Exercising Power on Behalf of the People', *Beijing Review*, no. 52, Dec. 27, p. 31.

Yi, Mengchun (1990), 'Zeng Guofan zai banli Tianjin jiaoan zhong de xinli maodun' (Zeng Guofan's psychological conflicts in handling the Tianjin riots), *Jindaishi yanjiu*, vol. 1, Beijing, pp. 84-97.

Yin, Wan-Lee (1995), 'On "Taiwan in the China Circle"', *Journal of Contemporary China*, no. 8, Winter-Spring, pp. 102-105.

Yu, Ying-shih (1998), *Xiandai Ruxuelun (On Modern Confucianism)*, Shanghai Renmin chubanshe, Shanghai.

Zha, Jianying (1995), China Pop: How Soap Operas, Tabloids, and Bestsellers Are Transforming a Culture, The New Press, New York.

Zhang, H. (1997), 'Bochi "gaobie geming" de miushuo' (Refuting the absurd slogan of 'farewell to revolution'), *Zhongliu*, vol. 2, Beijing, pp. 28-31.

Zhang, Qinghua (1996), 'Fanguan yu dingwei: ershi shiji zhongguo wenxue de wenhua jingyu' (Retrospection and Relocation: The

Cultural Environment of Chinese Literature in the 20th Century'), *Wenyi pinglun*, Jan., pp. 42-51.

Zhang, Weiping (1995), *A New Work Manual for Party Affairs*, Zhongguo yanshi chubanshe, Beijing.

Zhang, Wenbiao (1996), 'Zhonghua minzu yishi yu shehui fazhan' (National consciousness of China and society development), *Fujian luntan: Wenshizhe ban* , 1, Fuzhou, pp. 15-21.

Zhao, Q. (1988), 'A Proposed Model of Unification and Plural Politics', *China Forum*, vol. 26, no. 5, pp. 54-5.

Zhong, Weiguang (1997), 'Minzu zhuyi he zhongguo wenti' ('Nation, Nationalism and the China Problem'), *Modern China Studies*, no.2, pp. 128-2.

Zhou, Enlai (1949), 'Report to the CPPCC', *China Digest*, 5 Oct., pp. 3-11, Hong Kong.

Zhou, Yi (1996), 'Before and After the Publication of *China Can Say No*', *China Strategic Review*, vol. 1, no. 7, p. 20.

Zhou,Yangshan (1995), 'New Thinking on the "Chinese Commonwealth"', *Modern China Studies*, no. 6, pp. 19-24.

Zhu, Andong (1988), 'Ping Zeng Guofan zai jindaishi shang de zuoyong he yingxiang' (Zeng Guofan's role and influence in modern Chinese history), *Qiusuo*, vol. 1, pp.112-21.

Zhu, X. (1996), 'Jiushi niandai: changpian junlu xiaoshuo de chaodong' (The 90s: Novels with Military Themes), *Wenxue pinglun*, Jan., pp. 49-59.

Zhu, Zhenhua (1984), 'Zeng Guofan he jindai keji' (Zeng Guofan and modern science and technology), *Jianghuai luntan*, vol. 1, Hefei, pp. 116-20.

Zi, Zhongjun (1996), 'Aiguo de zuobiao' (The criteria for patriotism), *Dushu*, vol. 6, Beijing, pp. 57-65.

Zimmern, A. (1939), *Modern Political Doctrines*, Oxford University Press, London.

Zuckerman, M.B. (1994), 'Dangers on the Russian Front: Nationalism in Russia', *U. S. News and World Report* , vol. 116, no. 12.

Index

For Product Safety Concerns and Information please contact our EU
representative GPSR@taylorandfrancis.com Taylor & Francis Verlag GmbH,
Kaufingerstraße 24, 80331 München, Germany

Printed and bound by CPI Group (UK) Ltd, Croydon, CR0 4YY
01/05/2025
01859204-0001